P9-AFZ-082

WALLA WALLA
RURAL LIBRARY DISTRICT

The Great Big
CHEESE
COOKBOOK

Foreword by James Robson, CEO,
Wisconsin Milk Marketing Board

RUNNING PRESS
PHILADELPHIA · LONDON

© 2009 by Wisconsin Milk Marketing Board
Photographs © 2009 by Wisconsin Milk Marketing Board
All rights reserved under the Pan-American and International Copyright Conventions

Printed in China

This book may not be reproduced in whole or in part, in any form or by any means, electronic or mechanical,
including photocopying, recording, or by any information storage and retrieval system now known
or hereafter invented, without written permission from the publisher.

9   8   7   6   5   4   3   2
Digit on the right indicates the number of this printing

Library of Congress Control Number:
ISBN 978-0-7624-3497-8

Cover and interior design by Amanda Richmond
Edited by Geoffrey Stone
Recipe development by Wisconsin Milk Marketing Board and Monica Parcell
Typography: Avenir and Berkeley

Running Press Book Publishers
2300 Chestnut Street
Philadelphia, PA 19103-4371

Visit us on the web:
www.runningpress.com

The authors and publisher of this book assume no liability for, and are released by readers from, any injury
or damage resulting from the strict adherence to, or deviation from, the directions and/or recipes herein.

CONTENTS

FOREWORD

WISCONSIN AND CHEESE are synonymous. With 160 years of cheese-making experience, our state has an unexcelled American heritage. Many of our cheesemakers come from a lineage of artisans—four generations have been making cheese from Wisconsin's exceptional milk.

Wisconsin's geography has been blessed with lush, rolling pasturelands and spring-fed water sources. These superb conditions beckoned to nineteenth-century European immigrants from cheesemaking countries—Switzerland, Germany, and the Netherlands. In more modern times, they have been joined by Mexican, Italian, and French cheesemakers. The result is a Wisconsin renaissance in cheesemaking—more varieties, more specialty cheeses, more artisan styles—and an incomparable number of awards in national and international competitions.

The Great Big Cheese Cookbook will help you discover the very wide world of Wisconsin cheese, with recipes that showcase a multitude of varieties, types, and styles, from Wisconsin classics such as Muenster and Colby, to more recent specialties, such as asadero and Burrata. You'll find basic, everyday recipes, as well as sophisticated, chef-inspired creations, all made at their best with Wisconsin cheese. The Wisconsin Milk Marketing Board is pleased to be a part of this volume with Running Press.

James Robson
Chief Executive Officer
Wisconsin Milk Marketing Board

ACKNOWLEDGMENTS

THANKS TO THE many recipe contributors and chefs who gave their time, talents, and expertise to *The Great Big Cheese Cookbook*. Special gratitude goes to the Wisconsin Milk Marketing Board staff for their tireless efforts in making this book a reality—Marilyn Wilkinson, LuAnn Lodl, Mary Litviak, and Heather Porter Engwall. And especially, deep appreciation goes to Running Press for publishing this homage to cheese.

WHERE IT COMES FROM MATTERS

IT WAS MORE than 160 years ago when European settlers first brought their time-honored cheesemaking techniques to Wisconsin. Their traditions, combined with the high-quality milk that came from Wisconsin's pasture-fed cows, marked the beginning of the state's passion for cheese—and its reputation for making the best.

Today, Wisconsin is home to some of the world's most celebrated cheesemakers. Some pay homage to the early settlers, staying true to the ways of their ancestors. Others have veered from tradition to develop innovative techniques that are all their own. Although methods may have changed over the last two centuries, the flavor and quality of the milk are still excellent. (In fact, the quality of today's milk is even better due to improved nutrition and housing for dairy cows.) Many Wisconsin artisans still use milk exclusively from cows that graze on lush, rolling pastures and drink from the area's pristine, limestone-filtered waters. That's one reason why Wisconsin cheese is like no other, and why so many cheesemakers have honed their craft in what has come to be known as America's Dairyland.

With the very best production techniques, the finest raw ingredients, and a steadfast commitment to excellence, it's no wonder that Wisconsin cheeses consistently win more awards than cheeses from any other state or nation. It's also no wonder that more than six hundred varieties, types, and styles hail from the state.

When you enjoy Wisconsin cheese, you can taste the quality and craftsmanship in every bite. And the more you compare it to other cheeses, the more it becomes clear—where it comes from really does matter.

For more information on Wisconsin cheese, visit www.EatWisconsinCheese.com.

COOKING WITH CHEESE

CHEESE IS A FAVORITE recipe ingredient. Not only does it add immeasurably to the flavor of a dish; it also lends a creamy density to the texture. The versatility of cheese, available in so many varieties, types, and styles, also makes it a great addition to recipes for virtually any part of the meal. And of course, cheese is also wonderful to serve on its own. See the appendix for suggestions for wines and beers to pair with cheeses.

CHOOSING

Start by choosing the best-quality cheese, no matter what variety you're buying. Here are some tips:

- Cheese should have a fresh, clean appearance, with no cracks or surface mold. Be sure the packaging is sealed properly, without any openings or tears that expose the cheese.

- Buy cheese at a store or market where frequent shipments of fresh cheese are delivered. Check the use by or sell by dates on packaged cheese. If buying fresh-cut cheese, ask the clerk how best to wrap the cheese for storage and how long the cheese can be kept.

- Look for the Wisconsin cheese identification. You'll know you are buying a product that has met the highest of cheesemaking standards.

HANDLING

After arriving home with your cheese, remember the three Cs of cheese handling:

- **Clean:** Because cheese easily absorbs other flavors, keep it away from other aromatic foods in the refrigerator.

- **Cold:** Refrigerate cheese between 34° and 38°F.

- **Covered**: Cheese loses flavor and moisture when it's exposed to air, so make sure to wrap hard cheeses, such as Parmesan, in tightly drawn plastic wrap. Soft or fresh cheeses, such as mascarpone, are best stored in clean, airtight containers. Semihard cheeses, including Cheddar and Gouda, can be wrapped in plastic wrap as well as a lighter wrapping paper, such as parchment.

STORING

If you are lucky enough to have leftover cheese, store your opened cheese using these suggested guidelines. Proper storage will preserve a cheese's original flavor, appearance, and quality.

- Once a cheese is opened, it's imperative to minimize moisture loss by keeping it covered in the refrigerator. For covering suggestions, see the Handling section above.

- Natural and pasteurized process cheese should last about four to eight weeks in the refrigerator, while fresh and grated hard cheese with higher moisture content should be used within two weeks.

- If cheese develops surface mold, simply cut off about ¼ to ½ inch from each affected side and use the remaining cheese within one week.

FREEZING

Cheese can be frozen, but we do not recommend it. A cheese that has been frozen is best used as an ingredient. The best candidates for freezing are firm cheeses, such as Swiss, and hard cheeses, such as Parmesan.

• When freezing cheese, wrap the pieces tightly in weights of one pound or less.

• Label and date your cheese before storing it at temperatures around 0°F.

• It's best to thaw cheese in the refrigerator and use your cheese within a couple of days.

• Freezing cheese will change the texture. Semisoft and hard cheeses will be more crumbly, while softer cheeses will separate slightly. The nutritional value will remain stable.

CUTTING AND TRIMMING

Make cutting blocks of cheese easier by using these tips:

• Most cheese is easiest to cut when chilled. However, some hard cheeses, such as Parmesan or Asiago, cut better when they are brought to room temperature.

• A chef's knife works well for cutting most cheeses. If the cheese has a wax or rind, score it before you begin, ensuring a clean cut line.

• Before eating or serving, trim off any dry edges or surface mold.

GENERAL RULES FOR COOKING WITH CHEESE

Cheese is easy to use in recipes and calls for just a few techniques. When you are adding cheese to a sauce or soup, be sure to shred or grate it first. It will blend and melt into the liquid more quickly. Soups, sauces, and casseroles that contain a starch, such as flour, are "cheese friendly." The starch helps keep the cheese from curdling during long cooking or prolonged higher heat.

When you are grating or shredding cheese to add to a recipe, be sure the cheese is cold. It will shred or grate more easily. Some cooks like to place the desired size chunk of cheese in the freezer—just briefly—so it's good and cold before shredding or grating.

Generally speaking, 4 ounces of hard cheese, such as Cheddar and Swiss, will yield 1 cup of shredded cheese. There are exceptions, however. Moist, crumbly cheeses, such as feta or blue, will measure differently. These varieties yield approximately ⅓ cup of crumbled cheese per 2 ounces.

Cheese can stiffen and curdle when exposed to high direct heat, so it's best to add cheese to a sauce or soup over low heat—or to remove the pan from the heat, add the cheese, and stir.

Be careful, too, when you're browning a dish with a cheese topping. Wait until the end of the cooking time to sprinkle the cheese on top. Melt the cheese just until it starts to brown and bubble, usually under 5 minutes. Higher-fat cheeses, such as whole-milk mozzarella, will have a flowing melt, with little browning. Lower-fat cheeses, such as part-skim mozzarella, will brown more quickly and flow less. Watch carefully. Overbrowning will cause toughness. And it won't taste very good!

CHEESE SUBSTITUTIONS

Is this a situation you've ever experienced? You have several cheeses in the refrigerator, and you're in the mood for a particular recipe, but you don't have the cheese the recipe calls for. You don't want to buy more cheese until your current "stock" diminishes a bit. What to do? Fear not! It's possible—even easy—to substitute some cheeses for others, with very good results.

Here are our suggestions for cheese substitutions to make when preparing the recipes in this book or any other recipes. We're not promising the dishes will taste the same, but we think they will taste very good and the texture of the suggested cheeses will be appropriate as well. Certainly, not having a specific cheese shouldn't prevent you from creating a winning dish for an everyday occasion. However, when ethnic authenticity is important or you want to emulate exactly a chef's dish, it's best to buy the specified cheese.

Cheese Specified in Recipe	Cheese You Can Substitute
American	Mild Cheddar
Asadero (also called Oaxaca or Chihuahua) or queso quesadilla	Mozzarella, Muenster, or Monterey Jack
Asiago	Parmesan
Brick	Muenster or Havarti
Burrata	Fresh mozzarella
Butterkäse	Havarti
Camembert	Brie
Colby	Mild Cheddar or CoJack
Cotija	Romano or Parmesan
Farmer cheese	Light-tasting Havarti
Fontina	Mild provolone or Muenster
Gorgonzola	Creamy, mild blue
Gouda	Edam
Gruyère	Swiss (preferably aged)

Cheese Specified in Recipe	Cheese You Can Substitute
Justo Liepa	Bread cheese
Manchego	Fontina of similar age, or Gouda
Mascarpone	Whipped cream cheese
Muenster	Monterey Jack or Gouda
Parmigiano-Reggiano or Grana Padano	Parmesan
Pepato	Parmesan or Romano, plus black peppercorns
Queso blanco or queso fresco	Feta or salty farmer cheese
Raclette	Gruyère or aged Swiss
Roquefort	Pungent, salty blue
Scamorza	Whole-milk mozzarella

Wisconsin cheesemakers make a number of Wisconsin Originals (cheeses created only in Wisconsin), and some of them are featured in the recipes in this book. We've listed some that are widely available and also given alternatives in case you want to prepare recipes calling for these cheeses and cannot find them.

Wisconsin Originals Cheese	Alternative
American Grana	Parmesan
Bellavitano	Young, creamy Asiago
Emmentaler	Swiss
Gran Canaria	Another aged Wisconsin mixed milk cheese (cow's and/or goat's and sheep's milk)
Gran Queso	Italian-style fontina
Les Frères	Limburger
Pleasant Ridge Reserve	Gruyère or aged Swiss
SarVecchio Parmesan	Parmesan
Vintage Van Gogh	Aged Gouda

BREAKFAST

Baked Vegetable and Gruyère Omelet

1 medium onion, chopped

1 cup sliced fresh mushrooms

2 tablespoons olive oil

1 cup chopped asparagus, cooked

1 cup chopped green beans, cooked

½ teaspoon salt

⅛ teaspoon pepper

1 cup (4 ounces) grated Gruyère cheese

1 cup milk

4 eggs, lightly beaten

⅓ cup breadcrumbs

Preheat the oven to 350°F. Coat an 8-inch square baking pan with cooking spray. Set aside.

In a small skillet, sauté the onion and mushrooms in olive oil about 5 minutes, until the onion is tender. Pour into a large bowl. Add the asparagus, green beans, salt, pepper, and cheese. Combine. Add the milk and the eggs; mix well.

Pour into the prepared pan. Sprinkle with the breadcrumbs. Bake about 25 minutes, or until the top of the omelet is golden.

Arepas with Sunny-Side-Up Eggs, Wisconsin Cheese, and Salsa Fresca

CHEF GUILLERMO PERNOT

MAKES 6 SERVINGS

SALSA FRESCA

1 cup roughly chopped fresh cilantro

5 Roma (plum) tomatoes, roughly chopped

½ red onion, coarsely chopped

2 serrano chiles, split with seeds removed, coarsely chopped

¼ cup fresh lime juice

1½ tablespoons extra-virgin olive oil

Salt and pepper, to taste

AREPAS

1 cup canned hominy

¾ cup fresh or frozen, thawed corn kernels

¼ cup sugar

½ cup milk, divided

1 cup (4 ounces) shredded aged Gouda, queso quesadilla, or asadero cheese

½ cup cornmeal

1 teaspoon kosher salt

2 tablespoons all-purpose flour (optional)

Olive oil for frying

12 eggs

For the salsa fresca, pulse the cilantro, tomatoes, red onion, and chiles in a food processor until chopped. Place in a bowl. Stir in the lime juice and olive oil. Season with salt and pepper. Set aside.

For the arepas, combine the hominy, corn, sugar, and ¼ cup of the milk in the food processor. Purée until medium ground. Transfer to a medium bowl. Stir in the remaining ¼ cup of milk, the cheese, the cornmeal, and the salt. If the mixture is too thin to form cakes, add 2 tablespoons of flour. Let rest 20 minutes. Form the dough into 12 (2½-inch) cakes, ½-inch thick. Heat a thin layer of oil in a large nonstick skillet. Fry the arepas until golden brown, about 2 minutes on each side. Keep warm.

Fry the eggs, sunny-side up (or poach, if preferred). Into each of six shallow soup bowls, spoon ⅓ to ½ cup of the salsa fresca. Top with 2 arepas and 2 eggs. Serve immediately.

Gouda, Asparagus, and Mushroom Omelet

CHEF GOVIND ARMSTRONG

MAKES 2 SERVINGS

4 medium-size, fresh morel mushrooms*

3 spears jumbo asparagus

4 eggs

2 tablespoons crème fraîche or sour cream

Salt and pepper, to taste

4 teaspoons grapeseed or canola oil, divided

2 teaspoons unsalted butter, divided

4 thin slices Gouda cheese, ½ ounce each

* Substitute shiitake or portobello mushrooms if morels are unavailable.

Preheat the oven to broil.

Clean the mushrooms and cut into ¼-inch rings (strips if using shiitakes or portobellos). Trim the asparagus, peel the bottom 4 inches, and cut thinly on the bias. In a medium bowl, whisk together the eggs, crème fraîche, salt, and pepper (makes about 1 cup).

In a nonstick skillet, heat 2 teaspoons of the oil over medium-high heat. Sauté the mushrooms until fully cooked, about 2 minutes. Season with salt and pepper; set aside. Repeat the process with the asparagus. Set aside.

In an 8-inch nonstick omelet pan, melt 1 teaspoon of the butter over medium-high heat. Add half of the egg mixture. Using a rubber spatula, lift the cooked egg at the edges, tilting the pan so the uncooked egg flows to the exposed pan surface. Cook until the eggs are set but still shiny. Remove from the heat. Spoon half of the vegetables onto one half of the cooked eggs. Flip the uncovered half over the vegetables. Roll onto a small baking pan. Repeat with the remaining egg mixture and vegetables.

When both servings have cooked, place two thin slices of cheese on top of each omelet. Place the pan under the broiler until the cheese is just melted. Serve immediately.

Gorgonzola, Tomato, and Spaghetti Squash Frittata

CHEFS MARY AND GREG SONNIER

MAKES 4 TO 6 SERVINGS

SQUASH

½ small yellow onion, diced

¼ small red bell pepper, diced

4 tablespoons extra-virgin olive oil, divided

1 cup cooked spaghetti squash, completely drained of any liquid*

1½ teaspoons salt, divided

¾ teaspoon freshly ground pepper, divided

FRITTATA

8 eggs

½ cup heavy cream

1½ teaspoons Worcestershire sauce

4 shakes Tabasco sauce

1 medium tomato, thinly sliced

⅔ cup (4 ounces) Gorgonzola cheese, broken into 8 chunks

* To cook the squash, preheat the oven to 350°F. Cut the squash straight through the middle, scrape out the seeds with a spoon, and discard the seeds. Put the squash halves cut side down in a baking pan with about 1 to 2 inches of water. Cover with foil; bake for 30 to 50 minutes, depending on the size of the squash, until you can easily insert and remove a knife or fork. Remove from the oven; cool briefly. With a fork, pull the squash strands from the skin and place on paper towels to absorb moisture.

For the squash, in a small skillet, sauté the onion and bell pepper in 2 tablespoons of the olive oil until soft, 2 to 3 minutes. Stir in the squash, ½ teaspoon of the salt, and ¼ teaspoon of the pepper. Remove from the heat and set aside to cool.

For the frittata, heat the oven to 350°F. In a large bowl, whisk together the eggs, the remaining salt and pepper, the cream, and the Worcestershire and Tabasco sauces. Drain any liquid from the squash mixture and stir the squash mixture into the eggs. Set aside.

In a 10-inch ovenproof skillet, heat the remaining 2 tablespoons of olive oil to smoking point. Pour in the squash mixture. Remove from the heat. Top with the tomato slices and cheese. Bake 25 to 30 minutes or until the custard is set and slightly browned. Let rest 10 minutes.

To serve, slide onto a serving plate. Cut into wedges.

Hash Brown Frittata

MAKES 6

1 cup (4 ounces) shredded Gouda cheese

1 cup refrigerated shredded hash brown potatoes

8 crisply cooked bacon slices, crumbled

½ cup chopped green or red bell pepper

¼ cup green onion slices

5 eggs

1 cup milk

¼ teaspoon black pepper

1 small tomato, sliced

Preheat the oven to 350°F.

Combine the cheese, potatoes, bacon, bell pepper, and onion; toss lightly. Spoon into a well-buttered 9-inch pie plate.

In a medium bowl, beat the eggs; stir in the milk and the black pepper. Pour over the potato mixture; top with the tomato slices. Bake for 45 to 50 minutes or until the center is set. Allow to stand 5 minutes before serving.

Variations: Edam may be used in place of Gouda. The frittata can be baked in individual ramekins.

Queen Anne's Wild Rice Quiche

1 unbaked 9-inch pastry shell, prepared or homemade

1 tablespoon butter

1 cup cooked wild rice

⅓ cup diced baked ham

1 cup (4 ounces) finely shredded Monterey Jack cheese

½ cup minced white onion

3 eggs, well beaten

1 cup whipping cream

½ cup half-and-half

Preheat the oven to 425°F and bake the pastry shell for 5 minutes. Remove the shell from the oven and dot with butter, while the shell is still hot. Fill the shell with the rice, ham, cheese, and onion.

Beat the eggs in a mixing bowl with an electric mixer; blend in the cream and the half-and-half. Pour over the ingredients in the pastry shell. Reduce the oven temperature to 350°F and bake the quiche for about 50 minutes or until firm.

Cut into wedges and serve warm.

Ina's Pasta Frittata

INA PICKNEY

MAKES 6 TO 8 SERVINGS

Vegetable oil

¾ cup chopped onion

2 garlic cloves, minced

1 tablespoon olive oil

¾ cup julienned red bell pepper

1½ cups sliced mushrooms

1½ cups julienned zucchini

1 teaspoon dried oregano

1½ teaspoons salt

1 teaspoon pepper

10 eggs

1¼ cups whole milk

1½ cups (6 ounces) shredded sharp Cheddar cheese

½ cup (about 2 ounces) grated Parmesan cheese

2 (8-ounce) packages cream cheese

3 cups cooked spaghetti

2⅔ cups prepared tomato sauce, warmed

Preheat the oven to 350°F.

Lightly brush a 10-inch round pan with vegetable oil. Cut a piece of parchment, place in the pan, brush again with oil, and set aside.

Sauté the onion and garlic in the olive oil until soft. Add the red bell pepper, mushrooms, and zucchini, and continue to cook until all the vegetables are soft. Drain the liquid and add the oregano, salt, and pepper. Set aside to cool slightly.

In a large mixer bowl, beat the eggs, milk, Cheddar, and Parmesan cheeses on low speed. When combined, add the cream cheese in small, bite-size bits (pull off the pieces by hand).

Put the cooked spaghetti into the baking pan. Add the vegetables. Pour in the egg mixture, and mix with your hands to equally distribute the ingredients. Pat down so the liquid covers the solids.

Bake for 30 to 40 minutes until firm to the touch and lightly brown. The frittata will puff and settle. Cut into six to eight wedges and serve immediately on a pool of warm tomato sauce.

Tip: If you want to serve the frittata the next day, bake for only 25 minutes, cool, and then refrigerate. When ready to serve, cut into slices and reheat for 10 minutes at 400°F.

Southwestern Spinach Quiche

²/₃ cup cornmeal

1 tablespoon butter

³/₄ teaspoon salt, divided

1²/₃ cups cold water

1¹/₂ cups (6 ounces) shredded asadero or queso quesadilla cheese

2 tablespoons all-purpose flour

2 eggs

1 cup milk

¹/₂ of a 10-ounce package frozen chopped spinach, thawed and squeezed dry

¹/₂ cup chopped red bell pepper

1 tablespoon minced jalapeño pepper

1 garlic clove, minced

Preheat the oven to 350°F.

Stir together the cornmeal, butter, ¹/₂ teaspoon of the salt, and the water in a 1¹/₂-quart casserole; cover. Microwave on high for 3 minutes; stir. Continue microwaving for 4 to 5 minutes or until the batter is very thick, stirring every 2 minutes. Spread the batter onto the bottom and sides of a 9-inch pie plate, to form a crust.

In a small bowl, toss the cheese with the flour. In a separate bowl, beat the eggs; stir in the milk, spinach, bell pepper, jalapeño, garlic, the remaining ¹/₄ teaspoon salt, and the cheese mixture. Pour over the crust. Bake for 50 to 55 minutes or until set.

Cheesy Wisconsin Soufflé

4 tablespoons (½ stick) butter

¼ cup all-purpose flour

1½ cups milk

¼ teaspoon salt

⅛ teaspoon cayenne pepper

2 cups (8 ounces) shredded Colby cheese

6 eggs, separated

2 tablespoons chopped fresh parsley

¼ teaspoon thyme (optional)

Preheat the oven to 325°F.

In a 2-quart saucepan, melt the butter and stir in the flour. Gradually add the milk; stirring until smooth. Cook, stirring constantly, until the sauce is thickened. Stir in the salt and cayenne. Add the cheese and heat, stirring just until the cheese melts. Remove the cheese sauce from the heat.

In a small bowl, beat the egg yolks slightly. Add a small amount of hot cheese sauce to the egg yolks; beat. Return the saucepan to the heat and slowly add the egg mixture, sitrring constantly to prevent lumping. Stir in the parsley and thyme. Set aside.

Beat the egg whites until stiff peaks form. Gently fold the cheese mixture into the egg whites. Pour into a 2-quart soufflé dish or straight-sided casserole. With the tip of a spoon, make a slight indentation, or "track," around the top of the soufflé, 1 inch from the edge of the dish, to make the crown that will rise on the soufflé surface. Bake for 45 to 60 minutes or until deep golden brown and the center is set.

Wisconsin Cheese Pie

2 eggs, well beaten

1 cup milk

¾ cup all-purpose flour

1 cup ham, chopped

½ cup (2 ounces) shredded Muenster cheese

½ cup (2 ounces) shredded Cheddar cheese

1 tablespoon chopped onion

½ cup chopped black olives or mushrooms (optional)

Preheat the oven to 400°F.

Grease a 9-inch pie pan. Set aside.

In a medium bowl, combine the eggs, milk, and flour; beat until smooth with a rotary beater. Stir in the ham, Muenster and Cheddar cheeses, and onion. Pour into the pie pan. Top with black olives or mushrooms, if desired. Bake for 30 to 35 minutes until light brown and puffy. Serve at once.

Golden Crêpe Lorraine Cups

12 (4-inch) crêpes*

2 eggs

⅛ teaspoon ground nutmeg

¼ teaspoon white or black pepper

1 cup milk

½ cup diced white onion

½ cup shredded Gruyère cheese

1 cup diced ham

* These can be purchased frozen, or use your favorite crêpe batter recipe.

Preheat the oven to 350°F.

Coat a 12-cup muffin pan with cooking spray. Line each cup with a crêpe.

In a medium mixing bowl, beat the eggs, nutmeg, and pepper together. Add the milk and mix. In the bottom of each crêpe cup, place an equal amount of the diced onion. Repeat with the cheese and then the ham. Pour an equal amount of the egg mixture into each of the crêpe cups (about ⅔ ounce). Bake for 25 minutes, or until the filling has set and is slightly brown. Cool briefly and serve.

New Glarus Cheese and Onion Pie

MAKES 6 SERVINGS

1½ cups sliced onion

1 tablespoon butter

4 eggs

1 unbaked 9-inch pie crust

1½ cups half-and-half

½ teaspoon salt

⅛ to ¼ teaspoon nutmeg

⅛ teaspoon pepper

2 cups (8 ounces) shredded
   Swiss or baby Swiss cheese

1 tablespoon cornstarch

Preheat the oven to 400°F.

In a medium skillet, sauté the onion in butter until transparent, about 5 minutes; set aside. In a small bowl, beat the eggs; brush a small amount on the inside of the pie crust. Add the half-and-half, salt, nutmeg, and pepper to the remaining beaten eggs; beat to blend thoroughly. Toss the cheese with the cornstarch. Cover the bottom of the pie crust with the onion and the cheese. Pour the egg mixture over the top. Dust with additional nutmeg. Bake in the center of the oven for 35 to 45 minutes until set, browned, and puffy. Cool slightly. Cut into wedges to serve.

Wisconsin Cheese and Sausage Strata

MAKES 8 SERVINGS

12 slices white bread, cubed

1⅓ cups (about 8 ounces) cubed Cheddar cheese

⅔ cup (about 4 ounces) cubed mozzarella cheese

8 ounces Polish sausage or cubed cooked ham, or 16 ounces bacon, cooked and crumbled

1 (4-ounce) can mushroom stems and pieces, drained

6 eggs

2 cups milk

¼ teaspoon salt

¼ teaspoon pepper

¼ teaspoon dry mustard

Grease a 13 x 9-inch baking dish. Place half the cubed bread in the prepared baking dish. Cover with the cheeses, meat, and mushrooms. Top with the remaining cubed bread.

Beat the eggs with the milk and seasonings. Pour over the bread, making sure to coat all of the cubes. Cover and refrigerate overnight or at least 4 hours.

To complete the strata, preheat the oven to 350°F. Remove the strata from the refrigerator. Bake for 1 hour or until a knife inserted in the center comes out clean.

Gruyère and Provolone–Stuffed French Toast

FRUIT SALSA

4 cups ¼-inch diced fresh mango

2 cups ¼-inch diced fresh pineapple

1 cup chopped fresh cilantro

1 or 2 jalapeño peppers, finely chopped

¼ cup fresh lime juice

¼ cup firmly packed light brown sugar

FRENCH TOAST

24 slices homemade quality white or multi-grain bread

8 ounces Gruyère cheese, thinly sliced or shaved

8 ounces aged provolone cheese, thinly sliced or shaved

4 large fresh Anjou pears

¾ cup coarsely chopped pecans

12 eggs, beaten

¾ cup milk or water

12 tablespoons (1½ sticks) butter, softened

Additional butter and maple syrup, for serving

For the fruit salsa, combine all the salsa ingredients; keep refrigerated until ready to serve.

For the French toast, lay out 2 slices of bread per serving. Arrange the Gruyère cheese on one of the slices of bread, and the provolone on the other. Divide the cheese equally between the 12 servings.

Cut the pears into ⅛-inch slices from top to bottom. Place a layer of pear slices on top of the cheese on one side of the sandwich. Sprinkle with the pecans. Cover with the other half of the sandwich, so that the pears and nuts are sandwiched between the Gruyère and the provolone.

Beat the eggs and milk together. Dip the sandwiches in the mixture, allowing the mixture to soak in for a minute or two. Spread the griddle with the butter. Grill the French toast sandwiches until golden brown on both sides and the cheese is melted. Cut into quarters and serve with additional butter and maple syrup, with fruit salsa spooned on the side.

French Toast with Peaches and Wisconsin Mascarpone Cream

CHEF RHYS LEWIS

MAKES 12 SERVINGS

FRENCH TOAST

4 eggs

1 cup milk

1 tablespoon cardamom, ground

Butter for cooking

12 slices high-quality white bread

SYRUP

1 cup water

¾ cup firmly packed light brown sugar

1 tablespoon finely chopped fresh ginger

Butter for cooking

8 peaches, peeled and sliced

MASCARPONE CREAM

1 cup (8 ounces) heavy (whipping) cream

1 tablespoon sugar

1 teaspoon pure vanilla extract

1 (8-ounce) container mascarpone cheese, at room temperature

For the French toast, combine the eggs, milk, and cardamom in a large bowl. Over medium heat, melt about 4 tablespoons of butter in a large skillet. Dip the bread slices into the mixture and fry a few slices for 2 to 3 minutes on each side, until golden brown. Reserve in a warm place. Repeat until all the bread is used, adding more butter as necessary.

For the syrup, combine the water, brown sugar, and ginger. Bring to a boil and simmer 5 minutes. Strain the syrup through a wire sieve. This step may be done in advance. In a sauté pan, melt a small portion of butter and sauté the peaches until just warm. Add the reserved ginger syrup and bring to a simmer. Turn off the heat.

For the mascarpone cream, in a stainless steel bowl, whip the cream with the tablespoon of sugar and the vanilla extract until it has soft peaks.

Place the cheese in a second bowl and blend in one-third of the cream mixture. Add the remaining cream and blend. Avoid overmixing. Chill the cream until serving time.

To serve the French toast, cut the toast slices diagonally and arrange on twelve plates. Spoon the peach compote onto the toast. Top with the cream.

Lemon Ricotta Pancakes with Warm Blueberry Compote

CHEF MINDY SEGAL

MAKES 18 PANCAKES

BLUEBERRY COMPOTE

4 cups (2 pints) blueberries,
    fresh or frozen

2 teaspoons cornstarch

1 cup sugar

½ cup water

¼ cup prepared lemon curd
    (from 10- to 12-ounce jar)

1 tablespoon fresh orange juice

Pinch of salt

1 tablespoon butter

½ teaspoon pure vanilla extract

PANCAKES

2 cups all-purpose flour

2 teaspoons baking powder

½ teaspoon salt

2 tablespoons sugar

Grated zest of 1 lemon

2 eggs, separated

1 cup (8 ounces) ricotta cheese,
    preferably whole-milk

1½ cups milk, preferably whole

Prepared lemon curd (from
    10- to 12-ounce jar)

Confectioners' sugar

For the blueberry compote, in a large sauté pan, combine the blueberries, cornstarch, sugar, water, lemon curd, orange juice, and a pinch of salt. Gently cook over medium heat until the blueberries are tender but not broken down and the mixture simmers and thickens. Remove from the heat; stir in the butter and vanilla. Set aside to cool slightly.

For the pancakes, in a medium bowl, sift the flour, baking powder, salt, and sugar. Stir in the lemon zest. Set aside. In a large bowl, mix the egg yolks and the cheese. Fold in the dry ingredients alternately with the milk. In a separate bowl, whip the egg whites until medium-stiff peaks form. Fold into the batter.

Heat a buttered nonstick skillet or griddle over medium-high heat or to 350°F (water drops on the skillet should skitter or sizzle when hot). For each pancake, pour ¼ to ⅓ cup batter and cook until bubbles form on top. Turn and cook until the bottom is golden brown and the pancake is cooked through.

To serve, stack three pancakes on each plate with a dollop of lemon curd between pancakes. Sprinkle with confectioners' sugar and pour the compote over the pancakes.

Wisconsin Swiss Pancakes

2 cups buttermilk baking mix

1½ cups milk

½ cup sour cream

1 egg, beaten

¼ teaspoon nutmeg

1½ cups (6 ounces) shredded
    Swiss cheese

Butter, for griddle

Sautéed apple slices (optional)

Combine all of the ingredients except the cheese and apple slices in a large mixing bowl. Blend at low speed until the ingredients are just combined (do not over-mix). Stir in the cheese. Allow the batter to stand while preheating the griddle.

Lightly butter the griddle; then heat the griddle until a few drops of water dance on the surface, or set the automatic temperature control to 375°F. When the griddle is hot, pour the batter onto the griddle, using a scant ¼ cup of batter for each pancake. Cook each pancake until bubbles break on the surface and the edges are cooked; turn and cook the other side until golden. Serve warm with sautéed apple slices.

Breakfast Polenta Crostini
with Ham and Wisconsin Asiago

MAKES 12 SERVINGS

2 (11-ounce) tubes prepared polenta with sun-dried tomato

¾ cup (3 ounces) shredded Asiago cheese

1 large Roma tomato, seeded and chopped

2 tablespoons pine nuts, toasted and coarsely chopped

2 tablespoons chopped fresh basil or ½ teaspoon dried basil

2 tablespoons mayonnaise

1½ teaspoons finely diced oil-packed sun-dried tomatoes

9 thin slices cured ham

Preheat the oven to 400°F.

Coat a baking sheet with cooking spray. Slice each tube of polenta into six slices. Arrange the slices on the baking sheet. With a small spoon, scoop out a shallow depression in each slice. Spray the slices lightly with cooking spray. Bake for 20 minutes.

In a small bowl, combine the cheese, Roma tomato, pine nuts, and basil. Set aside. In another small bowl, combine the mayonnaise and sun-dried tomatoes. Set aside. Stack three slices of ham and cut into quarters, keeping the stacks intact. Repeat twice.

To assemble, spoon some of the cheese mixture into the depressions in the polenta slices. Top each polenta slice with about ½ teaspoon of the mayonnaise mixture. Add a stack of ham slice quarters to each polenta slice. Top each ham slice with some of the remaining cheese mixture.

Return the crostini to the oven, and heat 2 to 3 minutes or until the cheese is slightly melted.

Savory Bread Pudding with Wisconsin Colby

MAKES 24 SERVINGS

1 pound pork sausage

1 cup chopped onion

8 cups seven-grain bread, cut into 1-inch cubes

1½ cups (6 ounces) shredded Colby cheese, divided

4 eggs, slightly beaten

3¼ cups milk

2 tablespoons chopped fresh sage or 1 teaspoon dried sage, crushed

½ teaspoon salt

½ teaspoon freshly ground pepper

In a large skillet, brown the sausage and the onion; drain. In a large bowl, combine the cooked sausage, onion, bread cubes, and 1 cup of the cheese; toss to combine.

In a medium bowl, beat the eggs, milk, sage, salt, and pepper. Pour over the bread mixture; mix well. Cover and let stand for 30 minutes, or cover and refrigerate overnight.

Preheat the oven to 350°F. Lightly grease a 13 x 9-inch baking dish. Pour the bread mixture into the baking dish. Bake for 35 to 45 minutes, or until golden brown and the center is set. Sprinkle with the remaining cheese. Bake another 2 minutes, or until the cheese is melted. Let stand 10 minutes before serving.

Wisconsin Cheese Danish Pinwheels

MAKES 8 PINWHEELS

1½ cups all-purpose flour

¾ cup whole wheat flour

3 tablespoons sugar

2 teaspoons baking powder

½ teaspoon baking soda

⅛ teaspoon salt

¼ teaspoon cinnamon

1 cup plain low-fat yogurt

2 tablespoons butter, melted

CHEESE FILLING

½ cup (4 ounces) part-skim ricotta cheese

2 teaspoons sugar

Grated zest of 1 lemon

GLAZE

½ cup confectioners' sugar

1¾ teaspoons milk

½ teaspoon vanilla extract

Preheat the oven to 400°F.

In a large bowl, combine the flours, sugar, baking powder, baking soda, salt, and cinnamon. In a smaller bowl, combine the yogurt and the melted butter. Add the yogurt mixture to the dry mixture. Turn out onto a floured board and knead several times to make a soft dough.

Divide the dough in half. Roll half of the dough into an 8-inch square. Cut the square into 4-inch squares. Repeat with the remaining half of the dough. Form a pinwheel with each square by cutting a slit 1 inch from the center to each corner diagonally. Use a spatula to transfer the dough to an ungreased baking sheet.

For the cheese filling, in a small bowl, combine the cheese filling ingredients.

Place a heaping spoonful of filling in the center of the dough square. Lift and fold every other point over the filling. Press the center to hold the points in place. Repeat with the remaining dough. Bake for about 10 to 12 minutes until golden brown, while preparing the glaze.

For the glaze, in a small bowl, mix the glaze ingredients until smooth. Set aside until the pinwheels are baked. Remove the baked pinwheels from the oven and place on a a wire rack. Drizzle immediately with the glaze. Transfer to a serving plate and serve warm.

Colby Cheese Scones

MAKES 16 SCONES

2 cups all-purpose flour

2 tablespoons sugar

1 tablespoon baking powder

¼ teaspoon baking soda

½ teaspoon salt

1¼ cups (5 ounces) shredded Colby cheese

½ cup sour cream

3 tablespoons milk

1 egg, beaten

¼ cup oil

Additional milk, for brushing scones

Preheat the oven to 425°F.

In a large bowl, combine the flour, sugar, baking powder, baking soda, and salt. Add the cheese to the combined dry ingredients; mix lightly.

In a small bowl, combine the sour cream with 3 tablespoons of milk; blend in the egg and oil. Add to the flour mixture; stir until the mixture forms a ball. Pour onto a floured surface.

Knead the dough 15 times and divide the dough in half. Pat each half into a 7-inch circle. Brush the tops with milk. Cut each piece of dough into eight wedges. Place 2 inches apart on a greased baking sheet. Bake for 10 to 12 minutes, or until the bottoms are golden brown.

APPETIZERS

Baby Swiss Croutons with Double Pestos ...48

Bruschetta with Goat Cheese and Fresh Peach Chutney ...49

Bruschetta with Wisconsin Cheese Toppings ...51

Bruschetta with Wisconsin Limburger, Figs, and Grilled Onions ...52

Wisconsin Cheesy Bagels ...53

Fontina-Gorgonzola Crostini with Exotic Mushrooms ...54

Inside-Out Grilled Cheese with Red Onion Jam ...56

Salmon Gravlax on Wisconsin Havarti Crostini...57

Mascarpone Crostini and Mother's Tomato Conserve ...59

Pistachio–Wisconsin Peppercorn Feta Crostini ...60

Rhubarb Compote with Wisconsin Pleasant Ridge Reserve on Toast ...62

Artichoke, Spinach, and Pepper Jack Quesadillas ...65

Black Bean Quesadillas ...66

Corn Nachos with Wisconsin Muenster and Salsa Cruda ...67

Asiago Cheese Puffs ...68

Wisconsin Blue Cheese Cheesecake ...71

Borek (Flaky Cheese-Filled Pastry with Herbs) ...72

Wisconsin Cheese Straws ...74

Wisconsin Brie en Croûte ...76

Wisconsin Feta Triangles ...77

Goat Cheese Turnovers with Smoked Salmon and Leeks ...78

Heirloom Tomato and Asiago Tart ...79

Miami Spice Napoleons with Wisconsin Queso Fresco Cheese ...81

Wisconsin Cheese Tart with Apple-Walnut Salad ...82

Crumbled Feta Salad Tarts ...84

Gruyère and Onion Tart ...85

Manchego with Quince Paste ...86

Red Pepper and Cumin–Marinated Manchego ...87

Baby Swiss Croutons with Double Pestos

MAKES 12 CROUTONS

MINT PESTO

8 ounces fresh mint

2 tablespoons honey

1 ounce pecans

1 ounce dessert wine

Olive oil, to taste

ARUGULA PESTO

8 ounces fresh arugula

Olive oil, to taste

CROUTONS

1 loaf French bread, sliced into 12 thin croutons

2 Granny Smith apples, cored and thinly sliced

16 ounces baby Swiss cheese, thinly sliced

Preheat the oven to 350°F.

For the mint pesto, place the mint, honey, pecans, and wine in a food processor. While processing, slowly add the olive oil until the pesto is emulsified.

For the arugula pesto, process the arugula, slowly adding the olive oil until pesto forms. (This pesto will be thicker and not emulsified.)

To assemble the croutons, spread a thin layer of the arugula pesto over each crouton top. Add 1 apple slice and 1 slice of cheese to each crouton. Bake until the cheese is melted.

To serve, arrange the croutons on a serving dish. Accent each with a dollop of mint pesto.

Bruschetta with Goat Cheese and Fresh Peach Chutney

MAKES 8 TO 10 SERVINGS

CHUTNEY

2 ripe but firm medium peaches, peeled, halved, pitted, thinly sliced

½ cup finely chopped golden raisins

½ fresh jalapeño, seeded and finely chopped

2 teaspoons finely chopped peeled fresh ginger

2 teaspoons finely chopped shallot

1 tablespoon sugar

2 tablespoons fresh orange juice

Fine sea salt or kosher salt and freshly ground pepper, to taste

ROASTED GARLIC

2 large heads garlic

2 tablespoons olive oil

Fine sea salt or kosher salt and freshly ground pepper, to taste

ASSEMBLY

1 French bread baguette, cut into ⅓-inch-thick slices

Olive oil

1 (8- to 11-ounce) log soft fresh goat cheese

Fresh cilantro sprigs (optional), for garnish

For the chutney, place the peaches, raisins, jalapeños, ginger, shallots, sugar, orange juice, and salt and pepper in a medium bowl; toss gently to combine. Cover and chill for 1 to 2 hours before serving, tossing occasionally. Allow the chutney to come to room temperature before serving.

For the roasted garlic, preheat the oven to 350°F. Cut the top ¼ inch off of the heads of garlic to expose the cloves. Place the garlic in a small baking dish. Add the oil, and sprinkle with salt and pepper; toss to coat. Turn the garlic cut side up. Cover the baking dish tightly with aluminum foil. Bake the garlic for about 1 hour, or until the skins are golden brown and the cloves are tender. Allow the garlic to cool. When the garlic is cool enough to handle, squeeze the garlic cloves from the skins into a small bowl; discard the skins.

To assemble the bruschetta, preheat the oven to 450°F. Arrange the baguette slices on a baking sheet and brush both sides with olive oil. Bake for about 8 minutes, or until golden. (Bruschetta toasts can be prepared 1 day ahead. Let them cool; then seal them in an airtight container or resealable plastic bag and keep at room temperature.) Spread each toast with some roasted garlic; top with some goat cheese and chutney. Garnish with fresh cilantro, if desired.

Bruschetta with Wisconsin Cheese Toppings

MAKES 24 BRUSCHETTA

TUSCAN TOPPING

1 cup sun-dried tomatoes in oil, drained and chopped

½ cup toasted pine nuts, coarsely chopped

½ cup green onions, minced

1 cup (abour 4 ounces) grated Asiago cheese

2 cups (8 ounces) shredded Provolone cheese

PESTO TOPPING

4 cups fresh basil

2 cups fresh parsley

4 garlic cloves

¼ cup pine nuts, toasted

1 cup (about 4 ounces) grated Asiago cheese

1 cup olive oil

HILLS OF ROME TOPPING

3 tablespoons olive oil

2 large yellow onions, chopped

4 garlic cloves, minced

1 tablespoon dried rosemary

2 cups (8 ounces) shredded mozzarella cheese

1 cup (about 4 ounces) grated Asiago cheese

Freshly ground pepper

BRUSCHETTA

Italian bread loaves, split and cut into 24 4-inch pieces

For the Tuscan topping, mix all of the ingredients.

For the pesto topping, in the bowl of a food processor, combine the basil, parsley, garlic, and pine nuts. Process until smooth. Add the cheese and process 30 seconds. Slowly add the oil while the motor is running.

For the Hills of Rome topping, in a large skillet, heat the oil. Add the onions and sauté 5 minutes. Add the garlic and sauté an additional 8 minutes or until caramelized, stirring often. Stir in the rosemary and cook 1 minute. Remove from the heat and cool completely. In a separate bowl, mix the cheeses and pepper.

For the bruschetta, preheat the oven to 400°F.

Place the bread slices on a baking sheet. Top with your choice of toppings. For Tuscan and pesto toppings, spread 1 to 2 tablespoons on each slice of bread. For Hills of Rome topping, spread 1 tablespoon of the onion mixture on each slice of bread, and then spread 2 tablespoons of the cheese mixture on top of the onion mixture. Bake for 6 to 8 minutes, or until the bread is golden brown and heated through. Serve immediately.

Note: Each topping recipe makes 3 cups. These toppings may also be used to top focaccia or pizza, or they can be rolled into bread dough before baking.

Bruschetta with Wisconsin Limburger, Figs, and Grilled Onions

CHEF SUSAN GOSS

MAKES 24 BRUSCHETTA

FIG TOPPING

½ cup olive oil, divided

½ red onion, chopped

Salt and freshly ground pepper, to taste

½ tablespoon minced garlic

6 dried black figs, stems trimmed, cut into sixths

1 cup seeded and diced tomatoes

1 tablespoon cream sherry

¾ cup chicken stock

2 teaspoons minced fresh thyme, or ½ teaspoon dried

BRUSCHETTA

12 ounces Limburger cheese

24 slices crusty dark rye bread

Freshly ground pepper, to taste

For the fig topping, in a medium skillet heat 1 tablespoon of the olive oil over medium-low heat and sauté the onion until tender, about 10 minutes. Season with salt and pepper. Add the garlic and sauté until fragrant. Add the figs and tomatoes and sauté for 3 to 4 minutes.

Increase the heat to high and add the cream sherry, stirring until the sherry is absorbed. Add the chicken stock and bring to a boil. Lower the heat and simmer until the figs are tender and the liquid has reduced. Add the thyme and remove from the heat. Let cool to room temperature.

For the bruschetta, Preheat the oven to broil.

Cut the cheese into 12 equal slices, and cut each slice in half to make 24 pieces. Set aside.

Brush the bread slices with the remaining olive oil and place them on the broiler rack. Toast the bread lightly, at least 4 inches under the heating element. Remove from the oven.

To serve the bruschetta, top each piece of toast with one slice of cheese, and spoon approximately 1 tablespoon of the fig topping on top. Sprinkle the pepper over the figs and serve.

Wisconsin Cheesy Bagels

1 cup (4 ounces) shredded Cheddar cheese

1 cup (4 ounces) shredded Swiss or Monterey Jack cheese

¼ cup slivered almonds, toasted

¼ cup real bacon bits

¼ cup mayonnaise

¼ cup chopped green onions

¼ cup sour cream

2 egg whites, stiffly beaten

1 (11-ounce) package frozen miniature bagels, thawed, split, and toasted

Preheat the oven to broil.

Combine the cheeses, nuts, bacon, mayonnaise, green onions, and sour cream; mix well. Fold in the egg whites. Spread the mixture on the bagel halves. Place the bagels on a baking sheet. Broil until bubbly, about 3 minutes.

Fontina-Gorgonzola Crostini with Exotic Mushrooms

CHEF TOM CATHERALL

MAKES 8 CROSTINI

1 tablespoon extra-virgin olive oil

1 tablespoon butter

8 ounces fresh exotic mushrooms (such as shiitake or oyster), sliced

8 ounces portobello mushrooms, sliced

1 teaspoon minced mixed fresh herbs, such as thyme, rosemary, and basil

1 tablespoon minced fresh Italian parsley

Salt and freshly ground pepper, to taste

8 slices country bread, toasted

2 garlic cloves, peeled and halved

1 cup (4 ounces) grated fontina cheese

½ cup (3 ounces) crumbled Gorgonzola cheese

Juice of ½ lemon

Whole fresh Italian parsley leaves, for garnish

Preheat the oven to broil.

Heat the olive oil and butter in a large skillet over medium-high heat. Add the mushrooms and cook until the liquid has evaporated and the mushrooms are dry, about 10 minutes. Add the mixed herbs and parsley, and toss to mix. Season with salt and pepper. Remove from the heat.

Rub both sides of the toasted bread lightly with the garlic. Divide and distribute the warm mushrooms on top of the bread slices. Combine the cheeses and sprinkle the mixture evenly over the mushrooms. Place the mushroom toasts under the hot broiler. Broil until the cheese melts, 30 to 60 seconds. Place the toast slices on a serving platter and drizzle with the lemon juice. Garnish with the parsley leaves. Serve immediately.

Inside-Out Grilled Cheese with Red Onion Jam

CHEF TODD DOWNS

MAKES 12 SANDWICHES

RED ONION JAM

2 red onions, peeled and cut in very thin, match-size strips

¼ cup vegetable oil

½ cup rice vinegar

¼ cup grenadine syrup

Juice of 1 lemon

½ cup golden raisins

1 tablespoon fresh thyme leaves or ½ teaspoon freshly ground pepper, to taste

SANDWICHES

12 slices seeded, whole-grain bread, such as sunflower seed, 2 x 2 inches square and ⅛ inch thick, crusts removed

6 tablespoons butter, melted

24 slices queso blanco or queso blanco con frutas cheese, 2 x 2 inches square and ¼ inch thick

For the red onion jam, sauté the onion in the oil, cooking slowly until wilted, about 20 minutes. Do not brown. Add the remaining jam ingredients. Cook for about 20 minutes, or until thickened.

For the sandwiches, brush the bread slices on both sides with the melted butter. Toast until golden brown.

Heat a large, nonstick skillet over medium-high heat. Lightly grill the cheese squares until golden brown on both sides.

Place 12 of the cheese squares on a cutting board. Top each with a teaspoon of red onion jam and then a slice of the toasted bread. Top the bread with another teaspoon of jam. Top each sandwich with a slice of the remaining cheese. Press the sandwich together.

If preparing ahead, warm the sandwiches in a 350°F oven just before serving.

Salmon Gravlax on Wisconsin Havarti Crostini

MAKES 54 CROSTINI

DILL MUSTARD

½ cup Dijon mustard

1 ounce white wine

1 tablespoon chopped fresh dill

½ teaspoon black pepper

CROSTINI

3 multi-grain baguettes (about 1 pound each)

8 ounces Havarti cheese

1 pound salmon gravlax (smoked salmon may be substituted), sliced paper thin

1 bunch fresh dill

Preheat the broiler.

For the dill mustard, combine all of the ingredients.

For the crostini, cut each baguette on the bias into 18 crostini. Place the bread slices on the broiling rack. Broil the bread at least 4 inches below the heating element, until lightly browned on both sides, turning once. Remove and cool.

Thinly slice the cheese into triangles approximately the size of the crostini. On each baguette slice, spread a small amount of the dill mustard, and then place one slice of cheese. Follow with a rolled or folded slice of gravlax. Garnish with a small sprig of fresh dill.

Mascarpone Crostini and Mother's Tomato Conserve

CHEF RHYS LEWIS

MAKES 24 CROSTINI

CROSTINI

¼ pound (1 stick) unsalted butter, clarified*

24 thin slices French bread

TOMATO CONSERVE

6 cups ½-inch-diced peeled blanched tomatoes**

4 cups sugar

2 cinnamon sticks

1 tablespoon whole cloves

2 lemons, peeled, seeded, and cut into ¼-inch dice

1 orange, peeled, seeded, and cut into ¼-inch dice

TOPPING

2 cups (about 1 pound) mascarpone cheese, at room temperature

12 sprigs fresh cilantro, for garnish

* To clarify the butter: Melt the butter over medium heat. Stir without allowing it to boil. The butter will form three layers: milk solids on top, clarified butter in the middle, and milk solids on the bottom. As the butter continues to warm, skim off the top layer and discard. Carefully pour off the clear melted butter into a separate container and discard any remaining milk solids.

** To blanch the tomatoes: Immerse the tomatoes in boiling water for 15 to 30 seconds. Plunge into cold water to stop the cooking process. The tomatoes will then be easy to peel.

For the crostini, preheat the oven to 350°F. Meanwhile, warm the clarified butter and pour it out on a jelly-roll pan. Dip the top side of each slice of bread in the butter and place, unbuttered side down, on a separate baking sheet. Bake for 7 to 10 minutes, until golden brown and crisp. Remove the pan from the oven and cool the bread to room temperature on a wire rack.

For the tomato conserve, in a noncorrosive saucepan combine the tomatoes, sugar, cinnamon, cloves, lemons, and orange. Simmer gently for 30 minutes over low heat. Drain the conserve, reserving the juice and setting aside the tomato mixture. Place the juice in a heavy-bottomed saucepan and cook until reduced by half. Pour the juice over the tomato mixture and refrigerate until chilled.

For the topping, use a pallet knife to spread an equal portion of the cheese onto each of the crostini. Follow with an equal portion of the tomato conserve on each.

To serve the crostini, arrange two crostini on each of twelve plates, and garnish each plate with a sprig of cilantro.

Tip: The tomato conserve may be prepared in advance.

Pistachio–Wisconsin Peppercorn Feta Crostini

1 cup (6 ounces) crumbled feta cheese with peppercorns (or 1 cup regular feta cheese mixed with 1 teaspoon cracked peppercorns)

1 (8-ounce) package cream cheese, softened

⅓ cup chopped pistachios

1 loaf French bread (12 inches long), cut in ½-inch slices

⅓ cup extra-virgin olive oil

Preheat the broiler.

Combine the cheeses and nuts; mix well. Set aside.

Brush both sides of the bread slices with olive oil, and place the bread on the broiling rack. Broil the bread at least 4 inches below the heating element, until lightly browned on both sides, turning once. Spread each slice with the cheese mixture.

Rhubarb Compote with Wisconsin Pleasant Ridge Reserve on Toast

CHEF TORY MILLER

MAKES 20 SERVINGS

¼ pound sliced bacon, diced

1 sweet onion, thinly sliced

2 stalks red rhubarb, diced

3 tablespoons apple cider vinegar

½ cup firmly packed light brown sugar

Pinch of ground cinnamon

Pinch of ground cardamom

1 teaspoon chopped fresh chives

1 teaspoon chopped fresh parsley

20 slices whole-grain bread

20 ounces Pleasant Ridge Reserve cheese*

* Gruyère or Alpine-style aged Swiss may be substituted for the Pleasant Ridge Reserve cheese.

Heat a large skillet over medium-high heat. Add the bacon and cook until brown and crisp. Add the onion, stirring to pick up the browned bacon bits on the bottom of the pan. Reduce the heat to medium-low; cook 8 to 10 minutes, until the onions are soft and slightly caramelized. Stir in the rhubarb. Add the vinegar, brown sugar, cinnamon, and cardamom. Cook 5 to 8 minutes or until the rhubarb is soft. (If the rhubarb is very tart, add 1 to 2 additional tablespoons of brown sugar.) Spoon the compote into a container and refrigerate until cool. When the compote is cool, remove from the refrigerator and stir in the chives and parsley.

For each serving, toast a slice of whole-grain bread. Remove the crusts and cut the bread into two triangles. Cut the cheese into 1-ounce wedges, and place one wedge on each bread triangle. Top each cheese wedge with about 1 tablespoon of the compote. Serve at room temperature.

Artichoke, Spinach, and Pepper Jack Quesadillas

CHEF DEAN FEARING

MAKES 8 QUESADILLA WEDGES

SALSA

2 jalapeño peppers

2 unpeeled garlic cloves

1 unpeeled white onion

4 cups diced tomatoes

1 tablespoon chopped fresh cilantro

1 tablespoon fresh lime juice

Salt and pepper, to taste

GUACAMOLE

1 jalapeño pepper

3 large avocados

¼ cup diced white onion

¼ cup diced tomato

1 tablespoon lime juice

Salt and pepper, to taste

QUESADILLAS

1 tablespoon vegetable oil

1 white onion

½ cup canned artichoke hearts, sliced

1 cup fresh spinach

4 (8-inch) flour tortillas

1 cup (4 ounces) shredded pepper Jack cheese

For the salsa, preheat the oven to 350°F. Place the jalapeños, garlic, and onion on a baking sheet. Roast for 15 to 20 minutes, turning, until the peppers are soft. Trim, seed, and chop the jalapeños. Peel and chop the onion and garlic. In a food processor, finely chop the jalapeños and garlic. Turn the processor off, and add the onion, tomatoes, and cilantro. Season with the lime juice, salt, and pepper.

For the guacamole, trim, seed, and mince the jalapeño. Peel, seed, and mash the avocados with a fork, leaving some chunks. Add 1 tablespoon of the jalapeño (or to taste), the onion, the tomato, the lime juice, and the salt and pepper. Stir to blend. Cover and set aside for at least 30 minutes to allow the flavors to blend.

For the quesadillas, heat the oil in a nonstick skillet over medium-low heat. Cut the onion in half lengthwise, and thinly slice. Add the onion to the skillet and cook for 15 to 20 minutes, until golden brown. Add the artichoke hearts and spinach. Sauté for 1 to 2 minutes. Spread the mixture evenly on two of the tortillas. Sprinkle evenly with the cheese. Top with the remaining tortillas; press down. Heat a griddle or heavy skillet over medium-high heat; place the tortillas on the griddle. Flip the tortillas when crisp and brown, about 1 to 1¼ minutes, and then brown the other side. Remove the quesadillas from the skillet. To serve, cut each quesadilla into four wedges. Serve with the salsa and guacamole.

Black Bean Quesadillas

MAKES 16 QUESADILLA WEDGES

1 cup canned black beans, rinsed and drained

2 tablespoons sliced green onions

2 tablespoons chopped roasted red peppers

2 tablespoons chopped red onion

1 tablespoon lime juice

1 tablespoon chopped fresh cilantro or parsley

1 garlic clove, minced

4 burrito-size (10-inch) flour tortillas

1 cup (4 ounces) grated asadero cheese or shredded Muenster cheese, divided

In a small bowl, slightly mash the beans with a fork. Stir in the green onions, peppers, onion, lime juice, cilantro or parsley, and garlic. Set aside.

Preheat the oven to 200°F.

In a lightly greased large skillet over medium-high heat, cook the first tortilla for 15 seconds or until softened; turn over. Spread $\frac{1}{4}$ cup bean mixture over half of the tortilla; top with $\frac{1}{4}$ cup of the cheese. Fold the tortilla in half over the filling. Cook for 2 minutes on each side or until the cheese melts. Place the cooked quesadilla on a baking sheet, and set the baking sheet in the oven to keep warm as you prepare the remaining quesadillas. Then, beginning with a fresh tortilla, repeat the process, placing each quesadilla in the oven after cooking, until all of the quesadillas have been assembled.

To serve, cut each quesadilla into four wedges.

Corn Nachos with Wisconsin Muenster and Salsa Cruda

MAKES 8 SERVINGS

NACHOS

2 cups top-quality crisp corn tortilla pieces

1 tablespoon butter

½ cup diced white onion

1½ cups fresh corn kernels, cut from the cob (2 to 3 ears)

1 (4-ounce) can mild green chiles, drained

1 teaspoon mild or hot pure chili powder

½ teaspoon ground cumin

2 tablespoons water

1 cup canned black beans, drained

1 cup cubed smoked turkey breast

2½ cups (10 ounces) shredded Muenster cheese

SALSA CRUDA

2 cups finely chopped fresh tomatoes

Juice of 1 lime

¼ cup finely chopped onion

2 tablespoons diced fresh jalapeño pepper, or to taste

½ cup finely chopped fresh cilantro

Salt and pepper, to taste

TO COMPLETE THE RECIPE

Sour cream

For the nachos, preheat the oven to broil.

Spread the tortilla pieces on a baking sheet. Set aside.

Heat the butter in a skillet over medium heat and sauté the onion for 3 minutes. Add the corn kernels, green chiles, chili powder, cumin, and water. Bring to a boil, cover, and cook at a gentle boil for 5 to 7 minutes. Remove from the heat. Stir in the black beans and turkey cubes. Spoon evenly over the tortilla pieces. Spread the cheese over all. Place under the broiler for about 3 minutes, or until the cheese melts and browns slightly. Remove from the oven.

For the salsa cruda, combine the tomatoes, lime juice, onion, jalapeño, cilantro, and salt and pepper in a glass or pottery bowl. Stir. To serve, top the nachos with the sour cream and salsa.

Tip: Your favorite prepared salsa can be substituted for the salsa cruda. Also, instead of being broiled, the nachos can be baked in a 400°F oven for 5 to 7 minutes, or microwaved on high for 1½ minutes or until the cheese melts.

Asiago Cheese Puffs

1 tablespoon butter

1 tablespoon olive oil

½ teaspoon salt

Cayenne pepper, to taste

1 cup water

1 cup all-purpose flour

4 eggs

½ cup (about 2 ounces) finely shredded Asiago cheese

½ cup (about 2 ounces) grated aged Parmesan cheese

½ cup (2 ounces) shredded pepato cheese

Preheat the oven to 400°F. In a small saucepan, combine the butter, oil, salt, cayenne. and water; bring to a boil. Add the flour all at once; stir until the mixture forms a smooth ball. Cook over low heat, until the mixture is drier, but still smooth. Pour into a mixing bowl. Beat in the eggs, one at a time; stir in the cheeses.

Drop tablespoonfuls of the batter onto greased baking sheets. Bake for 20 minutes, or until lightly browned and firm. Serve immediately.

Wisconsin Blue Cheese Cheesecake

MAKES 6 TO 8 SERVINGS

2 (8-ounce) packages cream cheese, at room temperature

2 cups (12 ounces) finely crumbled blue cheese, at room temperature

3 eggs, at room temperature

¼ cup sour cream

2 tablespoons clover or orange blossom honey

Pinch of kosher salt

Pinch of fresh cracked pepper

½ cup caramel topping

Water crackers (optional)

Heat the oven to 300°F. Spray an 8-inch springform pan with cooking spray. Line the bottom with parchment paper and spray again.

In a large bowl, beat the cream cheese until smooth. Measure out ¼ cup of the blue cheese and set aside. To the remaining blue cheese, add the eggs, one at a time, beating well after each addition. Scrape the mixture off the sides of the bowl. Add the sour cream, honey, salt, and pepper. Beat until combined. Pour into the pan.

Place a shallow pan of water on the bottom rack in the oven, and place the cheesecake on the rack above it. (Steam from the water will help prevent cracks in the cheesecake.) Bake 40 minutes.

Remove the cheesecake from the oven. Sprinkle the reserved blue cheese over the top of the cheesecake and bake 10 to 15 minutes more, until lightly browned. Cool in the pan, to room temperature.

To serve, cut the cheesecake into wedges. Drizzle each plate with caramel; place the wedge on the plate. Serve with crackers, if desired.

Borek (Flaky Cheese-Filled Pastry with Herbs)

CHEF TOM CATHERALL

MAKES 25 TO 30 PASTRIES

FILLING

2 cups (12 ounces) crumbled feta cheese

4 tablespoons grated Parmesan cheese

1 egg, lightly beaten

Pinch of nutmeg

2 tablespoons chopped fresh chives

2 tablespoons chopped fresh dill

2 tablespoons chopped fresh mint

2 tablespoons chopped fresh parsley

4 tablespoons toasted pine nuts

Salt, to taste

Freshly ground pepper, to taste

PASTRY

8 ounces phyllo dough (about 20 sheets, 14 x 9 inches)

¼ pound (1 stick) butter, melted

For the filling, combine the cheeses, egg, nutmeg, chives, dill, mint, parsley, pine nuts, salt, and pepper in a large bowl and mash with a fork. Set aside.

For the pastry, with scissors, cut a stack of phyllo sheets into 3 x 14-inch strips. Place the strips on top of one another and cover with a slightly dampened towel.

Preheat the oven to 375°F.

Place one strip of phyllo on the work surface. Brush lightly with the butter. Place another strip on top and brush lightly with butter. (Keep the remaining strips covered.) Place a heaping teaspoon of the filling at one end, about 1 inch from the edge. Fold one corner over the filling to meet the opposite corner, forming a triangle. Lift the triangle and continue to fold as you would a flag, until the whole strip is folded into a small, triangular parcel. Make sure there are no holes in the dough.

Brush the top of the parcel with butter; place it on a buttered baking sheet. Repeat with the remaining filling and phyllo strips.

Bake for 15 to 20 minutes, until golden brown and crisp. Serve hot, warm, or at room temperature.

Tip: The unbaked borek can be prepared 2 weeks in advance and stored in the freezer until you are ready to use them. Defrost before baking.

Wisconsin Cheese Straws

CHEFS MARY AND GREG SONNIER

MAKES 64 STRAWS

4 cups (about 1½ pounds) grated aged Cheddar cheese

¼ pound (1 stick) butter, softened

1⅓ cups all-purpose flour

½ teaspoon ground cayenne pepper

1 teaspoon garlic powder

1 to 2 tablespoons water, if needed

Preheat the oven to 350°F. Line baking sheets with parchment paper.

In a food processor, combine the cheese and the butter; process well. Add the remaining ingredients and pulse until dough forms. Add water, if necessary. Cover the dough and chill in the refrigerator for 1 hour.

On a clean countertop or cutting board, use your fingers to gently roll 1 tablespoon of dough into a rope. When it is 8 to 10 inches long, cut it in half and continue rolling each rope until it is 6 to 8 inches long. Twist both ropes together and place on a baking sheet. Repeat with the remaining dough.

Bake for 15 to 17 minutes, until set and starting to brown. Cool on a wire rack; serve with your choice of dip.

Wisconsin Brie en Croûte

MAKES 12 SERVINGS

1 egg yolk

1 tablespoon water

1 (17¼-ounce) package frozen puff pastry sheets

1 wheel Brie or Camembert cheese (about 2 pounds)

Preheat the oven to 375°F.

Beat the egg yolk with 1 tablespoon of water. Set in the refrigerator until ready to use.

Thaw the puff pastry for 20 minutes, and then unfold. Roll out one pastry square until it is approximately ½ inch larger than the circle of cheese. Place the Brie in the center of the circle and trim the edges, leaving a ½-inch border. Brush the border with the egg mixture.

Roll the second square of pastry until it is large enough to fit over the cheese, again allowing the ½-inch border. Place the pastry over the circle of cheese and press the two pastry circles together to seal. If desired, decorate with cutouts made from pastry scraps (heart shapes, crescents, twists, etc.) and apply with the egg mixture. Brush the top of the Brie en croûte with the egg mixture and place on an ungreased baking sheet in the middle of the oven.

Bake for 20 minutes, or until golden brown. Serve warm or at room temperature.

Wisconsin Feta Triangles

MAKES 24 SMALL TRIANGLES (FOR APPETIZERS)
OR 12 LARGE TRIANGLES (FOR LUNCHEON SERVINGS)

FILLING

3 tablespoons olive oil

2½ cups chopped green onions

2 cups thawed chopped frozen spinach, squeezed dry

⅔ cup ricotta cheese

1 cup (6 ounces) crumbled feta cheese

¾ cup (about 3 ounces) grated Parmesan cheese

2 eggs

Salt and freshly ground pepper, to taste

¼ to ½ teaspoon ground nutmeg

¾ cup pine nuts, toasted

PASTRY

16 phyllo dough sheets

Butter, clarified, as needed (see note on page 59)

For the filling, in a large skillet, heat the oil. Add the green onions and sauté 1 minute to soften. Stir in the spinach and cook until dry. Remove from the heat and set aside to cool.

In a bowl, combine the cheeses, eggs, salt, pepper, and nutmeg. Mix well. Stir in the reserved spinach mixture and blend well. Stir in the nuts. Cover and refrigerate. Makes approximately 4½ cups.

For the pastry, Create four phyllo stacks: butter one sheet of phyllo, stack another sheet on top, and butter. Repeat until there are a total of four sheets forming each stack. Preheat the oven to 350°F.

To prepare as appetizers, cut the first phyllo stack into six even strips widthwise. Place a scant tablespoon of spinach filling at the bottom of each strip and fold up to form triangles. Butter both sides and place on a buttered baking sheet. Repeat with the remaining phyllo stacks to make 24 triangles.

Bake for 20 minutes, or until golden brown. Serve hot. Triangles may be cooled and reheated to serve.

To prepare as luncheon servings, cut the first phyllo stack into three rectangles widthwise and use a scant ½ cup of filling per piece, folding up to form triangles. Repeat with the remaining phyllo stacks to make 12 triangles. Butter and bake as directed above.

Goat Cheese Turnovers with Smoked Salmon and Leeks

MAKES 4 TO 6 SERVINGS

2 teaspoons olive oil

1 small leek, halved, thinly sliced crosswise

¼ cup whipping cream

½ cup (3 ounces) soft fresh goat cheese, at room temperature

2 tablespoons chopped fresh herbs (choose from thyme, dill, or oregano)

1 teaspoon finely grated lemon zest

½ teaspoon sea salt or kosher salt

¼ teaspoon freshly ground pepper

1 sheet frozen puff pastry, thawed overnight in the refrigerator*

3 slices thinly sliced smoked salmon, each slice cut cross-wise into ¼-inch-thick pieces

* Be sure to thaw the frozen puff pastry overnight in the refrigerator before you plan to make these.

Position a rack in the center of the oven and preheat the oven to 400°F.

In a small skillet, heat the olive oil over medium heat. Add the leek and sauté until soft, about 5 minutes. Add the whipping cream and simmer until the mixture is reduced slightly, about 5 minutes. Let the mixture cool.

In a medium bowl, mash the goat cheese with a fork. Stir in the leek mixture; then add the chopped fresh herbs, lemon zest, salt, and pepper. Stir to combine.

On a lightly floured surface, unfold the pastry sheet and lightly dust it with flour. Using a rolling pin, roll the sheet into a 12-inch square. Cut the dough into 9 squares. Put equal amounts of the filling (about 1 table-spoon) onto the center of each square. Top with equal amounts of the sliced salmon. Moisten the edges of a square with a fingertip dipped in water. Fold the dough over to form a triangle, gently pressing around the fill-ing and pressing the edges of the dough together. Use the tines of a fork to crimp and seal the edges of the turnover. Repeat with the remaining dough squares. (You can fill and shape the turnovers up to 2 hours ahead of cooking. Cover the unbaked turnovers tightly with plastic wrap or brush them with melted butter before chilling.)

Place the turnovers on a baking sheet and bake until the turnovers are puffed and golden, about 15 minutes. Transfer the turnovers to a cooling rack and cool slightly. Serve turnovers warm.

Heirloom Tomato and Asiago Tart

CHEF MICHAEL SYMON

MAKES 6 TO 8 SERVINGS

DOUGH*

1⅔ cups all-purpose flour

¼ pound (1 stick) butter

1 egg yolk

Pinch of salt

¼ cup ice water, approximately

¾ to 1 cup dried beans, for baking weights

FILLING

2 large tomatoes, preferably heirloom

1½ cups heavy cream

3 eggs

4 garlic cloves, roasted and puréed**

1½ cups (about 6 ounces) grated Asiago cheese

20 fresh basil leaves, for garnish

* Instead of making the dough, you can use a 9- or 10-inch prepared, unbaked pie crust.

** To roast and purée the garlic: Choose plump cloves. Scatter, unpeeled, in a baking pan. Salt and drizzle with olive oil. Bake at 375°F for 25 minutes. Peel the cloves and mash, adding a little olive oil if too dry.

For the dough, mix the flour, butter, egg yolk, and salt with a pastry blender until the mixture forms crumbs. Add the water, 1 tablespoon at a time. Incorporate quickly, just until the dough forms a ball. Wrap the dough in plastic and refrigerate at least 1 hour.

Preheat the oven to 350°F.

Roll the dough in a circle ⅛ inch thick. (If you are using a 9-inch prepared crust, you may have to roll it a bit thinner than packaged.) Line the bottom and sides of a 9-inch pie pan, crimping the crust around the top. Place foil over the bottom crust. Spread the beans over the foil to prevent the dough from rising. (Or generously prick the crust, bottom and sides, with a fork.)

Bake for about 10 minutes. Remove the beans and the foil. Place the crust on a wire rack to cool.

For the filling, preheat the oven to 375°F.

Peel and seed the tomatoes, and cut each vertically into eighths. Pat dry with paper towels.

Mix together the cream, eggs, roasted garlic purée, and cheese. Pour the mixture into the baked pie crust. Top with tomato pieces. Bake 30 minutes, or until firm in the center and lightly colored. (Bake 5 to 10 minutes longer, if necessary.) Remove from the oven and let the pie cool on a wire rack for 20 minutes.

Garnish the tart with basil leaves and serve.

Miami Spice Napoleons
with Wisconsin Queso Fresco Cheese

MAKES 12 NAPOLEONS

NAPOLEONS

2 tablespoons olive oil

2 garlic cloves, crushed

12 baby portobello mushrooms
  (about 2 inches in diameter)

2 large red bell peppers

3 cups (18 ounces) crumbled
  queso fresco cheese

LIME-CILANTRO DRESSING

6 tablespoons extra-virgin
  olive oil

2 tablespoons fresh lime juice

3 tablespoons finely chopped
  fresh cilantro

1 teaspoon salt

GARNISH

4 limes, quartered, or edible
  flowers

For the napoleons, prepare the grill according to the manufacturer's directions, or preheat the oven to broil.

Mix the oil and the garlic, and brush it on the mushrooms. Set the remaining garlic mixture aside.

Grill or broil the mushrooms until they begin to brown and the juices just begin to exude. Remove from the heat and set aside to cool. Brush the peppers with the garlic mixture, and place them on the grill or under the broiler. Cook the peppers, turning as necessary, until the skins are blackened. Remove from the heat and place the peppers into a paper bag to steam and cool. When cool, peel off the skins and discard the seeds and membranes.

Lightly oil 12 (2-inch) ring molds. Cut the mushrooms diagonally into thin slices to expose the interior surface. Trim the mushrooms and peppers to fit the diameter of the mold. Place a layer of mushrooms in the bottom of each mold. Top with an even, thin layer of cheese. Top with a layer of peppers, then another layer of cheese. Continue layering until you have four layers of vegetables and three layers of cheese, ending with a layer of peppers. Repeat for all 12 napoleons. Press down firmly, cover, and chill at least 30 minutes.

For the dressing, whisk together all four ingredients.

To serve, invert the napoleons onto twelve serving plates, loosening the edges with a knife. Drizzle with the dressing and garnish with limes or edible flowers.

Wisconsin Cheese Tart with Apple-Walnut Salad

CHEF RHYS LEWIS

MAKES 12 SERVINGS

TART

1 tablespoon chopped fresh basil

1 tablespoon chopped fresh thyme

1 tablespoon chopped fresh rosemary

8 eggs

2 cups heavy cream

1 cup ((4 ounces) Roth Käse Grand Cru Gruyère cheese

¼ cup (about 2 ounces) crumbled creamy Gorgonzola cheese

1 (16-ounce) box phyllo dough

¼ pound (1 stick) unsalted butter, clarified (see note on page 59)

SALAD

⅛ cup extra-virgin olive oil

⅛ cup aged Modena balsamic vinegar

Turbinado sugar, to taste

12 ounces mixed baby salad greens

¼ cup black walnuts

3 Gala apples, cored and finely sliced

Kosher salt and pepper

For the tart, preheat the oven to 375°F.

Combine the chopped herbs, eggs, and cream in a mixing bowl. Blend until smooth. Stir in the cheeses. Season to taste and refrigerate.

Remove the phyllo dough from the packaging. While it is still rolled up, trim a quarter inch off each end of the dough. Unroll the dough and cover with a towel to prevent drying.

On a cutting board, spread flat one layer of phyllo dough and brush with some of the clarified butter. Top with a second layer of phyllo and butter. Continue until four layers are completed. (Refrigerate the remaining phyllo for another use.)

Using a sharp knife, cut 12 (4-inch) phyllo squares, and put each square into an ungreased standard-size muffin tin, shaping into a cup. Fill the cups two-thirds full with the cheese mixture. Bake until the phyllo is crisp and the custard is set. When cool, carefully remove the tarts from the muffin tins. Place one on each of twelve serving plates.

For the salad, in a bowl, mix the oil, vinegar, and turbinado sugar for salad dressing. Blend well. Toss the greens, walnuts, and apple slices with the dressing. Arrange a portion of salad beside each tart. Season to taste and serve.

Crumbled Feta Salad Tarts

30 small phyllo pastry tart shells

SALAD

½ medium cucumber, peeled, seeded, and diced (about ½ cup)

½ cup diced tomato, seeded

¼ cup diced red onion

1 cup (6 ounces) crumbled feta cheese

¼ cup sliced ripe olives

DRESSING

1 teaspoon prepared mustard

1 teaspoon honey

¼ teaspoon pepper

¼ teaspoon dried oregano

1 tablespoon red wine vinegar

2 tablespoons extra-virgin olive oil

GARNISH

Fresh parsley sprigs

Thaw the phyllo tart shells according to the package instructions.

For the salad, in a medium bowl, combine the cucumber, tomato, onion, cheese, and olives. Set aside.

For the dressing, in a small bowl, mix together the mustard, honey, pepper, oregano, and vinegar; add the oil and mix well. Pour the dressing over the salad mixture; toss well. Allow the mixture to marinate ½ hour before serving.

To serve, fill the phyllo shells with the salad mixture and garnish with parsley sprigs.

Gruyère and Onion Tart

2 tablespoons butter

3 large onions, thinly sliced (about 6 cups)

1 refrigerated pie crust

2 cups (8 ounces) grated Gruyère cheese

1 tablespoon all-purpose flour

½ teaspoon dried thyme leaves

½ teaspoon salt

¼ teaspoon ground nutmeg

¼ teaspoon ground white pepper

2 eggs, at room temperature

½ cup half-and-half

Preheat the oven to 425°F.

In a large skillet, heat the butter over medium heat. Cook the onion, stirring occasionally, for 20 minutes, or until very soft and golden.

Prepare the pie crust according to the package directions for a single crust; refrigerate the remaining crust for a later use. Gently press the crust into the bottom and up the sides of an 11-inch tart pan with a removable bottom. Place the cheese in the pan; sprinkle the flour, thyme, salt, nutmeg, and pepper over the top. Toss lightly to combine; smooth to make an even layer.

Transfer the cooked onion to the tart pan; arrange to make an even layer. In a small bowl, whisk together the eggs and the half-and-half; pour evenly over the cheese mixture.

Place the tart on a baking sheet, and bake 10 minutes. Reduce the oven temperature to 375°F; bake 30 minutes longer, or until the filling puffs and is just set. Cool slightly. Serve warm or at room temperature.

Manchego with Quince Paste

MAKES 4 TO 6 SERVINGS

6 ounces Manchego cheese, rind trimmed, at room temperature

6 ounces quince paste (membrillo)*

* Quince paste (*membrillo*), a dense jelly made from the quince fruit, is available at some super-markets and specialty food markets and online at tienda.com and spanishtable.com.

Cut the Manchego wedge into 8 wedges; arrange each wedge on a serving plate. Cut the quince paste into eight ⅛-inch-thick slices; top each cheese wedge with a slice of the quince paste and serve.

Red Pepper and Cumin–Marinated Manchego

1 tablespoon cumin seeds

1 small dried red chile, cut into 3 pieces

2 garlic cloves, minced

1 tablespoon chopped fresh thyme leaves or chopped fresh oregano

2 teaspoons grated orange zest

1 cup extra-virgin olive oil, plus additional if needed

8 ounces Manchego cheese, rind cut off and discarded, cheese cut into ½-inch cubes*

* Manchego is an aged sheep's milk cheese from the La Mancha region of Spain. In tapas bars there (and in this country), it's often paired with slices of cured chorizo sausage, but another popular tapa is marinated cubes of the cheese, served on toothpicks.

In a small, heavy skillet, toast the cumin seeds and dried red chile over medium-high heat, shaking the pan gently to ensure even cooking, until fragrant, about 1 minute. Transfer the spices to a medium mixing bowl. When the spices have cooled slightly, add the minced garlic, chopped thyme, and grated orange zest. Pour in the olive oil, and stir gently to combine. Stir in the cheese. Add more oil to cover the cheese, if needed. Cover and refrigerate overnight. Remove the cheese from the refrigerator a few hours before serving to return the oil to room temperature.

To serve, transfer the cheese mixture with the flavored olive oil to a serving bowl; place toothpicks alongside for spearing the cheese. (The cheese will keep for up to three days in the fridge.) If you can't find Manchego, use cubes of firm feta cheese.

Pane Pomodoro with Fresh Wisconsin Mozzarella

MAKES 18 SERVINGS

1 to 1½ loaves day-old French baguette, cut into 1-inch cubes

4 ounces fresh basil, finely shredded

15 Roma tomatoes, quartered

1 cup toasted pine nuts

1 pound fresh mozzarella cheese, sliced (½ inch thick)

2 teaspoons roasted garlic purée*

1 cup olive oil

½ cup white balsamic vinegar

1 teaspoon salt

1 teaspoon cracked pepper

* Use prepared roasted garlic purée or follow the instructions on page 79.

Preheat the oven to 350°F.

Lightly toast the bread cubes for 7 minutes.

In a large mixing bowl, toss together the toasted bread cubes, basil, tomatoes, pine nuts, and cheese. Set aside.

Whisk the roasted garlic purée into the olive oil. Combine with the bread and cheese mixture. Sprinkle balsamic vinegar over the mixture and season with salt and cracked pepper.

Baked Feta with Red Onion Relish

MAKES 6 TO 8 SERVINGS

3 tablespoons extra-virgin olive oil, divided

½ medium fennel bulb, cored and cut into ¼-inch dice (about 1¼ cups)

½ medium red onion, cut into ¼-inch dice (about ¾ cup)

Fine sea salt or kosher salt and freshly ground pepper

12 pitted kalamata olives, quartered (about ⅓ cup)

1 teaspoon finely grated lemon zest

⅓ cup minced fresh mint or dill

2 (8-ounce) packages feta cheese

Additional chopped fresh mint or dill, for garnish

1 French bread baguette, sliced

Preheat the oven to 450°F. Heat 2 tablespoons of the oil in a heavy, medium skillet over medium heat until hot. Add the fennel and onions and cook, stirring occasionally, until the vegetables begin to soften (do not allow to brown), about 5 minutes. Reduce the heat to medium-low, add ¼ teaspoon salt and ¼ teaspoon pepper, and continue to cook until the vegetables soften completely, about 5 minutes. Reduce the heat to low and stir in the olives, lemon zest, mint, and the remaining 1 tablespoon of oil. Remove from the heat and cover to keep warm.

Cut each block of feta horizontally in half to make four ½-inch-thick pieces. Coat a nonstick rimmed baking sheet or glass baking dish with nonstick cooking spray (or coat very lightly with olive oil). Arrange the cheese squares on the baking sheet and bake until heated through, about 10 minutes. Remove the cheese from the oven.

Preheat the broiler. Return the cheese to the oven and broil until golden brown, about 5 minutes.

Spoon the warm relish onto a serving platter; arrange the cheese over the relish. Drizzle the cheese with a little olive oil, if desired, and sprinkle with chopped fresh herbs. Arrange the bread slices around the cheese and serve.

Camembert Beignets with Red Wine Reduction

CHEF KEN ORINGER

MAKES 12 BEIGNETS

BEIGNETS

1 wheel (2.2 pounds) Camembert cheese, cut into 2-inch chunks

1 cup all-purpose flour

8 eggs, beaten

2 cups panko breadcrumbs

Vegetable oil for frying

RED WINE REDUCTION

2 cups Cabernet Sauvignon

1 teaspoon red wine vinegar

¼ cup sugar

1 bay leaf

HERB SALAD

2 teaspoons lemon juice

2 tablespoons olive oil

4 cups herb salad mixture (chervil, tarragon, parsley, and dill)

Sea salt, to taste

For the beignets, roll each cheese chunk in flour, dip it in the eggs, and then coat it with breadcrumbs. Place the coated beignets on wax paper and set aside. Pour the oil into a large skillet to the depth of 2 inches, and heat on medium high to 350°F. Fry the cheese chunks until golden, but soft in the center. Drain on paper towels. Keep warm.

For the red wine reduction, combine all of the ingredients in a saucepan. Cook over medium heat until reduced to the consistency of syrup. Remove the bay leaf and discard.

For the herb salad, whisk together the lemon juice and olive oil for the dressing. Toss with the herb salad mixture and season with the sea salt.

To serve the beignets, drizzle the wine reduction syrup on each of twelve serving plates. Place one beignet on each plate. Slice the tops of the beignets and turn on their sides to expose the molten centers. Garnish each plate with ⅓ cup of the herb salad and serve.

Grilled Queso Fresco with Black Olive Mojo

CHEF JAMES CAMPBELL

MAKES 8 TAPAS

MOJO

½ cup pitted kalamata olives

½ cup chopped fresh parsley

1 tablespoon chopped fresh mint

2 garlic cloves

1 tablespoon crushed red chile flakes

1 teaspoon ground coriander

1 teaspoon smoked paprika

½ teaspoon ground cumin

1¼ cups extra-virgin olive oil

QUESO FRESCO

¼ cup vegetable oil

8 pieces (1 x 3 x ½-inch rectangles) queso fresco or queso blanco cheese

Salt and pepper, to taste

8 lemon wedges

16 caperberries

For the mojo, in a food processor, combine all of the ingredients and process until finely chopped. Set aside.

For the queso fresco, in a cast-iron skillet, heat ¼ cup vegetable oil over medium-high heat. Sprinkle the cheese with salt and pepper and add it to the skillet. Sear each cheese slice for about 1 minute on each side. The cheese will soften, but hold its shape.

To serve the tapas, transfer the seared cheese slices to a serving platter. Top with the black olive mojo. Garnish with the lemon wedges and caperberries.

MAKES 12 SERVINGS

12 petite Brie wheels (4 to 6 ounces each)

24 garlic cloves, peeled and halved

9 cups honey

Salt, to taste

Freshly cracked pepper, to taste

3 French baguettes, cut in fourths

Preheat the oven to 350°F.

Place one Brie wheel on each of 12 small baking dishes or on a baking sheet. Place 4 garlic halves in each dish, around the cheese. Pour ³/₄ cup of honey over each Brie. Season with salt and pepper, and place the baking dishes in the oven.

Bake for 15 minutes. Remove from the oven.

Quickly heat the baguette slices in the oven until crisp, about 5 minutes.

Serve the Brie hot with one crispy baguette quarter on the side.

Pan-Fried Haloumi with Lemon, Chile, and Olives

MAKES 4 TO 6 SERVINGS

1 (8-ounce) package haloumi cheese, cut into ¼- to ⅜-inch-thick slices

10 pitted large green olives, chopped into small pieces

Zest of 1 lemon

1 small fresh red chile, cut into small pieces

2 tablespoons lemon juice

2 tablespoons chopped fresh parsley

Set a large (preferably 12-inch) nonstick skillet over medium-high heat (no oil is necessary) until hot, about 1 minute. Working in batches, if necessary (do not crowd the cheese, which will cause it to steam), cook the haloumi until golden in spots, about 2 minutes. Flip and cook until the second side of each slice is golden, about 2 minutes more. Reduce the heat as needed if the haloumi is browning too fast.

Shingle the haloumi on a serving platter.

While the pan is still hot, add the olives, lemon zest, red chile, and lemon juice. Stir just to warm through. Immediately pour over the haloumi, sprinkle with the chopped parsley, and serve.

Queso Blanco Fruit Compote

JOHN ESSER

MAKES 6 SERVINGS

1 cup fresh blueberries

1 cup fresh raspberries

1 cup sliced fresh strawberries

1 cup diced apple

1 cup diced fresh pineapple

3 tablespoons blackberry jam

6 ounces queso blanco cheese, sliced into 12 (½-inch-wide) strips

1 ounce shelled, salted sunflower seeds

Combine the berries, apple, pineapple, and jam in a medium bowl and gently mix.

Heat a nonstick fry pan to medium-high heat, and fry the cheese strips for 30 seconds on each side. Remove from the pan and cut the strips into cubes.

Divide the fruit mixture among six salad plates, and top with the fried cheese cubes. Top each serving with sunflower seeds and serve immediately, while the cheese is warm.

Queso Blanco with Roasted Tomato Sauce

MAKES 8 SERVINGS

ROASTED TOMATO SAUCE

1 (14.5-ounce) can diced fire-roasted tomatoes*

2 unpeeled garlic cloves

1 jalapeño pepper

Salt, to taste

1 teaspoon dried Mexican oregano

2 tablespoons olive oil

CHEESE

1 (12-ounce) square or package queso blanco, cut horizontally in three pieces (4 ounces each)

ACCOMPANIMENTS

Fresh hot tortillas or tortilla chips

* Several brands make fire-roasted tomatoes, including Progresso and Muir Glen.

For the sauce, place the tomatoes in the bowl of a food processor or the beaker of a blender. Heat a heavy skillet, such as cast iron, until very hot. Place the garlic cloves and jalapeño in the skillet. Grill until "roasted" and the skin turns black in places, turning as necessary.

Peel the garlic and chop roughly. Add to the tomatoes. Cut the jalapeño in half. Stem and seed. Roughly chop half of the jalapeño. Add to the tomatoes. Blend, leaving a rough texture. Taste for salt, adding some if necessary. Add more chopped reserved jalapeño if a hotter flavor is preferred. Stir in the oregano.

Heat the olive oil in a medium skillet until hot. Add the sauce (it will splatter). Stir and cook at a low boil for about 5 minutes until it thickens and reduces slightly. Keep warm.

For the cheese, heat a large, nonstick skillet over medium-high heat. Lightly grill the cheese slices until golden brown on all sides, 5 to 6 minutes.

To serve, transfer the slices to serving plates and spoon the warm sauce over each slice. Serve with fresh hot tortillas or crisp tortilla chips.

Chèvre with Pesto and Balsamic-Roasted Tomatoes

MAKES 6 TO 8 SERVINGS

BALSAMIC-ROASTED TOMATOES

1 (10-ounce) basket cherry or grape tomatoes (about 1⅔ cups)

1 tablespoon olive oil

Pinch of fine sea salt or kosher salt

1 tablespoon balsamic vinegar

PESTO

4 cups (loosely packed) fresh basil leaves

½ cup olive oil

⅓ cup pine nuts

2 small garlic cloves

Juice of ½ lemon

Pinch of crushed red pepper flakes

½ cup (2 ounces) freshly grated Parmesan cheese

1 teaspoon sea salt or kosher salt

ASSEMBLY

1 (8- to 11-ounce) log soft fresh goat cheese

Fresh basil or thyme sprigs (optional), for garnish

For the balsamic roasted tomatoes, preheat the oven to 350°F.

In a medium mixing bowl, combine the tomatoes with the olive oil and salt. Transfer the tomato mixture to a small baking dish, and roast in the oven until the tomatoes are softened, slightly browned, and release some juices, 35 to 45 minutes. Remove the tomatoes from the oven, and stir in the balsamic vinegar.

For the pesto, combine the basil, olive oil, pine nuts, garlic cloves, lemon juice, and crushed red pepper flakes in the bowl of a food processor or blender. Blend until a paste forms, stopping to scrape down the sides of the processor or blender. Add the cheese and salt, and blend until smooth. (If the pesto is too thick, add a little a water by tablespoonfuls until it reaches a smooth consistency.) Taste and adjust the seasonings as desired.

To assemble and serve, place the goat cheese log on a large serving plate or small platter. Drizzle ½ cup of the pesto over half of the goat cheese. Spoon ½ cup of the roasted tomatoes over the remaining half of the goat cheese. (Reserve the remaining pesto and tomatoes for another use; cover separately and refrigerate.) Garnish the cheese with fresh herb sprigs, if desired.

Buffalo Wings with Blue Cheese Dipping Sauce

MAKES 8 SERVINGS

2½ to 3 pounds chicken wings

MARINADE
3 tablespoons vegetable oil
1 tablespoon hot pepper sauce
1 teaspoon paprika

DIPPING SAUCE
⅔ cup (4 ounces) crumbled
   blue cheese
⅔ cup reduced-fat sour cream
4 teaspoons white wine vinegar
3 tablespoons finely chopped
   green onions, including green
   tops, divided
½ teaspoon coarsely ground
   pepper
1 to 2 tablespoons milk

TO COMPLETE THE RECIPE
Hot pepper sauce, to taste
3 celery stalks, cut into sticks

For the chicken, prepare the grill according to the manufacturer's directions.

Chop off the wing tips; cut the wings in half at the joint. Place the cut wings in a shallow dish.

For the marinade, combine the oil, hot pepper sauce, and paprika. Add to the chicken, turning to coat the pieces evenly. Set aside to marinate while making the sauce.

For the dipping sauce, in a small bowl, combine the cheese and the sour cream. Stir in the vinegar, 2 tablespoons of the green onions, and the pepper, mashing with a wooden spoon to combine. Whisk in the milk (or pulse in a food processor) until the sauce is smooth. Sprinkle the top with the remaining 1 tablespoon of green onions. (Refrigerate if not using immediately.)

To complete the recipe, grill the wings for about 15 minutes, until lightly charred and no longer pink inside, turning occasionally and brushing with any remaining marinade. Remove to a platter and sprinkle with a few more dashes of hot pepper sauce. Serve with the celery sticks and the dipping sauce.

Gran Queso Crab Cakes

CHEF JAMES CAMPBELL

MAKES 6 CRAB CAKES

CRAB CAKES

4 tablespoons (½ stick) butter

¼ cup finely chopped celery

¼ cup finely chopped onion

1 tablespoon finely chopped red bell pepper

½ small garlic clove, finely minced

12 ounces lump crabmeat

2 cups (8 ounces) shredded Gran Queso cheese*

2 green onions, finely chopped

2 eggs, lightly beaten

3 tablespoons mayonnaise

1 teaspoon sherry vinegar

1½ cups soft breadcrumbs

¼ teaspoon cayenne pepper

4 tablespoons olive oil

AÏOLI

2 garlic cloves

½ cup roasted red peppers

1 teaspoon fresh lemon juice

½ cup fresh basil

⅓ cup mayonnaise

2 tablespoons olive oil

Salt, to taste

Freshly ground black pepper, to taste

* Italian-style fontina may be substituted for the Gran Queso cheese.

For the crab cakes, in a sauté pan, melt the butter over medium heat. Add the celery, onions, chopped bell pepper, and minced garlic. Cook until soft, 3 to 4 minutes. In a large bowl, mix the crabmeat, cheese, green onions, eggs, 3 tablespoons mayonnaise, the sherry vinegar, the breadcrumbs and the cayenne. Stir in the sautéed vegetables. Cover and refrigerate for about 2 hours.

For the aïoli, while the crab mixture is chilling, combine the garlic, roasted red pepper, lemon juice, basil, mayonnaise, and olive oil in a food processor bowl with a metal blade. Process until finely chopped. Season with salt and pepper.

To complete the recipe, remove the crab mixture from the refrigerator and form 6 round cakes, 3 x 1 inch thick. Heat 4 tablespoons of olive oil in a large skillet over medium heat. Cook the crab cakes 3 to 4 minutes per side, or until golden brown and thoroughly heated. Serve with the aïoli.

Smoked Gouda–Baked Oysters and Chorizo

¾ cup (3 ounces) shredded smoked Gouda cheese

⅓ cup (2 ounces) cooked chorizo (smoked Spanish-style sausage), finely chopped*

10 shucked fresh oysters in half shell

* If chorizo is unavailable, substitute a flavorful smoked sausage.

Preheat the oven to 350°F.

In a small bowl, mix the cheese and the chorizo. Top each oyster with equal amounts of the cheese mixture. Place the oysters on a 9 x 9-inch baking pan or small baking sheet. Bake for 10 to 12 minutes, or until hot and the cheese has melted. Serve hot or warm.

Pepper Jack Shrimp Cocktails

1 pound (26 to 30 count) frozen shrimp, cooked and deveined

½ pound pepper Jack cheese

1 bunch kale, rinsed

½ cup prepared cocktail sauce

Toothpicks, frilled or fancy

1 lemon, cut into wedges, for garnish

Thaw the shrimp under cold running water. Cut the cheese into ½-square cubes. Line a serving platter with kale. Pour cocktail sauce in a serving dish and place it in the center of the kale-lined platter. Place a cube of cheese in the center of each shrimp where the natural curve occurs. With a toothpick, skewer the shrimp, first through the tail, then through the cheese cube, then into the shrimp again. Place the skewered shrimp on the platter. Continue until all of the shrimp are skewered. Arrange the lemon wedges on the platter to garnish. Chill the shrimp platter about ½ hour before serving.

Black Bean Tortilla Pinwheels

1 (8-ounce) package cream cheese, softened

1 cup sour cream

1 cup (4 ounces) shredded Monterey Jack cheese

¼ cup chopped pimento-stuffed green olives

¼ cup chopped red onion

½ teaspoon seasoned salt

⅛ teaspoon garlic powder

1 (15-ounce) can black beans, drained

5 (10-inch) tortillas

Salsa

Combine the cream cheese and sour cream; blend well. Stir in the Monterey Jack cheese, the olives, the onions, and the seasonings. Chill for 2 hours.

Purée the beans in a food processor or blender. Spread a thin layer of beans over each tortilla. Spread the cream cheese mixture over the beans. Roll up tightly. Chill for 30 minutes. Cut into ¾-inch slices. Serve with salsa.

Sea Scallops with Orange-Parsnip Purée and Wisconsin Gran Queso

CHEF JAMES CAMPBELL

MAKES 8 TAPAS

SCALLOPS

½ cup olive oil

¼ cup fresh orange juice

1 crushed bay leaf

½ teaspoon toasted coriander seed, ground

½ teaspoon crushed sea salt

¼ teaspoon cracked black pepper

16 large sea scallops

ORANGE-PARSNIP PURÉE

1 pound parsnips, peeled, cut in 2-inch pieces

Juice of 1 orange

Zest of 1 orange

¼ pound (1 stick) butter

Salt and pepper, to taste

HAZELNUT BUTTER

1 cup toasted hazelnuts

2 tablespoons sugar

1 teaspoon salt

TO COMPLETE THE RECIPE

1½ cups (6 ounces) shredded Gran Queso cheese*

* Italian-style fontina may be substituted for the Gran Queso cheese

For the scallops, in a glass dish or a plastic bag, mix the olive oil, orange juice, bay leaf, coriander, sea salt, and pepper. Add the scallops; stir to coat. Cover and refrigerate 1 hour to marinate.

For the orange-parsnip purée, cook the parsnips in boiling water until tender, 10 to 15 minutes. Drain. While still hot, combine the parsnips with the juice, orange zest, butter, salt, and pepper. Process until smooth. Keep warm.

For the hazelnut butter, in a food processor, combine the hazelnuts, sugar, and salt. Process until a very smooth paste forms (the mixture is quite thick).

To complete the recipe, heat the oven broiler to high. Heat a large sauté pan on high heat. Drain and sear the sea scallops about 3 minutes per side. Cover with the cheese. Place the pan under the broiler until the cheese is bubbling, about 1 minute. Serve 2 scallops per plate, with parsnip purée and hazelnut butter.

Serrano, Arugula, and Manchego Rolls

MAKES 6 TO 8 SERVINGS

3 tablespoons olive oil

1 tablespoon fresh lemon juice

⅛ teaspoon Spanish smoked paprika (pimentón)

18 thin slices serrano ham*

1 (5-ounce) bag arugula

4 ounces Manchego cheese, shaved into strips using a vegetable peeler

Freshly ground pepper

* Along with the Spanish smoked paprika, serrano ham is available at some specialty markets and supermarkets. If you can't find serrano ham, use prosciutto instead.

In a small bowl, whisk together the olive oil, lemon juice, and paprika; set aside.

On a work surface, arrange 1 slice of ham so that one long side is parallel to the edge of the work surface. Place 3 arugula leaves at one short end, perpendicular to a long end (the leaves will extend past one long side). Top with 2 strips of cheese. Season with pepper and drizzle with a little of the lemon vinaigrette. Starting at the end with the filling, roll up the ham to enclose the filling. Place the roll, seam side down, on a plate. Repeat with the remaining ingredients. (Rolls can be refrigerated, covered, several hours before serving; bring to room temperature before serving.)

Goat Cheese–Stuffed Fried Squash Blossoms

MAKES 4 TO 6 SERVINGS

Vegetable oil for frying

1 cup (8 ounces) soft fresh goat cheese, at room temperature

¼ cup finely chopped fresh mixed herbs (thyme, chives, and oregano)

1½ teaspoons minced shallots

Large pinch of salt

12 fresh open zucchini blossoms*

2 large eggs

1 cup all-purpose flour

½ teaspoon salt

Pinch of freshly ground white pepper

* Squash blossoms are available throughout the summer at farmers' markets. Use them within a day of purchase.

Pour 2½ inches of vegetable oil into a large, heavy skillet. Heat the oil over high heat until very hot (to 350°F, if using a deep-fry or candy thermometer).

In a small bowl, combine the goat cheese, herbs, shallots, and salt; stir to blend. Open up each squash blossom widely enough to insert a teaspoon or so of the cheese mixture. Gently twist the ends of each blossom together.

In a medium bowl, whisk the eggs. In another medium bowl, mix together the flour, salt, and pepper; transfer the seasoned flour to a wide, shallow bowl. Dredge the stuffed blossoms in the flour, gently shaking off any excess, and dip in the egg mixture to coat. Dredge the blossoms in the flour again. Fry the blossoms in batches (do not crowd), turning frequently, until they are crisp and begin to turn light golden brown, 3 to 5 minutes. Transfer the fried blossoms to a baking rack lined with paper towels to drain. Sprinkle with salt, and serve immediately.

Grilled Goat Cheese–Stuffed Grape Leaf Rolls

MAKES 4 TO 6 SERVINGS

ROLLS

1 (8-ounce) log soft fresh goat
cheese, at room temperature

1 tablespoon mixed chopped
fresh mint and dill

3 teaspoons olive oil, plus
additional for grilling

1 teaspoon finely grated
lemon zest

¼ teaspoon fine sea salt or
kosher salt

12 large grape leaves from jar,
rinsed, patted dry, stemmed

VINAIGRETTE

¼ cup extra-virgin olive oil

2 tablespoons red wine vinegar

1 medium tomato, seeded and
diced

⅓ cup coarsely chopped, pitted
oil-cured kalamata olives

Fine sea salt or kosher salt and
freshly ground pepper

For the rolls, in a medium mixing bowl, combine the goat cheese, chopped herbs, olive oil, lemon zest, and salt. Using a fork, mash the ingredients together to blend.

Arrange the grape leaves, vein side up, on a work surface. Place 1 heaping tablespoon of goat cheese mixture in the center of 1 grape leaf. Fold up the bottom of the grape leaf over the goat cheese. Fold the sides of the leaves over the cheese and continue to roll up, enclosing the cheese completely. Repeat with the remaining cheese and grape leaves. Arrange the wrapped cheeses, seam side down, on a plate. Brush the grape leaf rolls lightly with oil. Cover and refrigerate at least 1 hour. (Grape leaf rolls can be prepared 1 day ahead; keep chilled.)

Heat a gas grill to medium or prepare a medium-hot charcoal fire.

For the vinaigrette, in a small bowl, whisk together the olive oil and vinegar to blend. Whisk in the tomato and olives. Season the vinaigrette with salt and pepper.

To complete the recipe, place the grape leaf rolls on the grill, seam side down. Grill until the cheese softens and the leaves begin to char, about 2 minutes per side. To serve, arrange the cheeses on a serving platter and drizzle with the kalamata olive vinaigrette.

Grilled Portobellos with Sun-Dried Tomato Dressing

MAKES 12 SERVINGS

GRILLED MUSHROOMS

2 tablespoons olive oil

2 garlic cloves, crushed

12 portobello mushrooms, 3 inches in diameter

4 cups (16 ounces) shredded queso quesadilla or anejo enchilado cheese

SUN-DRIED TOMATO DRESSING

1 cup extra-virgin olive oil

$\frac{1}{2}$ cup sun-dried tomatoes, drained

$\frac{1}{2}$ cup roasted red peppers, drained

$\frac{1}{2}$ cup white wine vinegar

1 to 3 teaspoons chipotle chili powder, to taste

1 teaspoon salt and pepper

CHEESE CRISPS

4 cups (16 ounces) grated Parmesan cheese

1 cup masa harina

1 to 2 tablespoons ancho or Chimayo (New Mexican) chili powder

12 cups baby lettuce

For the mushrooms, prepare the grill according to the manufacturer's directions, and preheat the oven to broil.

Mix the olive oil and garlic. Brush the mushrooms with the oil mixture. Grill or broil the mushrooms for 1 minute on each side until darkened and juicy. Turn the mushrooms bottom side up and fill each with 1 ounce of the cheese. Place the filled mushrooms under the broiler for 1 minute, until the cheese is melted.

For the dressing, combine the dressing ingredients in a blender; process until smooth. Refrigerate.

For the cheese crisps, heat an 8-inch, nonstick omelet pan over medium heat until hot, and a drop of water sizzles in the pan. In a bowl, mix the cheese, masa harina, and chili powder. Sprinkle $\frac{1}{4}$ cup of the cheese mixture evenly over the bottom of the pan. Tilt and shake the pan to cover the bottom evenly. Toast for 1 to $1\frac{1}{2}$ minutes until the cheese is melted. Push the edges down gently with a rubber spatula to loosen from the sides of the pan. When the entire surface is bubbly, invert the cheese crisp onto an upside-down custard cup. The cheese crisp will take on the shape of the cup. Repeat the procedure to yield 12 crisps.

To serve, place each cheese crisp on a plate, and fill each cheese crisp with one cheese-filled mushroom. Arrange lettuce around each crisp, and drizzle with the dressing. Sprinkle with the remaining shredded cheese.

Wisconsin Jalapeño Jack Empanadas

EMPANADA DOUGH

12 ounces flat stout (beer),
  at room temperature

⅛ ounce dry yeast
  (half of a ¼-ounce packet)

2 teaspoons sugar

2 teaspoons olive oil

4 cups all-purpose flour

1 teaspoon salt

FILLING

1 bunch fresh cilantro, washed,
  dried, stems removed

2½ cups shredded jalapeño
  Jack cheese

4 ounces roasted pork loin,
  shredded

2 egg yolks, lightly beaten

ACCOMPANIMENTS

Salsa or guacamole

For the dough, combine the stout, yeast, sugar, and oil. Let sit 10 to 15 minutes. Add the remaining ingredients. Using a heavy-duty mixer, mix until the dough is smooth and elastic. Add more flour, if necessary, until the dough is easy to handle. Place the dough in a greased bowl, cover, and let rise in a warm place for 1 hour. Punch down and let rise an additional ¼ hour.

For the filling and assembly, preheat the oven to 350°F. Separate the prepared dough into two portions. For each portion, roll the dough to ¹⁄₁₆-inch thickness. Using a cookie cutter or a glass of 3 inches diameter, cut into circles. On one half of each circle, stack 3 to 4 cilantro leaves, a scant tablespoon of cheese, and a sprinkling of pork shreds. Brush the egg yolk around the rim of the circle. Fold in half. Seal the edges, using the tines of a fork. Place on a baking sheet. Brush the tops with the egg yolk.

Bake for 15 to 17 minutes. Serve with fresh salsa or guacamole for dipping.

Variation: Salsa Jack, pepper Jack, or regular Monterey Jack may be used in place of jalapeño Jack. If using regular Monterey Jack, add a few chopped jalapeño peppers in escabèche to the filling.

Wisconsin Pesto Jack–Stuffed Mushrooms with Tomato Concassé

MAKES 6 SERVINGS

STUFFED MUSHROOMS

¾ pound hot Italian sausage, casing removed

¼ cup pine nuts

2 tablespoons diced sun-dried tomatoes

1 cup (4 ounces) shredded pesto Jack cheese

6 large (12 ounces) portobello mushrooms, stems removed

TOMATO CONCASSÉ*

2 tablespoons olive oil

2 garlic cloves, minced

1 shallot, diced

4 large Roma tomatoes, diced

2 tablespoons chopped fresh basil

½ cup chopped roasted red peppers

¼ teaspoon salt

¼ teaspoon pepper

* Instead of making the tomato concassé, you can use a 14- to 16-ounce jar of chunky Italian-style tomato sauce.

For the mushrooms, preheat the broiler. In a skillet, cook the sausage over medium heat, breaking apart until fully cooked; remove from the heat and drain fat. Add the pine nuts, sun-dried tomatoes, and cheese. Mix well; set aside.

In the preheated broiler, broil the mushroom caps, rounded side up, for 3 to 5 minutes. Remove from the oven; turn the caps over, and carefully spoon the warm sausage stuffing into each cap. Return to the oven and broil 3 to 5 minutes.

For the concassé, heat the olive oil over medium heat in a small saucepan. Add the garlic and the shallot; sweat 1 minute to release the flavors. Add the remaining ingredients and cook until softened, 6 to 8 minutes. Cool slightly.

In a food processor, pulse the tomato mixture to the desired consistency. Spoon onto the tops of the filled mushrooms and serve immediately.

Honeyed Cantaloupe with Prosciutto and Wisconsin Blue Cheese

CHEF JAMES CAMPBELL

MAKES 8 TAPAS

1 cup honey

2 fresh rosemary sprigs

2 cups vegetable oil

8 thin slices prosciutto

2 ripe cantaloupes

¼ cup extra-virgin olive oil

Salt and pepper, to taste

1 cup (6 ounces) crumbled Virgin Pine Blue Cheese

Warm the honey and the rosemary in a small saucepan on low heat for 2 to 3 minutes. Remove from the heat and set aside for 2 to 3 hours. Remove the rosemary sprigs.

Heat the vegetable oil in a deep skillet on medium-high heat. Fry the prosciutto until crisp, about 1 minute. Drain and cool on a paper towel–lined plate.

Peel the cantaloupes. Cut in half and scoop out the seeds. With a very sharp knife, slice both cantaloupes as thinly as possible.

To serve the cantaloupe, arrange 4 or 5 slices on each of eight plates. Drizzle with the olive oil, and season with the salt and pepper. For each plate, crumble one piece of prosciutto and sprinkle over the cantaloupe slices. Top with the blue cheese. Drizzle with the rosemary honey.

Pepper Jack Bola de Queso

MAKES 30 SERVINGS

1½ cups tortilla chips (plain, jalapeño, ranch, or salsa flavored)

2 cups (8 ounces) shredded pepper Jack cheese

½ cup (2 ounces) shredded sharp Cheddar cheese

12 tablespoons (6 ounces) cream cheese, cut in chunks and at room temperature

¼ teaspoon Mexican hot pepper sauce, to taste (optional)

2 tablespoons grated white onion

½ teaspoon dried oregano, preferably Mexican

¼ cup finely chopped dried Spanish olives with pimientos

Fresh cilantro, red jalapeño pepper slices, or additional olives (optional), for garnish

Tortilla chips or crackers

Place the tortilla chips in the bowl of a food processor. Process to fine crumbs. Pour on waxed paper and set aside.

Place the pepper Jack, Cheddar, cream cheese, and hot pepper sauce in the bowl of a food processor. Process until well blended and smooth. Add the onion and oregano. Pulse briefly to incorporate. Add a little half-and-half if the mixture is too stiff. (You may also use a heavy-duty electric mixer to make the cheese mixture.) Stir in the olives or work in with your hands. Refrigerate at least 1 hour.

Form the mixture into a ball. Roll the ball in the tortilla crumbs. Garnish with fresh cilantro, slices of red jalapeños, and/or additional olives. Serve with tortilla chips or crackers.

Variation: Use salsa Jack (for a milder ball) or chipotle or habañero Jack (for a hotter ball). If using chipotle Jack, replace the Spanish olives with ripe black olives.

Miniature Blue Cheese Balls with Winter Fruit

MAKES 30 CHEESE BALLS

30 dried apricots

Water

4 teaspoons pure vanilla extract

²/₃ cup coarsely chopped pecans

8 tablespoons (4 ounces) cream cheese, cut in chunks and softened to room temperature

¾ cup (about 5 ounces) crumbled blue cheese

1 tablespoon French brandy*

½ tablespoon grated yellow onion

* If a non-alcoholic mixture is preferred, substitute sherry extract. Start with ¼ teaspoon and add to taste.

** This mixture is a terrific filling for stewed dried plums (prunes) and Med-jool dates. Make a party plate with all winter fruits—apricots, dried plums, and dates—for variety.

Preheat the oven to 375°F.

Place the apricots in a saucepan. Add enough water to barely cover. Stir in the vanilla. Bring the apricots to a boil, uncovered, and simmer until tender, 1 to 4 minutes, depending on the dryness of the apricots. Test with a fork. The apricots should be tender but not limp. Drain and dry well. Set aside.

Spread the pecans on a baking sheet, and toast for 4 to 5 minutes, until aromatic. Stir after 2 minutes and watch, so the nuts do not scorch. Remove from the oven and pour the pecans onto waxed paper to cool. When cooled, grind the pecans in a blender or food processor until very fine. Set aside.

Place the cheeses and brandy in the bowl of a food processor. Pulse until the ingredients are well blended. Add the onion and pulse briefly to incorporate. (You may also use an electric mixer, if you prefer.) Remove the mixture to a bowl and refrigerate at least 2 hours.**

Remove the cheese mixture from the refrigerator, and shape the cheese into miniature balls. Dip the tops in the pecans. Place each ball on a reserved apricot, nut side up. Repeat until all of the mixture is used. (If the mixture is too soft, spoon it onto the apricots, rounding the top. Sprinkle with the nuts.

** This mixture is a terrific filling for stewed dried plums (prunes) and Med-jool dates. Make a party plate with all winter fruits—apricots, dried plums, and dates—for variety.

Savory Italian-Style Wisconsin Cheese Ball

MAKES 25 TO 30 SERVINGS

¾ cup pine nuts

8 ounces (2 cups) shredded Asiago cheese

2 ounces (½ cup) shredded Fontina cheese,

1 tablespoon shredded or grated Parmesan cheese

8 tablespoons (4 ounces) cream cheese, cut in chunks and at room temperature

2 tablespoons prepared refrigerated basil pesto

2 tablespoons half-and-half, if needed

½ cup marinated sun-dried tomatoes, diced and dried well

Fresh basil (optional), for garnish

Sun-dried tomatoes, slivered (optional), for garnish

Crusty bread, Italian breadsticks, or crostini crackers

Preheat the oven to 375°F. Spread the pine nuts on a baking sheet and toast for about 5 minutes or until golden. (Check after 3 minutes and stir.) Pour onto waxed paper and cool.

Place the four cheeses into the bowl of a food processor, and process until well blended. Add the pesto (drain first if the pesto is runny). Pulse to incorporate. If the mixture is too stiff, add half-and-half to reach the desired consistency. Remove the mixture to a bowl and stir or work in the tomatoes with your hands. Refrigerate for at least an hour.

When ready to serve, shape the cheese mixture into a ball. Roll the ball in the toasted pine nuts, pushing the nuts into the ball, if necessary.

Garnish with fresh basil and slivers of sun-dried tomatoes. Serve with crusty bread, Italian breadsticks, or crostini crackers.

Wisconsin Three-Cheese Ball

1 (8-ounce) package cream cheese

1 (10-ounce) package sharp Cheddar cold pack cheese spread

$\frac{1}{3}$ cup (about 2 ounces) crumbled blue cheese

Pinch of celery salt

Pinch of onion salt

$\frac{1}{2}$ cup (4 ounces) chopped walnuts

In a small bowl, beat the cream cheese until softened and blended. Gradually stir in the cheese spread; mix well. Stir in the blue cheese, celery salt, and onion salt. Form into a ball. Roll in the chopped walnuts. Chill until firm. Serve with crackers or vegetables.

Apple and Wisconsin Cheddar Cheese Spread

MAKES 8 SERVINGS

2 tablespoons chopped onion

1 tablespoon butter or margarine

1 cup (about 1 medium) pared, chopped Golden Delicious apple

3 cups (12 ounces) finely shredded Cheddar cheese

1 (3-ounce) package cream cheese, at room temperature

In a nonstick pan, sauté the onion in butter until softened. Add the apples; cook and stir until tender. Cool.

Blend the cheeses in a large bowl, and stir in the apple mixture. Spoon the mixture into a serving bowl; chill until ready to serve.

Variations: Add 2 tablespoons of dry sherry, 1 teaspoon of caraway seeds, or ½ teaspoon of curry powder.

Wisconsin Cheese and German Beer Spread

2 cups (8 ounces) shredded sharp Cheddar cheese

2 cups (8 ounces) shredded Swiss cheese

1 teaspoon Worcestershire sauce

½ teaspoon dry mustard

1 garlic clove, minced

½ cup dark German or other beer or lager

Assorted rye or pumpernickel crackers, breadsticks, or rye bread rounds

Bring the cheeses to room temperature; place in a food processor bowl fitted with a metal blade. Add the Worcestershire sauce, mustard, and garlic. Pulse until combined. Add the beer and process until smooth, 2 to 3 minutes. Pack in crocks or decorative jars; refrigerate overnight to blend the flavors.

Bring to room temperature and serve with crackers or bread rounds.

Creamy Wisconsin Brick Spread

MAKES 8 TO 12 SERVINGS

1 (8-ounce) package cream
cheese, at room temperature

¼ cup milk

2 cups (8 ounces) shredded
brick cheese

1 tablespoon chopped fresh
chives

2 tablespoons minced onion

½ teaspoon hot pepper sauce

Rye or pumpernickel bread or
crackers, for serving

In a mixer bowl, beat together the cream cheese and milk until fluffy. Add the remaining ingredients; mix well. Serve with bread or crackers.

Garlic Cheese Log

2 cups (8 ounces) shredded
  Cheddar cheese

1 (8-ounce) package cream
  cheese, at room temperature

1 small garlic clove, minced

½ teaspoon salt

Poppy seeds

Combine the cheeses until smooth, using a mixer or blender. Add the garlic and salt; mix thoroughly. Divide into two parts; shape into logs, and roll in enough poppy seeds to coat. Chill and serve.

Herbed Goat Cheese Spread

1 (11-ounce) log soft fresh goat cheese (about 1½ cups), at room temperature

3 tablespoons heavy cream

3 tablespoons extra-virgin olive oil

1 tablespoon dry white wine

Juice and finely grated zest of ½ lemon

Salt and freshly ground pepper, to taste

1 tablespoon finely chopped oil-packed sun-dried tomatoes

1 tablespoon chopped fresh flat-leaf parsley

1 tablespoon mixed chopped fresh herbs (dill, chives, mint, thyme, and oregano)

Chopped fresh herbs, for garnish

In the bowl of a food processor, combine the goat cheese, cream, olive oil, wine, and lemon juice; pulse until just blended, smooth, and spreadable. (If the mixture is too thick, add cream by tablespoonfuls, and pulse to blend.) Season the spread with salt and pepper. Add the lemon zest, tomatoes, and fresh herbs. Pulse again a few times just to blend.

Line a small bowl with plastic wrap, allowing several inches of overhang; scrape the cheese mixture into the bowl. Cover and refrigerate for at least 30 minutes and up to 24 hours.

To serve, invert the bowl onto a serving platter and peel off the plastic. Sprinkle with chopped fresh herbs.

Gorgonzola Spread

MAKES 16 SERVINGS

2 cups (16 ounces) mascarpone cheese

½ cup (4 ounces) creamy Gorgonzola cheese

2 tablespoons chopped fresh basil

½ cup chopped walnuts

Sliced apples and pears

In a small bowl, combine the cheeses and basil; mix well. Transfer to a serving bowl, cover, and refrigerate at least 2 hours or overnight.

Before serving, cover the spread with the chopped walnuts; arrange the apple and pear slices around the bowl.

Wisconsin Gouda and Beer Spread

1 ball (2 pounds) Gouda cheese*

12 tablespoons (1½ sticks) butter, cubed and softened

2 tablespoons snipped fresh chives

2 teaspoons Dijon mustard

½ cup amber or dark beer, at room temperature

Cocktail rye or pumpernickel bread slices

* Edam can be substituted for Gouda. If the cheese is not available in ball form, this spread may be served in your favorite serving bowl.

Cut ⅕ off the top of the cheese to create a flat surface. With a butter curler or melon baller, remove the cheese from the center of the ball, leaving a ½-inch-thick shell. Shred enough removed cheese to measure 4 cups. Reserve the remaining cheese for another use.

In a large bowl, blend the shredded cheese, butter, chives, and mustard. Stir in the beer until blended. Spoon the spread into the hollowed cheese ball; reserve the remaining spread for refill. Chill until serving time. Serve as a spread with cocktail bread.

Green Olive, Walnut, and Pepato Spread

MAKES 6 SERVINGS

1 cup (4 ounces) finely grated pepato cheese

4 tablespoons (2 ounces) cream cheese, softened

¼ cup sliced green olives

1 tablespoon white wine

⅓ cup chopped walnuts

Sliced olives, for garnish

Melba toast

In a medium bowl, combine the cheeses, stirring until combined. Add the olives and wine; beat until smooth. Transfer to a small serving bowl and smooth the top. Refrigerate at least 1 hour or up to 2 days.

Return the cheese mixture to room temperature. In a small skillet, toast the walnuts about 5 minutes, or until one shade darker. Sprinkle over the cheese; garnish with sliced olives. Serve the spread surrounded by pieces of melba toast.

Pecan, Bacon, and Wisconsin Cheese Spread

MAKES 10 SERVINGS

1 (8-ounce) package cream cheese, softened

3 tablespoons milk

4 slices crisply fried bacon, crumbled

2 tablespoons pecans

1 teaspoon garlic powder

1 teaspoon onion salt

Combine the cream cheese and milk in a blender. Add the remaining ingredients and blend until the pecans are chopped. Chill well; serve with whole wheat toast.

Variation: Substitute blue cheese for up to half of the cream cheese. The more blue cheese you use, the sharper the taste of the dip will be.

Cottage Blue Chip Dip

MAKES ABOUT 2 CUPS

1½ cups (12 ounces) cream-style small curd cottage cheese

⅓ cup (2 ounces) crumbled blue cheese

⅛ teaspoon pepper

½ teaspoon Worcestershire sauce

2 teaspoons finely chopped onion

3 tablespoons cream

Paprika, for coloring

Beat the cottage cheese with an electric mixer until smooth. Add the remaining ingredients and mix well. (More cream may be added for a thinner dip.) Serve chilled, with vegetables or crackers.

Wisconsin Swiss and Walnut Spread

MAKES 32 SERVINGS

1 (8-ounce) package cream cheese

1½ cups shredded Swiss cheese

½ cup sour cream

⅓ cup chopped walnuts

⅓ cup finely chopped fresh parsley

¼ cup chopped green onions

2 tablespoons Dijon mustard

Toasted pita triangles, assorted crackers or bagel chips

Combine the cheeses, sour cream, walnuts, parsley, green onions, and mustard in a medium-size bowl. Cover and refrigerate at least 1 hour to blend the flavors.

Serve with the pita triangles, crackers, or bagel chips.

Tavern Beer Cheese

CHEF SUSAN GOSS

MAKES 8 SERVINGS

3 cups (12 ounces) shredded aged Cheddar cheese

1½ cups (6 ounces) shredded Parmesan cheese

1½ teaspoons Tabasco sauce

3 tablespoons Worcestershire sauce

1 tablespoon pure chili powder blend, such as ancho and New Mexico

½ teaspoon garlic powder or granulated garlic

¼ to ⅓ cup beer

½ cup chopped fresh parsley

Crackers or toast slices

In large bowl, combine the cheeses. Add the Tabasco sauce, Worcestershire sauce, chili powder, and garlic powder. Mix well.

In a large food processor bowl with a metal blade, process the mixture, adding the beer to make a thick spread. Return to the serving bowl, and stir in the parsley. Serve at room temperature with crackers or toasts.

Creamy Gorgonzola Dip

1⅓ cups (8 ounces) creamy Gorgonzola cheese*

1 cup sour cream

½ teaspoon freshly ground black pepper

¾ cup coarsely chopped toasted walnuts**

* 1 to 1½ cups (6 ounces) of crumbled blue cheese may be substituted for the creamy Gorgonzola cheese.

** To toast the walnuts: Bake on a baking sheet for 8 to 10 minutes in a 350°F oven, checking and stirring frequently to prevent scorching.

In a medium bowl, combine the cheese, sour cream, and pepper; mix well. Cover and refrigerate until serving time. Just before serving, stir in the walnuts. Serve with sliced ripe pears or apples, breadsticks, or vegetables for dipping.

Asiago and Artichoke Dip

1½ cups (about 6 ounces) grated Asiago cheese

1 (8-ounce) package cream cheese, softened

¼ cup oil-packed sun-dried tomatoes, drained and chopped

2 tablespoons chopped fresh parsley

¼ teaspoon ground pepper

1 (14-ounce) can artichoke hearts, drained and chopped

Toasted French bread rounds

Preheat the oven to 350°F.

In a small bowl, mix the cheeses. Add the tomatoes, parsley, and pepper; blend. Stir in the artichokes. Place in a 1-quart ovenproof casserole dish; bake for about 25 minutes, or until bubbly. Serve with French bread rounds.

Hot Cheesy Spinach Dip

MAKES ABOUT 2 CUPS

1 (4-ounce) can chopped mild green chile peppers

1½ tablespoons chopped jalapeño peppers

¼ cup finely chopped onion

1 tablespoon vegetable oil

¾ cup chopped tomatoes

8 tablespoons (4 ounces) cream cheese, softened

½ cup half-and-half

1¾ teaspoons apple cider vinegar

2 ounces frozen chopped spinach, thawed and squeezed dry

1½ cups (6 ounces) shredded Cheddar cheese

Preheat the oven to 350°F.

Sauté the chiles, jalapeños, and onion in oil over medium heat for 4 minutes or until soft. Add the tomatoes and cook an additional 2 minutes, stirring frequently. Remove from the heat; reserve.

On medium speed, blend the cream cheese with an electric mixer until smooth. Gradually add the half-and-half and the vinegar; continue mixing until thoroughly blended. On low speed, gradually add the spinach and Cheddar cheese, mixing until thoroughly blended. Stir in the reserved chile mixture.

To serve, spoon the dip into ovenproof ramekins. Bake for 10 minutes or until warm. Serve as a dip for crackers and/or crudités.

Tangy Blue Cheese Whip

MAKES ABOUT $\frac{1}{2}$ CUP

1 cup whipping cream

$\frac{1}{2}$ cup (3 ounces) finely crumbled blue cheese

1 teaspoon dried basil, crushed

$\frac{1}{4}$ teaspoon garlic salt

$\frac{1}{2}$ cup almonds, toasted and chopped

Assorted fruits or raw vegetables

In a small mixing bowl, combine the whipping cream, cheese, basil, and garlic salt. Beat with an electric mixer on medium speed until slightly thickened. Gently fold in the chopped almonds. Serve with vegetables or fruit.

Layered Taco Dip

1 (8-ounce) container sour cream

8 tablespoons (4 ounces) cream cheese, softened

$2/3$ cup taco sauce

$1\frac{1}{2}$ cups torn iceberg lettuce

$1/3$ cup chopped green bell pepper

$1/2$ cup chopped onion

$3/4$ cup (3 ounces) shredded Cheddar cheese

$3/4$ cup (3 ounces) shredded Monterey Jack cheese

1 medium tomato, chopped

Tortilla chips

In a small mixing bowl, combine the sour cream and cream cheese; stir until smooth. On a large platter, spread the mixture to an 8-inch circle. Spread the taco sauce evenly over the top. Then layer with the lettuce, green pepper, onion, Cheddar cheese, and Monterey Jack cheese. Sprinkle the tomato on top. Serve with tortilla chips.

Mexican Cocktail Dip

MAKES 15 SERVINGS

BEANS

1 (15-ounce) can refried beans

½ teaspoon chili powder

½ teaspoon cumin

AVOCADOS

2 medium avocados, peeled, seeded, and chopped

2 teaspoons lemon juice

⅓ cup chopped onion

½ teaspoon sugar

½ teaspoon celery salt

⅛ teaspoon cayenne pepper

SOUR CREAM SAUCE

½ cup sour cream

¼ cup mayonnaise

2 teaspoons paprika

1 teaspoon cumin

½ teaspoon garlic powder

½ teaspoon chili powder

½ teaspoon hot pepper sauce

¼ teaspoon dried oregano

TO COMPLETE THE RECIPE

1 cup (4 ounces) shredded Cheddar cheese

1 cup (4 ounces) shredded Monterey Jack cheese

½ cup thinly sliced pitted ripe olives, drained

2 medium tomatoes, chopped

3 green onions, sliced

For the beans, in a small bowl, mix together the beans, chili powder, and cumin. Spread the bean mixture over the bottom of a serving dish 10 inches in diameter.

For the avocados, combine the avocados, lemon juice, onion, sugar, celery salt, and cayenne pepper in a blender container. Cover and blend until smooth. Spread on top of the bean mixture.

For the sour cream sauce, mix the sour cream, mayonnaise, paprika, cumin, garlic powder, chili powder, hot pepper sauce, and oregano. Spread this mixture on top of the avocado mixture.

To complete the recipe, mix the cheeses and sprinkle over the sour cream mixture. Arrange the olives in the center. Place the tomatoes around the olives and the onions around the tomatoes. Cover and refrigerate until serving time. Serve as a dip for tortilla chips or crackers.

Spicy Wisconsin Cheese and Veggie Dip

MAKES ABOUT 1¼ CUPS

YOGURT CHEESE*

1 (8-ounce) container plain
  lowfat yogurt

DIP

¼ cup (1 ounce) shredded sharp
  Cheddar cheese

⅔ cup finely shredded carrot

¼ cup prepared salsa

Pinch of salt

* Instead of making the yogurt cheese,
  you can use sour cream.

For the yogurt cheese, spoon the yogurt into a fine-mesh strainer. Set over a bowl and drain in the refrigerator for at least 4 hours. (The longer it is refrigerated, the firmer the cheese will be.) Discard the liquid. Store the cheese in the refrigerator in a tightly covered container until ready to use, up to 1 week. Makes 1½ to 2 cups.

For the dip, in a medium bowl, mix ⅓ cup of the yogurt cheese with the dip ingredients until blended. Transfer the dip to a serving dish and serve as a dip for crackers or pita chips.

Smoky Wisconsin Cheese Fondue

MAKES 4 TO 6 SERVINGS

1 cup (4 ounces) shredded smoked Cheddar cheese

¾ cup shredded Gruyère cheese

½ cup shredded pepato or Asiago cheese

2 tablespoons all-purpose flour

1 teaspoons dry mustard

1 cup dry white wine

1 teaspoon Worcestershire sauce

3 to 4 drops hot pepper sauce

1 teaspoon Dijon mustard

1 loaf sourdough bread, cut into cubes

In a small bowl, combine the cheeses, flour, and ground mustard. Toss to coat.

In a small saucepan, bring the wine to a simmer. Add a small handful of the cheese mixture to the simmering wine and stir until the cheese has melted. Repeat the process until all of the cheese has been melted. Add the Worcestershire, hot pepper sauce, and mustard, and cook on low until the mixture is thick and smooth. Transfer to a fondue pot and keep warm. Serve with fondue forks and the cubes of bread for dipping.

Wisconsin Cheddar Blue Fondue

1 (10½-ounce) can condensed tomato soup

1 teaspoon Worcestershire sauce

3 cups (12 ounces) shredded sharp Cheddar cheese

½ cup (3 ounces) crumbled blue cheese

2 tablespoons dry sherry

French bread or hard rolls, torn in bite-size pieces

In a fondue pot or heavy saucepan, heat the soup and the Worcestershire sauce. Stir in the cheeses, a little at a time, until they begin to melt. Add the sherry; stirring until the cheese is fully melted and the sherry is blended into the mixture. Serve over low heat with bread chunks or hard rolls.

Gorgonzola Fondue with Winter Vegetables

MAKES 10 SERVINGS

18 small red-skinned potatoes, rinsed, halved

3 large carrots, peeled, cut lengthwise into quarters, then into 1½-inch pieces

18 small Brussels sprouts

1 small cauliflower, separated into florets

2 tablespoons all-purpose flour

1 pound chilled Brie cheese

12 ounces chilled Gorgonzola cheese

1¾ cups dry white wine

2 garlic cloves, minced

Salt and pepper, to taste

1 crusty bread loaf (1½ pounds), cut into 1½-inch cubes

Steam the vegetables until tender, about 12 minutes for the potatoes, 10 minutes for the carrots and Brussels sprouts, and 8 minutes for the cauliflower. Arrange the steamed vegetables on a platter. Tent with foil to keep warm.

Meanwhile, place the flour in a large bowl. Cut the rind from the Brie cheese and cut into cubes. Drop the cubed cheese into the flour and toss to coat. Crumble the Gorgonzola cheese into the same bowl; toss again to coat. Combine the wine and garlic in a heavy medium saucepan. Simmer over medium heat for 2 minutes. Reduce the heat to medium low. Add the cheese by handfuls, stirring until melted after each addition. Stir until smooth. Season with salt and pepper. Transfer to a fondue pot. Set the pot over a candle or canned heat. Pierce the vegetables with fondue forks, and dip in the cheese. Serve with the cubed bread.

Traditional Wisconsin Cheese Fondue

2 cups dry white wine

1 tablespoon lemon juice

4 cups (16 ounces) shredded
　Gruyère cheese

4 cups (16 ounces) shredded
　fontina cheese

1 tablespoon arrowroot

2 ounces kirsch

Pinch of nutmeg

French bread cubes

Apples, cut in wedges

Pears, cut in wedges

Warm the wine and lemon juice to boiling in a fondue pot. Reduce the heat to low. Toss the cheeses with the arrowroot and gradually add the cheese mixture to the wine, stirring constantly. When the cheese is melted, stir in the kirsch. Sprinkle with nutmeg. Serve with French bread, apples, and pears.

Swiss Cheese Fondue

MAKES 6 SERVINGS

1¼ cups dry white wine, divided

1 large garlic clove, halved

5 cups (20 ounces) shredded Swiss or Gruyère cheese

4 teaspoons cornstarch

⅛ teaspoon nutmeg

1 loaf (1 pound) French bread, cut into 1½-inch chunks

In a 3-quart saucepan, combine 1 cup of the wine and the garlic. Bring just to simmering over low heat. Remove the garlic. Gradually stir in the cheese, waiting for each addition of cheese to melt before adding more; do not boil. When the cheese is completely melted, mix the cornstarch and nutmeg with the remaining wine. Add to the cheese mixture; stir until evenly smooth and thick. Transfer to a fondue pot or chafing dish, maintaining a temperature just below boiling for best consistency. Provide guests with fondue forks or bamboo skewers for dipping the bread chunks into the fondue. Fresh vegetable chunks can also be dipped into the fondue.

SOUPS AND SANDWICHES

Swiss Cheese and Shrimp Soup en Croûte

MAKES 6 SERVINGS

4 tablespoons (½ stick) unsalted butter

2 shallots, chopped

1 cup all-purpose flour

¾ cup Gewürztraminer wine

6 cups chicken stock

1 pound extra-large (16 to 20 count) shrimp, peeled and deveined

6 cups (1½ pounds) shredded baby Swiss cheese

Salt and freshly ground white pepper

6 (6-inch) disks puff pastry (about 1½ pounds)

1 egg, beaten

3 ounces grated Asiago cheese

1 cup pine nuts

Preheat the oven to 400°F.

In large pot over medium heat, melt the butter. Sauté the shallots. Stir in the flour, and add the wine. Simmer for 5 minutes to reduce. Stir. Add the chicken stock and shrimp, and cook 3 minutes longer. Whisk in the Swiss cheese. Add the salt and pepper. Remove from the heat and set aside.

Brush the pastry disks with beaten egg. Top the disks with Asiago cheese and pine nuts.

Pour the soup into six 5½-inch ovenproof bowls. Brush the rim of the bowls with egg. Place the pastry disks on top of the bowls. Press the rim to seal. Bake for 15 minutes until the pastry is golden brown.

Cheddar, Swiss, and Beer Soup

MAKES 12 SERVINGS

2 cups diced onion

2 tablespoons chopped garlic

½ pound (2 sticks) butter

½ cup all-purpose flour

2 quarts milk

2 bay leaves

3 cups (12 ounces) shredded
medium Cheddar

3 cups (12 ounces) shredded
aged Swiss

Salt and pepper, to taste

Pinch of nutmeg

1½ cups pale ale

Sauté the onion and garlic in butter until soft, about 5 minutes. Add the flour; cook, stirring frequently, over medium heat, about 5 minutes. Whisk in the milk. Add the bay leaves; cook, stirring constantly, over low heat until the mixture thickens, about 20 minutes. Stir in the cheese gradually; cook just until the cheese melts. Remove from the heat. Season with salt, pepper, and nutmeg; remove the bay leaves. Stir in the beer.

Monterey Jack Cheese Soup

MAKES 6 SERVINGS

½ cup finely chopped onion

1 large ripe tomato, peeled and diced

1 large can chopped green chiles

½ garlic clove, minced

1 cup chicken stock

1½ cups heavy white sauce*

1 cup half-and-half

Pinch of freshly ground black pepper

1½ cups (6 ounces) shredded Monterey Jack cheese

* To make heavy white sauce: Melt 4½ tablespoons butter in a small saucepan on medium heat. Stir in 4½ tablespoons flour and ⅛ teaspoon salt. Gradually add 1½ cups milk, stirring constantly. Cook and stir until thickened and bubbly.

In a large saucepan, combine the onion, tomato, chiles, garlic, and chicken stock. Bring to a boil; simmer until the vegetables are tender. Remove from the heat. Slowly stir in the white sauce, stirring constantly. Slowly add the half-and-half. Add the pepper. Gradually add the cheese, stirring constantly, until melted. Serve immediately.

Cheesy Corn Soup with Smoked Chiles

MAKES 6 SERVINGS

10 ears sweet corn in their husks

5 cups water, divided

2 to 4 canned chipotle chile peppers, deveined, seeded and finely chopped*

Salt, to taste

1 cup (6 ounces) crumbled feta cheese

* Chipotle chile peppers are available in Mexican markets and in some supermarkets; 1 to 1½ tablespoons minced, fresh, or canned jalapeño peppers can be substituted.

Preheat the oven to 400°F.

Cook the corn on an outdoor grill or boil on the stovetop. To grill, leave the husks on and remove the silks. Soak in a large bowl of cold water for at least 1 hour and drain. Grill on an outdoor grill over direct heat, turning often, for 15 to 25 minutes, or until cooked through. Cool and remove husks. To boil on the stovetop, husk the corn and place in a large pot. Cover with water and bring to a boil. Boil for 10 minutes. Drain and cool.

Cut the kernels from the ears (you should have 7 to 8 cups). With an electric blender, Purée 4 cups of the corn with 3 cups of the water.

In a 3- to 4-quart saucepan, combine the purée, the remaining 2 cups of water, and the peppers. Bring to a boil, reduce the heat, and simmer 15 minutes over low heat. Add the remaining corn; heat through. Season with salt. Ladle into bowls. Top with the crumbled cheese.

Tip: Since ears of corn vary in size, adjust the recipe by using a total of about 1 cup of water for every 1½ cups of corn. Adjust the amounts of peppers and salt accordingly.

Cabbage and Wisconsin Cheese Soup

CHEF ROBERTO DONNA

MAKES 6 SERVINGS

1 pound savoy cabbage

1 quart beef stock

2 mild Italian sausages
(½ pound)

1 (8-ounce) block aged
Wisconsin Cheddar cheese

6 tablespoons butter

6 slices country bread (about
½ inch thick), cut in half

Preheat the oven to 325° F.

Clean and wash the cabbage leaves. Cook in boiling water 5 minutes or until limp. Drain well and julienne the leaves. Set aside.

In a 2-quart saucepan, bring the beef stock to a boil with the sausages. Simmer 8 to 10 minutes until thoroughly cooked. Remove from the stock and cut into thin slices. Set aside.

Cut the Cheddar cheese into thin slices. Set aside.

Melt the butter over low heat. In an ovenproof casserole (preferably terra-cotta), arrange 3 of the bread slices. Layer with the cabbage, sausage, cheese, and remaining bread. Drizzle the top layer of the bread with melted butter. Gently pour the boiled stock over the top. Bake for about 30 minutes, until the top bread layer is crisp and the soup is thoroughly heated. Spoon into soup bowls. Season to taste.

Curried Carrot and Mascarpone Soup

CHEF MICHAEL SYMON

MAKES 4 SERVINGS

2 shallots, minced

1 garlic clove, minced

2 tablespoons olive oil

Sea salt

12 ounces (about 5) carrots, peeled and chopped

1 tablespoon Thai red curry paste*

3½ cups chicken stock

1 tub (8 ounces) mascarpone cheese, at room temperature

* The soup will have a definite "kick." Reduce the amount of curry paste if a milder flavor is preferred.

Place the shallots and garlic in olive oil in a deep saucepan, and lightly salt. Cover and cook gently for 3 to 4 minutes until limp but now brown. Add the carrots and continue to cook, covered, for 10 minutes over medium-low heat. Add the curry paste and chicken stock, and simmer, uncovered, for 1 hour.

Remove the soup from the heat and pour into a blender beaker or food processor bowl; blend until smooth. Return to the heat and bring to a simmer. Whisk in the mascarpone cheese. Serve immediately in soup bowls.

Cauliflower and Cheddar Cheese Soup

MAKES 8 SERVINGS

4 cups chicken stock or water

2 cups chopped potatoes

3½ cups cauliflowerets, divided

1 cup chopped onion

1 cup chopped carrot

3 garlic cloves, minced

1½ teaspoons salt

1½ cups (6 ounces) shredded
Cheddar cheese

¼ teaspoon dried dill

¼ teaspoon dry mustard

⅛ teaspoon pepper

¾ cup milk

1 tablespoon all-purpose flour

2 tablespoons butter

Combine the stock, potatoes, 2 cups of the cauliflowerets, onion, carrot, garlic, and salt in a large saucepan. Bring slowly to a boil, and simmer 15 minutes. Remove from the heat. Cool about 20 minutes. Purée.

Return the purée to the saucepan and over low heat, gradually add the cheese, dill, dry mustard, and pepper. Stir until the cheese melts.

In a small bowl, whisk the milk and flour together until smooth. Slowly pour into the hot soup, stirring until well blended, about 5 minutes.

Sauté the remaining 1½ cups of cauliflowerets in butter until crisp and tender. Add to the soup.

Creamy Cucumber Soup with Wisconsin Ricotta

MAKES 6 SERVINGS

1½ cups (12 ounces) ricotta cheese

3¼ cups peeled, seeded, and diced cucumber, divided

⅓ cup chopped onion

4 tablespoons chopped fresh dill, divided

2¾ cups buttermilk

⅓ cup thinly sliced green onion

Salt and red pepper sauce, to taste

Sesame bread sticks

In the bowl of a food processor, blend the cheese, 1¼ cups of the cucumbers, the onion, and 2 tablespoons of the dill until smooth. Pour the cheese mixture into a large container with a lid. Stir in the buttermilk, the remaining 2 cups of cucumber, the green onions, the remaining 2 tablespoons of dill, and the salt and red pepper sauce. Cover. Refrigerate at least 4 hours before serving.

To serve, ladle approximately 1 cup of chilled soup into each soup bowl. Serve with sesame bread sticks.

Tuscan Onion Soup with Shaved Wisconsin Parmesan

CHEF TOM CATHERALL

MAKES 6 SERVINGS

3 pounds white onions
(3 or 4 large)

4 medium leeks

4 ounces pancetta, in 1 piece

¼ cup extra-virgin olive oil

6 cups chicken stock

3 to 4 tablespoons balsamic
vinegar

¾ to 1 cup fruity red wine, such
as Merlot or Beaujolais

Salt and pepper, to taste

6 slices rustic country style
bread

2 garlic cloves, peeled and
halved

3 ounces Parmesan cheese,
in 1 chunk

2 tablespoons chopped fresh
parsley

Peel the onions and cut in half lengthwise. Thinly slice crosswise. Trim the leeks and cut in half lengthwise. Slice crosswise in ¼-inch slices, using 3 inches of pale green. Place the leeks in cold water, and rinse to remove the dirt. Drain. Reserve the onions and leeks.

Unroll the pancetta and dice into ¼-inch pieces. Heat the olive oil in a large soup pot over medium-high heat. Add the pancetta and cook until some of the fat has been rendered, about 5 minutes. Add the onions and leeks. Sauté for 20 minutes or until tender, stirring occasionally. Add the stock, and simmer 30 minutes. Stir the vinegar, wine, salt, and pepper into the soup. Cook until thoroughly heated.

Toast the bread slices, and rub with the peeled garlic clove halves.

To serve, spoon the soup into soup bowls. Float the bread croutons in the soup. Pare 4 or 5 shavings of the cheese on top of each serving. Garnish with the chopped parsley, and serve immediately.

Calabaza Soup with Wisconsin Limburger Cheese

CHEF GUILLERMO PERNOT

MAKES 6 SERVINGS

2 pound calabaza or butternut squash, peeled, chopped

2 tablespoons olive oil

1 tablespoon kosher salt

1 Spanish onion, chopped

1½ quarts rich chicken stock

½ cup heavy cream

6 slices Limburger cheese, ¼ inch thick, at room temperature

3 tablespoons pumpkin seeds (pepitas), toasted

2 teaspoons pumpkin seed oil

Preheat the oven to 400°F.

In a shallow baking pan, toss the squash with the oil and salt. Roast 20 minutes or until tender.

In a soup pot, combine the squash, onions, and chicken stock. Simmer until the onions are very tender, about 20 minutes. Purée the soup with an immersion blender until smooth. If too thick, add additional chicken stock. Adjust the seasonings and add the cream. Serve hot in soup bowls. Top each serving with a cheese slice, pumpkin seeds, and a drizzle of oil. Serve immediately.

Winter Squash Bisque and Apple-Ham Crostini with Cheddar

CHEF JAMES CAMPBELL

MAKES 6 SERVINGS

BISQUE

1 (2-pound) butternut squash

1 medium acorn squash

3 tablespoons butter

1 medium onion, finely chopped

4 garlic cloves, minced

1 tablespoon grated fresh ginger

1/4 cup sweet sherry

4 cups chicken stock

Salt and pepper

1 tablespoon finely chopped fresh sage

1 cup half-and-half

CROSTINI

6 slices French baguette, 1/2 inch thick

4 tablespoons olive oil, divided

2 Granny Smith apples, peeled, cored, diced

1/2 pound smoked ham, diced

1 teaspoon finely chopped fresh sage

1/3 to 1/2 pound aged Cheddar cheese, cut in 6 slices the size of the bread slices

For the bisque, preheat the oven to 350°F. Cut the butternut and acorn squashes in half; scoop out the seeds. Place on a baking sheet, cut side down. Bake 1 to 1 1/4 hours or until tender, turning to place the peel side down midway through baking. Remove from the oven, but keep the temperature at 350°F for the crostini. Scoop out the flesh and set aside.

In a large soup pot over medium heat, melt the butter. Sauté the onion until soft. Stir in the garlic and ginger. Deglaze the pan with sherry. Stir in the stock and cooked squash. Season to taste with salt and pepper. Cook until the mixture boils; reduce the heat to simmer, and cook about 15 minutes. Purée the soup, adding the sage and the half-and-half. Keep warm.

For the crostini, brush the bread slices with 2 tablespoons of the olive oil; place on a baking sheet. Bake 4 minutes.

In a medium sauté pan over medium heat, cook the apples, ham, and sage in the remaining 2 tablespoons olive oil until tender, about 3 minutes. Place 1 slice of cheese on each slice of bread, and top with a tablespoon of the apple-ham mixture.

Tomato and Basil Bisque

MAKES 8 SERVINGS

BISQUE

3¼ cups low-sodium chicken
   stock, divided

1 Spanish onion, diced

1 tablespoon chopped garlic

1 (28-ounce) can plum tomatoes
   with juice

¼ teaspoon red pepper flakes

½ cup (1½ ounces) grated
   Asiago cheese

½ cup julienned fresh basil

ASIAGO CROUTONS

1 tablespoon olive oil

2 teaspoons chopped garlic

12 to 16 thin slices of Italian
   bread

½ cup (about 2 ounces) grated
   Asiago

For the bisque, place ¼ cup of the chicken stock in a heavy-gauge nonreactive pot over medium heat. Add the onion, and sweat for 6 to 8 minutes, until the onion is limp. Add the garlic, and continue to cook 2 to 3 minutes. Add the tomatoes, the remaining stock, and the red pepper flakes. Bring the soup to a boil. Reduce the heat, and simmer for 35 to 40 minutes. Remove the soup from the heat and let it cool slightly. When cooled, purée the soup in a blender, in batches. Stir in the cheese and the basil, adjust the seasoning, and chill the soup.

For the Asiago croutons, preheat the oven to 400°F.

Combine the oil and the garlic, and lightly brush the Italian bread with this mixture. Place the bread slices on a baking sheet, and top each slice with the cheese. Bake the croutons for 8 to 10 minutes, or until the cheese is golden and bubbling. Cool.

To serve, ladle approximately 1 cup of soup into each bowl. Top each serving with two Asiago croutons. Serve immediately.

Cheddar Sausage Soup

MAKES 8 SERVINGS

4 tablespoons (½ stick) butter

⅓ cup chopped green onion

1 (8-ounce) package fresh cabbage, shredded for coleslaw

¼ cup all-purpose flour

2 (10 ¼-ounce) cans chicken stock

½ cup beer

1 tablespoon Dijon mustard

2 cups half-and-half, heated

2 cups (8 ounces) shredded sharp Cheddar cheese

1 pound precooked smoked sausage, cut into bite-sized chunks

Melt the butter in a large, heavy saucepan. Add the onion and cabbage. Cook and stir over medium-high heat until the vegetables become translucent. Stir in the flour; cook 1 minute. Add the stock, beer, and mustard. Cover and simmer 30 minutes. Add the hot half-and-half, cheese, and sausage. Warm gently until heated through and the cheese melts.

Artichoke, Goat Cheese, and Marinated Tomato Panini

MAKES 3 SANDWICHES

TOMATOES

2 medium tomatoes, peeled and finely chopped (about 2 cups)

1 garlic clove, pressed or minced

2 tablespoons extra-virgin olive oil

½ teaspoon fine sea salt or kosher salt

Freshly ground pepper, to taste

PANINI

¾ cup (6 ounces) soft fresh goat cheese, at room temperature

2 tablespoons finely chopped fresh basil

3 teaspoons extra-virgin olive oil

6 slices artisanal white bread or sourdough

1 (6-ounce) jar quartered marinated artichoke hearts, drained

Fine sea salt or kosher salt and freshly ground pepper, to taste

For the tomatoes, in a small bowl, combine the tomatoes, garlic, olive oil, and salt. Season with the pepper. Set the tomato mixture aside to allow the flavors to blend for at least 20 minutes, stirring occasionally.

For the panini, in another small bowl, combine the goat cheese, basil, and olive oil; stir until the cheese is well combined with the other ingredients.

Arrange the bread slices on a work surface, and spread some of the goat cheese mixture on 3 slices. Using a slotted spoon, spoon some of the tomato mixture atop the goat cheese. Top with some of the artichokes. Sprinkle with salt and pepper. Top each sandwich with the remaining bread slices.

If using a panini grill, cook each sandwich according to the manufacturer's instructions, until golden brown, about 7 minutes.

If using a nonstick skillet, heat the skillet over medium heat. Add a sandwich to the skillet; then top the sandwich with a second heavy skillet to press the sandwich. (To weigh the sandwich down even more, place canned goods atop the second skillet.) Grill the sandwich until golden brown, about 4 minutes per side. Repeat with the remaining sandwiches.

Portobello Reubens

8 large caps (about 2 pounds) portobello mushrooms

½ cup pastrami seasoning*

¼ cup olive oil

8 slices dark rye bread

½ cup Thousand Island dressing

2 cups (1 pound) sauerkraut

8 slices (8 ounces) Gruyère cheese

¼ pound (1 stick) unsalted butter, softened

* This seasoning includes garlic, cracked black pepper, allspice, clove, coriander, salt, and brown sugar.

Remove the gills from the mushroom caps. Liberally sprinkle the mushroom caps with the pastrami seasoning mixture. Cover and let the mushrooms stand for several hours, to marinate.

In a large skillet, heat the oil over medium-high heat. Add the mushrooms and sauté evenly on both sides for 6 minutes or until softened and lightly browned. Remove from the heat and cool. Slice and reserve.

On a clean, flat surface, lay out the bread slices. Spread each slice with dressing. Top 4 slices of bread with the sauerkraut and sliced mushrooms. Lay the cheese slices over the tops of the mushrooms, and top with the remaining slices of bread.

Spread the sandwiches with softened butter and cook in a nonstick skillet until golden and the cheese has melted. Cut each Reuben into 3 equal portions and keep warm until ready to serve.

Savory Wisconsin Three-Cheese Sandwich Spread

MAKES ABOUT 2 CUPS

⅔ cup ricotta cheese

½ cup (2 ounces) shredded Cheddar cheese

½ cup (2 ounces) shredded Swiss cheese

¼ cup finely chopped green onions

¼ cup finely chopped celery

1 teaspoon prepared mustard

⅛ teaspoon pepper

1 tablespoon milk

In a bowl mix all of the ingredients except the milk. Gradually mix in enough milk to make the mixture spreadable. Cover and store in the refrigerator for up to 3 days.

Variation: Other varieties of shredded cheese can be used with the ricotta.

Serving Suggestions: Halve crusty French rolls horizontally. Pull out the centers of the rolls to make shells about ½ inch thick. (Reserve the crumbs for another use.) Fill the roll halves with sandwich spread and press together; package individually in plastic wrap.

Make hearty main-dish sandwiches with whole-grain bread, sandwich spread, sliced tomatoes, and lettuce. For a picnic, pack the sandwich spread in a paper cup or plastic container. Cover securely. Serve with crackers or vegetable sticks.

Spiced Apple Grilled Havarti Sandwiches

MAKES 4 SANDWICHES

3 tablespoons butter

2 large Granny Smith apples, cored and thinly sliced

4 to 6 tablespoons sugar, to taste

½ teaspoon cinnamon

½ teaspoon cardamom

1 tablespoon apple brandy (optional)

8 thick slices day-old bread

8 thin slices Havarti cheese

¼ pound (1 stick) butter, softened

Melt the butter in a skillet over medium heat. Sauté the apples for 3 to 5 minutes. Add the sugar, cinnamon, cardamom, and brandy. Toss to coat the apple slices with the sugar and spices. Remove the pan from the heat. Set aside.

Lay four slices of the bread on a griddle. Top with one slice of Havarti, one-fourth of the spiced apples, and another slice of Havarti. Place the remaining slices of bread on top of all. Butter the sandwich tops. Turn over. Butter again. Place the griddle over medium heat. Brown the sandwiches on each side for 3 to 5 minutes, until golden and the Havarti is soft. Cool for 5 minutes before serving.

Note: Serve with hot mulled wine or spiked cider; or chilled sparkling cider, with or without alcohol.

Tip: Prepared apple-cinnamon pie filling can be used.

Tuscan-Style Wisconsin Grilled Cheese Sandwiches

2 pounds (about 18 spears) asparagus, grilled

½ cup prepared balsamic-garlic-olive oil vinaigrette

12 slices crusty sourdough bread

12 slices (12 ounces) fontina cheese

12 slices (1 pound from 4-ounce ovals) fresh mozzarella cheese

36 fresh basil leaves

1 cup roasted red pepper pieces

12 slices provolone cheese

Extra-virgin olive oil, as needed

6 fresh fruit kebabs, with fruits, such as melon, pineapple, and strawberries

In a large bowl, toss the grilled asparagus with vinaigrette. Cover and refrigerate for at least 2 hours before using.

Preheat the oven to 350°F.

Lay 6 slices of bread on a clean, flat surface. Top each slice with (in order): 2 slices of fontina cheese; 3 marinated, drained asparagus spears; 2 slices of fresh mozzarella; 6 fresh basil leaves; 2½ tablespoons of red pepper pieces; and 2 slices of provolone. Top with a second slice of bread. Brush both sides of each sandwich lightly with olive oil.

Heat a large nonstick skillet over medium heat and grill the sandwiches on both sides until golden brown. Transfer to a baking sheet and bake for 8 to 10 minutes or until heated through.

To serve, cut each sandwich on the diagonal and serve with a fresh fruit kebab.

Berry, Cucumber, and Brie Baguette

MAKES 6 SERVINGS

6 ounces Brie cheese, rind removed, cubed

⅓ cup prepared cucumber ranch dressing

1 (16-ounce) loaf sourdough French or Italian bread

Lettuce leaves

1 cup sliced cucumber

12 thin slices fontina, Havarti, Swiss, or Colby cheese (any combination)

¾ cups fresh raspberries

¾ cups sliced fresh strawberries

⅓ cup chopped pecans

In a medium bowl, combine the Brie and the dressing; mix to coat. Slice the bread in half horizontally. Hollow out the bottom half, leaving a ¾-inch shell. Spread the Brie mixture on the bottom. Top with the lettuce leaves, cucumber slices, cheese slices, raspberries, strawberries, and pecans. Replace the top of the bread; secure with long wooden picks. Slice into individual servings. Serve immediately, or pack the ingredients into containers to assemble later.

Chimichurri Burgers with Wisconsin Gouda Cheese

MAKES 4 BURGERS

CHIMICHURRI SAUCE

2 garlic cloves

1 jalapeño pepper, stemmed, halved, and seeded (or more to taste)

¾ cup packed fresh parsley leaves

½ cup olive oil

2 tablespoons red wine or sherry vinegar

¼ teaspoon salt

1½ teaspoons dried oregano

½ teaspoon red pepper flakes (optional)

BURGERS

1½ pounds ground beef chuck

½ teaspoon salt

¼ teaspoon freshly ground pepper

4 ounces Gouda cheese, diced

4 Kaiser rolls or hamburger buns, split

For the sauce, combine the garlic and jalapeño in a food processor. Process until finely minced. Add the parsley; process until finely minced. Scrape down the work bowl. Add the oil, vinegar, and salt; process until well combined. Transfer to a small bowl. Stir in the oregano and red pepper flakes. Let the sauce rest for 2 hours, if possible, to blend the flavors.

For the burgers, prepare a barbecue grill or preheat a ridged grill pan. Spoon 3 tablespoons of the chimichurri sauce into a large bowl. Add the meat, salt, and pepper; mix well. Divide the mixture into 8 balls. Form each ball into a thin patty, about 5 inches in diameter. Divide the cheese over four of the patties, and top with the remaining patties. Seal the edges well, enclosing the cheese.

Grill the patties over medium-hot coals (or follow ground meat directions if using a gas grill) or in the preheated grill pan for 5 minutes per side or until the internal temperature of the meat reaches 160°F. If desired, place the buns, cut sides down, on the grill during the last 1 minute of cooking, or toast the buns in the oven or under the broiler. Place the patties in the buns and serve with the remaining chimichurri sauce.

Note: If desired, additional Gouda cheese, thinly sliced, may be placed over the patties during the last minute of cooking.

Greek Cheeseburgers

1 pound ground beef

½ pound ground lamb

2 tablespoons finely chopped onion

½ teaspoon dried oregano, crushed

¼ teaspoon pepper

1 cup (6 ounces) crumbled feta cheese, plus additional for sprinkling

¼ cup chopped ripe olives

¾ teaspoon lemon-pepper marinade, divided

¾ cup plain yogurt

¼ cup shredded seeded cucumber, well-drained

4 pita bread rounds, cut in half

Combine the beef, lamb, onion, oregano, and pepper; mix well. Shape into eight 4-inch patties. Combine 1 cup of the cheese, the olives, and ½ teaspoon of the lemon-pepper marinade. Top four patties with the cheese mixture; cover with the remaining patties. Pinch the edges together to seal.

To broil indoors, preheat the oven to broil. Place the patties on the greased rack of a broiler pan. Broil both sides to the desired doneness. Sprinkle the patties with cheese; continue broiling until the cheese is melted.

To grill outdoors, place patties on a greased grill over medium coals (the coals will be glowing). Grill, uncovered, 5 minutes on each side, to desired doneness. Sprinkle the patties with cheese; continue grilling until the cheese is melted.

To serve, cut each cooked patty in half. Combine the yogurt, cucumber, and ¼ teaspoon of the lemon-pepper marinade. Spread the inside of each pita bread half with the yogurt mixture; fill with the patty half.

Italian Cheeseburgers

MAKES 4 CHEESEBURGERS

½ pound ground beef

½ pound Italian sausage, casings removed

½ cup dry breadcrumbs

½ cup tomato sauce

2 tablespoons finely chopped onion

2 tablespoons grated Parmesan cheese

¼ teaspoon pepper

4 (1-ounce) slices provolone cheese

8 Italian bread slices, toasted

Combine the beef, sausage, breadcrumbs, tomato sauce, onion, Parmesan cheese, and pepper; mix well. Shape into four 5-inch oval patties. Cook following one of the methods below.

To broil indoors, preheat the broiler. Place the patties on the greased rack of a broiler pan. Broil both sides to desired doneness. Top each with a slice of cheese; continue broiling until the cheese is melted.

To grill outdoors, place the patties on a greased grill over medium coals (coals will be glowing). Grill, uncovered, 5 minutes on each side, or to desired doneness. Top each with a slice of cheese; continue grilling until the cheese is melted.

To serve, place each patty on a bread slice; top with additional tomato sauce and a bread slice.

Pepper Jack–Stuffed Burgers

2 pounds ground beef

1½ teaspoon salt

½ teaspoon pepper

¼ cup minced onion

2 cups (8 ounces) shredded
  pepper Jack cheese*

6 tablespoons salsa

6 hamburger buns

* For a twist, substitute feta cheese and
  kalamata olives.

In a large bowl, combine the ground beef, salt, pepper, and onion, and mix thoroughly. Shape into 12 (¼-inch-thick) patties. Reserve ⅓ cup of the shredded cheese. Top six patties with the remaining cheese. Place the remaining patties over the cheese-topped patties, and firmly press the edges together. Refrigerate until ready to grill.

Spray the grate of an outdoor grill and utensils with cooking spray. Preheat the grill to medium.

Place the burgers on the heated grill and cook, covered, 7 to 8 minutes to medium (160°F) doneness, until the meat is no longer pink in the center and the juices show no pink color; turn occasionally. During the last 2 minutes of cooking, spoon 1 tablespoon of salsa on each burger and sprinkle with the remaining cheese. Place on the hamburger buns, and serve immediately.

Cheesy Meatloaf Sandwiches

MEATLOAF

1 pound ground beef

6 ounces ground pork

1 cup (4 ounces) grated Asiago cheese

1 egg

½ cup dried breadcrumbs

3 tablespoons minced fresh parsley

2 teaspoons grainy Dijon mustard

¾ teaspoon cracked black pepper

1 teaspoon salt

SANDWICHES

⅓ cup mayonnaise

3 tablespoons grainy mustard

8 French rolls

8 lettuce leaves

2 tomatoes, sliced

16 slices provolone cheese

For the meatloaf, preheat the oven to 375°F.

In a bowl, combine all of the meatloaf ingredients. Mix well and pack into a 9 x 5-inch loaf pan. Bake the loaf until cooked through and browned, 55 to 60 minutes.

Remove the pan from the oven and drain the excess grease. Let the loaf cool completely before slicing. Cut the loaf into 12 slices.

For the sandwiches, blend the mayonnaise and mustard. Split the rolls and top each bottom bun with 1 lettuce leaf, 2 tomato slices, 1 meatloaf slice, 2 provolone slices, and 1 tablespoon of the mayonnaise/mustard spread. Top with the roll tops, and serve the sandwiches with potato salad or french fries.

Wisconsin Cheese Steak Sandwiches

MAKES 6 SERVINGS

STEAK AND MARINADE

¾ cup red wine vinegar

6 tablespoons vegetable oil

1 teaspoon dry mustard

3 garlic cloves, minced

2 teaspoons dried oregano

2¼ pounds beef flank steak

CHEESE BREAD

¼ pound (1 stick) butter, softened

2 garlic cloves, minced

1 loaf French bread, split lengthwise

2 cups (8 ounces) shredded Muenster cheese

For the steak and marinade, in a small bowl, combine the vinegar, oil, mustard, garlic, and oregano. Place the steak in a nonmetal baking dish. Pour the marinade over the steak. Cover and marinate overnight in the refrigerator, turning the steak occasionally.

For the cheese bread, the next day, combine the butter and the garlic; spread on the cut bread. Sprinkle each half with 1 cup of cheese. Wrap the halves, side by side, in foil, 2 halves per packet.

Grease a grill rack, and grill the steak for 8 to 10 minutes on each side (medium). Remove the steak from the grill, put the wrapped bread on the grill, and cover the bread. Cook for 8 to 10 minutes. or until the cheese melts.

To complete the sandwiches, while the cheese bread is cooking, thinly slice the steak across the grain. Remove the bread from the grill. Cut each loaf into 6 pieces. Top the grilled bread with the sliced beef.

Moroccan Rollups

MAKES 10 SERVINGS

ROLLUPS

1 pound boneless leg of lamb or chicken, cut into ½-inch cubes

½ cup minced sweet onions

2 teaspoons ground cumin

1 teaspoon cinnamon

½ teaspoon cayenne

½ teaspoon salt

2 tablespoons olive oil

5 (6- or 7-inch) pita bread rounds

1 cup (4 ounces) coarsely grated pepato or Asiago cheese

1 cup (6 ounces) crumbled feta cheese

½ cup chopped ripe olives

½ cup chopped tomatoes

YOGURT SAUCE

1 cup low-fat plain yogurt

1 tablespoon chopped mint

½ cup chopped cucumber

For the rollups, preheat the oven to 400°F.

Combine the meat, onion, spices, and salt. Heat the oil in a large skillet over medium-high heat; add the meat mixture and cook for about 10 minutes (5 to 8 minutes for chicken) until cooked through.

To assemble, split each pita at the edges to yield two rounds. Place them with the insides facing up on the countertop. Sprinkle the rounds with the cheese, olives, and tomatoes. Spoon a strip of sautéed lamb across each round. Roll the pita round tightly around the filling and place seam side down in a baking dish. Bake for 10 minutes or until crispy. While the rollups are baking, prepare the yogurt sauce.

For the yogurt sauce, mix the yogurt, mint, and cucumber in a small bowl until blended. Serve with the rollups.

The New Yorker, Wisconsin-Style

GEORGE LACKEY

MAKES 6 SANDWICHES

HORSERADISH MUSTARD

½ cup Dijon mustard

¼ cup prepared horseradish

PICKLE SLAW

2 cups shaved cabbage

¾ cup dill pickle relish, drained

½ cup mayonnaise

SANDWICHES

12 slices pumpernickel bread

12 dill pickle sandwich slices, drained

6 slices (12 ounces) smoked Gouda cheese

12 slices (12 ounces) hard salami, thinly sliced

12 slices (1 pound 8 ounces) Gruyère cheese

1¼ pounds corned beef, thinly shaved

12 pickle slices, for garnish

24 large green olives, for garnish

For the horseradish mustard, combine the mustard and horseradish in a small bowl.

For the pickle slaw, combine the cabbage and pickle relish in a large bowl. Stir in the mayonnaise. Combine the slaw mix with the remaining horseradish mustard mixture, and toss well to coat. Cover and refrigerate at least 2 hours before using.*

For the sandwiches, on a clean, flat surface, lay out the bread slices. Spread each slice evenly with 1 tablespoon of horseradish mustard. Top 6 of the bread slices with 2 pickle slices. Layer 1 slice of smoked Gouda, 2 slices of hard salami and ⅓ cup of pickle slaw on top of the pickle slices. Set aside.

Top each of the remaining 6 bread slices with 2 slices of Gruyère cheese and an equal amount of the shaved corned beef. Pair each slaw-topped bread slice with a corned beef–topped bread slice to form closed sandwiches. Press the slices together to secure. Cover and refrigerate.

To serve, slice each sandwich in half diagonally. Skewer the top of each half with a toothpick speared with a pickle slice and an olive.

* This recipe makes more pickle slaw than is needed for the sandwiches. Save the leftover slaw to serve with other sandwiches.

Cheesy BLTs

CHEF MICHAEL SYMON

MAKES 6 SANDWICHES

1½ cups prepared roasted garlic purée

12 slices sourdough bread

24 slices jalapeño Jack cheese

24 slices vine-ripened tomatoes

24 fresh basil leaves

24 slices bacon, cooked crisp

Preheat the oven to 400°F.

Spread the roasted garlic purée on sourdough bread and top each slice with 2 slices of cheese. Place on a baking sheet and bake until the cheese is melted and the bread is toasted, about 5 minutes.

Remove from the oven. Layer 6 of the bread slices with equal parts of the remaining ingredients as follows: 2 slices of tomato, 2 basil leaves, 4 slices bacon, 2 additional basil leaves, 2 remaining tomato slices, and the remaining 6 slices of cheese-topped bread. Cut on the diagonal and serve.

Homestyle Ham and Wisconsin Cheese Pockets

MAKES 6 SANDWICHES

FOR 6 SERVINGS

12 puff pastry squares
  (5 x 5 inches each)

12 thin slices ham

6 teaspoons Dijon mustard

6 slices Swiss cheese

1 tablespoon water, and
  additional water, as needed

1 egg

Lettuce (optional), for serving

Tomato slices (optional), for
  serving

Preheat the oven to 400°F.

Lay the puff pastry squares out on a lightly floured surface. Place 2 slices of ham on half of the squares, leaving a ¼-inch border all the way around. Spread 1 teaspoon of Dijon mustard evenly over the ham, and top with 1 slice of Swiss cheese.

Lightly brush the border of each square with water. Place the remaining square evenly on top of the cheese. With the prongs of a fork, seal the pastry all the way around.

Combine the egg with the water, beat well. With a pastry brush, baste all of the squares with the egg wash, and prick the tops with a fork. Place the squares on a parchment-lined baking sheet and bake for 10 to 12 minutes, or until golden brown and puffy. Serve the pockets immediately. Garnish with the lettuce and tomato.

Note: Any type of meat can replace the ham.

Butterkäse Focaccia Antipasto Sandwiches

2 (14½-ounce) packages Italian flatbread (focaccia)

Romaine lettuce leaves

12 (1-ounce) slices thinly sliced baked ham

8 ounces butterkäse cheese, sliced

12 (6-ounce) slices thinly sliced salami (optional)

2 (6-ounce) jars marinated artichoke hearts, drained (reserving the marinade) and chopped

1 cup drained julienned roasted red peppers

1 medium red onion, thinly sliced

2 tomatoes, thinly sliced

8 ounces provolone cheese, sliced

Lightly brush the top of one of the Italian flatbreads with 1 tablespoon of the reserved artichoke marinade. Place the bread on a serving dish and layer with lettuce leaves, ham, cheese, salami (if desired), artichokes, peppers, onions, and tomatoes. Sprinkle with 2 to 3 tablespoons of the reserved marinade, and layer the top with provolone cheese slices. Brush the underside of the second Italian flatbread with the remaining marinade and place on top of the sandwich. With a bread knife, cut into 10 pie-shaped wedges and place a sandwich pick in each.

Fontina–Stuffed Pretzel Bread

GOVIND ARMSTRONG

MAKES 4 SERVINGS

½ cup (about ½ medium) julienned yellow onion

1 teaspoon olive oil

⅓ cup roasted red peppers, cut in ½-inch strips

2 teaspoons chopped fresh parsley

½ teaspoon chopped fresh thyme, or ¼ teaspoon dried

2 cups (8 ounces) shredded fontina cheese

1 cup diced smoked baked ham

Salt and pepper, to taste

4 (6-inch) pretzel rolls

Preheat the oven to 375°F.

In a small skillet, sauté the onion in oil until soft, 3 to 4 minutes. In a medium bowl, toss the sautéed onions with the peppers, parsley, thyme, cheese, and ham. Season with salt and pepper.

To hollow the pretzel rolls, cut off one end and set aside. Using a thin-bladed knife, gently cut the center out of each bread, leaving ⅜ inch around the edge. Use a small spoon to scrape out the inside of the bread, and discard or save for another use.

Stuff one-fourth of the filling mixture into the pretzel breads by using the end of a wooden spoon to gently push the filling into the bread. Replace the cut-off end, and wrap each bread with foil, leaving the foil open on top. Place the stuffed breads on a baking sheet. Bake for 10 to 15 minutes, until the bread is crisp and the filling is warm. Slice and serve.

Proscuitto Panini with Wisconsin Mozzarella and White Bean Purée

CHEF SETH BIXBY DAUGHERTY

MAKES 6 SERVINGS

2 cups white beans that have been cooked very soft, plus 1 to 2 tablespoons cooking liquid

1 tablespoon roasted garlic purée*

Salt and pepper, to taste

1 loaf French bread, split

8 ounces Crave Brothers fresh mozzarella cheese, sliced

10 slices shaved proscuitto

3 small roasted red peppers

2 Roma tomatoes, thinly sliced

10 large fresh basil leaves

* Use prepared roasted garlic purée or follow the instructions on page 79.

Purée the beans and liquid, garlic, salt, and pepper in a food processor until smooth. Microwave or heat on the stove until hot to the touch. Liberally spread the purée on one cut side of the bread. Top with the remaining ingredients, sprinkling the tomato layer with salt and pepper. Slice and serve.

Wisconsin Cheese and Salami Packets

MAKES 6 SERVINGS

2½ cups all-purpose flour, divided

1 package active dry yeast

1 teaspoon dried sage, crushed

½ teaspoon salt

¾ cup warm water (115°to 120°F)

2 tablespoons cooking oil

1½ cups (6 ounces) shredded mozzarella cheese

⅓ cup (about 1 ounce) freshly grated Parmesan cheese

6 ounces salami, chopped

1 small tomato, peeled, seeded, and chopped

1 egg

1 teaspoon water

In a large mixer bowl, combine 1 cup of the flour with the yeast, sage, and salt. Add the warm water and the oil. Beat with an electric mixer on low speed for 30 seconds. Beat on high speed for 3 minutes. Stir in as much of the remaining flour as you can. Turn out onto a floured surface.

Knead in enough of the remaining flour to make a moderately stiff dough that is smooth and elastic (6 to 8 minutes total). Place the dough in a greased bowl; turn once. Cover and let rise in a warm place until the dough has doubled (45 to 55 minutes).

Meanwhile, make the filling. In a small mixing bowl, combine the cheeses, salami, and tomatoes. Toss until well combined; set aside.

Punch the dough down; divide into 6 pieces. Cover and let the dough rest for 20 minutes.

Preheat the oven to 375°F.

Roll each piece of dough into a 7-inch circle. Spoon ½ cup of the filling onto half of each circle. Combine the egg and water, and brush over the outer edges of the dough, to moisten. Fold the circle in half; use the tines of a fork to seal the edges. Place on a greased baking sheet. Prick the tops and brush with more of the egg mixture.

Bake for 25 to 30 minutes, or until golden. Remove from the baking sheet; cool on a wire rack.

Brat Reubens

MUSTARD SAUCE*

¼ cup prepared mustard

¼ cup mayonnaise

1 tablespoon horseradish

SANDWICHES

1 tablespoon butter

6 bratwurst, precooked

6 rye buns

6 slices Swiss cheese

1½ cups sauerkraut, heated
and drained

* Instead of making the mustard sauce,
  you can use bottled Thousand Island
  dressing.

For the mustard sauce, mix the ingredients until well blended.

For the sandwiches, preheat the broiler.

Melt the butter in a large skillet. Add the bratwurst and cook over medium heat for 5 to 7 minutes, or until brown. (To prevent piercing of the sausage casings, use tongs to turn the brats.) When brown, slit open the brats, place on buns, and top with the cheese slices. Broil the sandwiches open faced, 5 inches from the heat, for 3 to 5 minutes or until the cheese melts. Top each with ¼ cup of the sauerkraut and 1 tablespoon of the mustard sauce. Put the bun halves together and serve.

Beer Garden Sandwiches

3 tablespoons mayonnaise

1 tablespoon prepared grainy mustard

2 teaspoons prepared horseradish

8 slices caraway rye bread

4 lettuce leaves

8 ounces Limburger cheese, sliced

8 ounces liverwurst, sliced

2 medium dill pickles, sliced lengthwise

1 small red onion, sliced into rings

In a small bowl, mix the mayonnaise, mustard, and horseradish; spread evenly on one side of 4 bread slices. Top each with equal portions of lettuce, cheese, liverwurst, pickles, and onion; cover with the remaining bread slices. Cut each sandwich in half and serve.

Open-Faced Pork Loin Sandwiches
with Smoked Baby Swiss

MAKES 4 SANDWICHES

1 (12-ounce) pork tenderloin

1 teaspoon dried rosemary

¼ teaspoon salt

⅛ teaspoon pepper

4 slices black bread, toasted

Herb mustard

8 ounces thinly sliced smoked baby Swiss cheese

Preheat the oven to 350°F.

Season the meat with rosemary, salt, and pepper. Place in a baking pan. Bake for 45 to 60 minutes or until the meat registers 165°F. Cool and cut into ¼-inch slices.

Preheat the oven to broil.

For each sandwich, spread one bread slice with mustard; top with one-fourth of the meat slices and one-fourth of the cheese slices. Broil the sandwiches until the cheese is melted.

Classic Cuban Sandwiches

MAKES 12 SANDWICHES

5 pounds pork shoulder or brisket

1½ teaspoons Cuban spice mixture (onion flakes, ground cloves, crumbled bay leaf, oregano, red pepper flakes, salt)

3 garlic cloves, mashed

1 tablespoon cracked black pepper

12 (5-inch) soft white rolls

¾ cup prepared mustard

12 slices from 4 large tomatoes (optional)

1½ cups sliced dill pickles

24 thin slices salami

24 slices Swiss cheese

Preheat the oven to 325°F.

Place the pork in a roasting pan and rub with the Cuban spice mixture, garlic, and pepper; cover with foil. Add ½ inch of water to the bottom of the pan, and roast for 4 hours or until very tender. Remove from the heat and cool to room temperature. Shred meat.

Place the shredded meat in a pot with the pan juices from the roasting pan, and simmer with additional seasonings, if needed, until moist but not runny. Keep warm.

To make a sandwich, lay the bottom of an opened roll on a clean surface. Spread with 1 tablespoon of mustard. Top with 1 thin tomato slice, 2 or 3 pickle slices, 4 ounces of pork, 2 thin slices of salami, and 2 slices of Swiss cheese. Top with the roll lid. Repeat with the remaining sandwiches. Each sandwich may be served immediately or griddled like a panini and served hot to melt the cheese.

Variation: Gruyère cheese may be used in place of Swiss.

Mexican Torta with Wisconsin Asadero Cheese

MAKES 4 SERVINGS

¼ cup vegetable oil

1 pound boneless, thin-sliced pork chops (8 pieces)

Salt and pepper

1 teaspoon dried oregano, preferably Mexican, crushed

1 cup canned refried beans (pinto or black)

4 French rolls

1⅓ cups shredded asadero or queso quesadilla cheese*

6 to 8 slices tomato

1 ripe Hass avocado, peeled and sliced

¼ cup sliced jalapeño peppers in escabèche (optional)

Shredded romaine lettuce

⅓ cup Mexican salsa, preferably chipotle (red or green may be substituted)

½ cup mayonnaise

* Muenster cheese may be substituted.

Heat the oil in a heavy skillet over medium-high heat. Quickly grill the pork chops, turning once, until cooked through. Remove from the heat. Salt and pepper to taste. Scatter the oregano over the chops while hot, pressing into the meat. Set aside.

Meanwhile, heat the refried beans in a microwave or on the stovetop. Split the rolls. Spread the bottom of each roll with ¼ cup of the hot refried beans. Cover with ⅓ cup of shredded asadero cheese. Top with 2 pieces of pork. Layer the tomatoes, avocados, jalapeños, and lettuce over the meat, dividing evenly among the sandwiches.

Mix the salsa and mayonnaise together in a small bowl. Spread the roll tops with the mixture, and place the tops on the sandwiches.

Pork Loin Sandwiches with Wisconsin Smoked Swiss

CHEF TREY FOSHEE

MAKES 6 SERVINGS

PORK LOIN

1½ pounds boneless center-cut pork loin

1 teaspoon vegetable oil

½ teaspoon salt

¼ teaspoon pepper

ONION JAM

½ cup sugar

½ cup cider vinegar

2 tablespoons honey

2 yellow onions, thinly sliced

HORSERADISH AÏOLI

½ cup mayonnaise

2 teaspoons fresh lemon juice

1 small garlic clove, minced

2 teaspoons prepared horseradish

Pinch of cayenne

1 tablespoon extra-virgin olive oil

SANDWICHES

6 hamburger buns

4 cups arugula, cleaned and dried

8 ounces smoked Swiss or smoked Gouda cheese, sliced

For the pork, preheat the oven to 425°F. Place the pork in a small roasting pan. Brush with oil; sprinkle with salt and pepper. Roast for 50 to 60 minutes until the center is only slightly pink.

For the jam, combine the sugar, vinegar, and honey in a medium saucepan. Simmer until the sugar is dissolved. Add the onions and cook over medium heat until the onions are tender and golden, and most of the liquid has been absorbed, 20 to 25 minutes. Set aside to cool.

For the aïoli, combine the mayonnaise, lemon juice, garlic, horseradish, cayenne, and olive oil in a small bowl. Set aside.

To assemble the sandwiches, slice the pork very thinly. Toast the buns. Spread both cut sides of the buns with the aïoli. Top with arugula, several slices of pork, the jam, and then the cheese. Serve warm, or grill as panini.

Spanish Hacienda Pork Wraps

MAKES 4 WRAPS

2 tablespoons vegetable oil

1 pound boneless pork loin, finely cubed

2 cups chopped sweet onions

1 cup green or red chile salsa

½ cup chopped ripe olives

2 teaspoons chili powder

1 teaspoon cornstarch

1 teaspoon sugar

½ teaspoon ground cumin

Hot pepper sauce, to taste

1⅓ cups hot cooked rice

4 burrito-size flour tortillas, steamed

1 cup (4 ounces) shredded brick cheese (or for more heat, use ½ cup shredded habañero Jack cheese)

Heat 1 tablespoon of oil in a large skillet, and sauté half of the pork and onion over high heat until browned; remove from the pan. Repeat with the remaining oil, pork, and onion; remove from the pan.

Combine the salsa, olives, chili powder, cornstarch, sugar, and cumin in the same skillet. Cook, stirring and scraping up the pork drippings, until the sauce is hot. Return the pork mixture to the pan; heat through. Season with hot pepper sauce, if desired.

To assemble, portion ⅓ cup of hot rice into the center of each tortilla; top with a generous ¾ cup of the pork mixture and ¼ cup of cheese. Fold in two sides, and then roll the tortilla around the filling.

Buffalo Chicken Wraps

JOHN ESSER

MAKES 6 WRAPS (FOR LUNCHEON SERVINGS) OR 30 SLICES (FOR APPETIZERS)

3 large flour tortillas or wraps

¼ cup prepared ranch dressing

12 ounces cooked chicken breasts, cut into strips

1 celery stalk, sliced thin

3 green onions, sliced

1 cup chopped lettuce

⅓ cup finely diced tomatoes

3 tablespoons dried cranberries

12 ounces (2 cups) crumbled blue cheese

Place the tortillas on a flat surface and spread the ranch dressing on the upper half of each tortilla. Divide each of the remaining ingredients into thirds and arrange along the middle of each tortilla. Roll the tortillas up tightly and slice in half for luncheon portions, or into 1-inch slices, secured with toothpicks, for appetizers.

Pesto Chicken Bruschetta

MAKES 4 SERVINGS

1 tablespoons olive oil

½ teaspoon coarsely chopped garlic

4 slices sourdough bread, cut diagonally, ¼ inch thick

½ cup (about 2 ounces) grated Asiago cheese, divided

2 tablespoons prepared pesto

¼ teaspoon pepper

4 boneless, skinless chicken breast halves

8 ounces fresh mozzarella cheese, cut into 12 (¼-inch-thick) slices

1 tomato, cut into 4 slices

In a 10-inch skillet, heat the olive oil and garlic. Add the bread slices. Cook over medium-high heat for 5 to 7 minutes or until toasted, turning once. Remove from the pan and place on a plate. Sprinkle ¼ cup of the Asiago cheese on the bread. Set aside.

In the same skillet, combine the pesto and pepper. Add the chicken, coating with the pesto. Cook over medium-high heat for 8 to 10 minutes, or until the chicken is brown, turning once.

To serve, place 3 slices of mozzarella on each bread slice; top with a tomato slice and then a chicken breast half. Sprinkle with the remaining Asiago cheese.

Grilled Turkey and Fontina Sandwiches

MAKES 4 SANDWICHES

CHERRY CHUTNEY

1 tablespoon olive oil

¼ cup chopped red onion

¼ cup apple cider vinegar

1 cup dried cherries, coarsely chopped

½ teaspoon kosher salt

¼ teaspoon dried tarragon

1½ tablespoons honey

1 cup water

SANDWICHES

¼ pound (1 stick) butter, room temperature

8 slices hearty bread

16 slices fontina cheese

1 pound smoked turkey, shaved

1 Granny Smith apple, sliced thin

For the chutney, heat the oil in a nonstick skillet over medium heat. Sauté the onion until it begins to brown. Deglaze the pan with vinegar. Add the cherries, salt, tarragon, honey, and water and simmer for 20 to 25 minutes; cool.

For the sandwiches, butter one side of each slice of bread. Place four slices of the bread, buttered side down, in a large, nonstick pan or griddle, on medium heat. Top each with fontina cheese, turkey, sliced apples, and 1 tablespoon of chutney. Top with the remaining four slices of bread, buttered side out. Grill each side until golden brown and the cheese is melted.

Smoked Turkey Cobb Sandwiches
with Wisconsin Blue Cheese Mayonnaise

WISCONSIN BLUE CHEESE MAYONNAISE

¼ cup blue cheese

¼ cup mayonnaise

AVOCADO PURÉE

1 cup puréed avocado

Salt and pepper, to taste

¼ teaspoon lemon juice

SANDWICH

8 slices sourdough bread

2 ounces mixed greens

8 slices tomato

8 slices smoked turkey

8 strips bacon, fried crisp

For the blue cheese mayonnaise, combine the cheese and mayonnaise in a small bowl, and mix well.*

For the avocado purée, in a small bowl or blender, blend the avocado purée, salt and pepper, and lemon juice.

To assemble the sandwiches, spread one bread slice with 1 to 2 tablespoons of the blue cheese mayonnaise. Layer the mixed greens, 2 tomato slices, 2 turkey slices, and 2 bacon strips on the bread. Spread another slice of bread with the avocado purée, and top the other half of the sandwich. Repeat, using all ingredients (there will be extra blue cheese mayonnaise).

* This recipe makes more blue cheese mayonnaise than is needed for the sandwich. Save the leftover mayonnaise for other sandwiches or to use on salads.

Poached Tuna Salad on Ciabatta with Wisconsin Havarti

CHEF MINDY SEGAL

MAKES 4 SERVINGS

3 cups extra-virgin olive oil

7 garlic cloves, divided

4 fresh thyme sprigs

2 pounds tuna loin trimmings, cubed (room temperature)

Salt and pepper, to taste

1 cup mayonnaise

4 ounces capers with brine

4 large ciabatta rolls, split

½ cup (2 ounces) shredded Havarti cheese, divided

In a large saucepan, combine the oil, 3 garlic cloves, and the thyme. Heat to a soft boil. Remove from the heat and add the cubed tuna. Poach the tuna for 20 minutes or until no longer pink, stirring occasionally. Remove the tuna from the oil to a medium bowl; reserve 1 cup of the oil. Season the tuna with salt and pepper, and let it cool completely. When cooled, mix with the mayonnaise and capers.

Preheat the oven to broil.

Meanwhile, in a small saucepan, bring the reserved oil and the remaining 4 garlic cloves to a soft boil. Brush the cut sides of the rolls with the garlic oil. Place the rolls on a baking sheet, cut sides up, and broil until toasted, about 2 minutes. Remove from the oven, and reduce the oven temperature to 350°F.

Spoon a rounded cup of the tuna mixture on the bottom half of each of the toasted rolls. Top each with 2 tablespoons of cheese. Place the baking sheet back in the oven and heat for 7 to 10 minutes or until the cheese is melted. Place the roll tops on the tuna; cut in half to serve.

Jumbo Lump Crab Melts

MAKES 12 SERVINGS

Sourdough baguettes, cut into 6 (4-inch) sections

½ cup olive oil, divided

⅓ cup chopped fresh herbs, such as tarragon, parsley, and thyme, divided

Salt and freshly ground pepper, to taste

2 cups (10 ounces) jumbo lump crabmeat, picked over

1 cup (6 ounces) crumbled Gorgonzola cheese

1 cup (8 ounces) mascarpone cheese

24 slices (2 pounds) ripe red tomatoes

2 cups micro greens

3 tablespoons prepared lemon vinaigrette

Preheat the oven to 350°F.

Split the baguette sections in half (as for sandwiches) and brush with ¼ cup of the olive oil. Sprinkle with 3 tablespoons of the fresh herbs, and salt and pepper. Toast until almost golden. Set aside.

In a bowl, combine the crabmeat, the cheeses, the remaining ¼ cup of olive oil, the remaining 3 table-spoons of chopped herbs, and salt and pepper.

Place 4 tomato slices on top of the toasted bottom half of each piece of baguette. Top each evenly with micro greens tossed with lemon vinaigrette and an equal portion of the crabmeat-Gorgonzola mixture. Place the top on each sandwich. Cut each melt in half for 12 equal servings. Place on a baking sheet and bake for 5 minutes or until the cheese melts. Serve warm.

New Age Egg Salad Sandwiches

MAKES 6 SERVINGS

EGG SALAD

6 large hard-cooked eggs, chopped

⅔ cup (about 3 ounces) shredded Cheddar cheese

¼ cup (scant 1 ounce) grated Asiago cheese

1 tablespoon grated yellow onion

⅓ cup mayonnaise

3 tablespoons plain yogurt or sour cream

1 tablespoon grainy mustard

¼ teaspoon ground white pepper

SANDWICHES

12 slices oatmeal bread, plain or toasted

24 thin cucumber slices

6 slices Colby, Monterey Jack, or Cheddar cheese

6 lettuce leaves

For the egg salad, in a bowl, combine the eggs, cheeses, and onion. Set aside.

In a separate bowl, combine the mayonnaise, yogurt, mustard, and pepper; mix well. Add to the egg mixture, and mix until combined. Cover and refrigerate at least 2 hours before using.

For the sandwiches, spread about ⅓ cup of the egg salad on 1 slice of bread, and top with 4 slices of cucumber. Top with 1 slice of cheese and 1 lettuce leaf. Top with another slice of bread. Repeat to make the remaining sandwiches. Cut and serve with your favorite homemade shredded carrot salad, lemon dressing, and sliced fruit.

Variations: Substitute smoked Cheddar for regular Cheddar in the salad. Other sliced cheeses may be substituted in the sandwich also. Try substituting chopped egg whites instead of whole eggs. Try low-fat or no-fat mayonnaise, instead of regular mayonnaise.

SIDES AND SALADS

Wisconsin Pepato and Carrot Bake

MAKES 8 SERVINGS

3 cups cooked, mashed carrots

3 eggs, lightly beaten

2 cups milk

1¼ cups (4 ounces) shredded pepato cheese

1 cup breadcrumbs

2 tablespoons unsalted butter, melted

Salt, to taste

1 teaspoon prepared horseradish

¼ cup chives, finely chopped

Preheat the oven to 350°F.

Coat a 9 x 9-inch baking pan with cooking spray. Set aside.

In a large bowl, combine all the ingredients. Transfer to the prepared pan. Bake for about 30 minutes, or until a knife inserted in the center comes out clean.

French Onion Casserole

8 teaspoons butter (for the bread)

8 (¾-inch) slices French bread

2 large onions, thinly sliced and separated into rings

2 tablespoons butter

2 cups (8 ounces) shredded Swiss cheese

1 (10¾-ounce) can condensed cream of chicken soup

1 (5-ounce) can evaporated milk (⅔ cup)

¼ teaspoon pepper

Preheat the oven to 350°F.

Spread 1 teaspoon of butter on each slice of French bread. Set aside.

In a large skillet over medium heat, cook the sliced onions in 2 tablespoons of butter for about 10 minutes, or until the onions are tender but not brown, stirring often. Transfer the cooked onions to a 12 x 7-inch baking dish. Sprinkle the cheese in a layer over the onions. Set aside.

In a small mixing bowl, combine the soup, evaporated milk, and pepper, stirring until well mixed. Pour the soup mixture into the baking dish, spreading evenly over the cheese layer.

Layer the bread slices, buttered side up, over the soup mixture. Bake for 30 minutes, or until the onion mixture is heated through and the bread slices are golden brown.

Sweet Red Peppers Stuffed with Haloumi

MAKES 6 SIDE DISH OR 3 MAIN COURSE SERVINGS

4 tablespoons olive oil

2 garlic cloves

½ cup pine nuts

3 extra-large sweet red bell peppers, preferably Holland bell peppers

6 to 8 mini sweet peppers, halved, seeded, cut into ½-inch pieces

1 (8-ounce) package haloumi cheese, cut into ½-inch pieces

Fine sea salt or kosher salt and freshly ground pepper

Pour the olive oil into a small bowl. Place the garlic cloves on a work surface. Place the flat side of a chef's knife atop the garlic and give it a good whack to smash the cloves in their skins. Remove and discard the skins; add the smashed garlic cloves to the olive oil and let soak in oil to infuse for at least 1 hour.

Preheat the oven to 425°F.

Heat a small, heavy skillet over medium-high heat. Add the pine nuts, and toast, shaking the pan occasionally for even cooking, until the pine nuts are light golden brown and fragrant, about 2 minutes. Remove from the heat immediately to prevent burning. Set the pine nuts aside.

Cut the bell peppers lengthwise in half and remove the seeds. Using a small, sharp knife, carefully remove the white membrane.

Arrange the bell pepper halves on a baking sheet. Fill the pepper halves with mini pepper pieces, dividing equally. Drizzle half of the garlic oil over the peppers and bake until the edges of the peppers begin to brown, about 25 minutes. Remove the peppers from the oven. Add the haloumi cheese pieces to the pepper halves, tucking them among the mini pepper pieces. Sprinkle the pine nuts over the cheese and peppers, and drizzle with the remaining garlic oil. Sprinkle with salt and pepper. Return to the oven and bake until the cheese is softened and golden brown, and the edges of the peppers are well browned, 15 to 20 minutes.

Roasted Peppers with Wisconsin Feta

5 medium red bell peppers, sliced

5 medium green bell peppers, sliced

4 medium onions, sliced

3 tablespoons olive oil

⅔ cup (4 ounces) crumbled basil and tomato feta cheese

Preheat the oven to 425°F.

In a large, shallow baking pan, toss the peppers, onion, and olive oil to combine. Bake for about 25 minutes, or until the vegetables are tender, stirring occasionally. Transfer the cooked vegetables to a serving platter. Sprinkle the crumbled feta cheese over the top.

Wisconsin Cheese and Broccoli Baked Potato

1 medium baked potato

¼ cup (2 ounces) shredded provolone, Cheddar, or Swiss cheese

¼ cup cooked broccoli

Salt and pepper, to taste

Split open the top of a medium baked potato. Pinch to bring up the pulp. Layer half of the cheese, then the broccoli, and then the remaining cheese. Season with the salt and pepper.

Greek Lemon New Potatoes with Wisconsin Feta

MAKES 4 SERVINGS

2 tablespoons olive oil

2 pounds small new potatoes, scrubbed, dried, and sliced

2 teaspoons freshly squeezed lemon juice

1½ teaspoons dried oregano

Salt, to taste

¼ teaspoon pepper

½ cup (3 ounces) crumbled feta cheese

2 teaspoons finely grated lemon zest

¼ cup chopped fresh Italian parsley

In a large skillet, heat the oil. Add the sliced potatoes in a single layer; cover and cook over medium-low heat for about 20 to 30 minutes, or until light golden brown, shaking the skillet occasionally.

Add the lemon juice, oregano, salt, and pepper. Cover and cook over low heat for 15 minutes, or until the potatoes are tender. Sprinkle the potatoes with the cheese, lemon zest, and parsley. Serve hot, warm, or at room temperature.

Pepper Jack Potatoes with Bacon and Onions

MAKES 4 SERVINGS

1 pound small red potatoes, washed well

4 ounces (about 6 slices) thick-cut applewood smoked bacon

2 tablespoon butter

Large pinch of kosher salt

Freshly ground pepper, to taste

1 medium yellow, white, or red onion, peeled and sliced thin

½ teaspoon whole cumin seeds

½ teaspoon chili powder

1½ cups (about 6 ounces) grated pepper Jack cheese (can substitute smoked Gouda)

Boil the potatoes in salted water until soft, about 25 minutes. Drain and cool slightly. Cut the potatoes in quarters and set aside.

Place a large nonstick sauté pan over medium heat, and cook the bacon until it reaches the desired doneness. Drain the bacon on paper towels and crumble slightly. Wash the pan.

While the potatoes are boiling, place the butter in the sauté pan over medium-high heat and sauté the onions with the salt, pepper, cumin seeds, and chili powder, stirring occasionally, until the onions are soft and aromatic. Add the quartered potatoes and combine, allowing the mixture to brown slightly.

Sprinkle the cheese and bacon over the mixture, turn heat to very low, and cover for 5 minutes, allowing the cheese to melt.

Romano and Roasted Garlic Mashed Potatoes

DAVID SCHY

MAKES 10 POTATOES

½ cup olive oil

15 garlic cloves

10 medium baking potatoes, peeled

1 gallon cold water

1 cup milk

¼ pound (1 stick) butter

Salt and pepper, to taste

½ cup (about 2 ounces) grated Romano cheese, plus additional for garnish

Chopped fresh parsley, for garnish

Place the olive oil and garlic cloves in a small pan and simmer slowly until the garlic is browned. Purée the garlic and oil, and reserve.

Cut the potatoes into medium-size chunks. Place the chunks in the cold water. Bring to a boil. Cook until the potatoes are just tender. Strain off all of the water and return the potatoes to the pot. Add the garlic purée, milk, butter, salt, pepper, and ½ cup of cheese; hand mash until smooth.

To serve, spoon into a serving bowl and garnish with cheese and parsley.

Potato Gratin with Wisconsin Sharp Cheddar and Blue Cheese

1 garlic clove, halved

1 cup chopped onions

6 medium-size baking potatoes, peeled and cut into ⅛-inch slices (about 2½ pounds)

¼ teaspoon salt

¼ teaspoon freshly ground pepper

¾ cup (3 ounces) shredded extra-sharp Cheddar cheese

¼ cup (about 2 ounces) crumbled blue cheese

1¾ cup low-sodium chicken stock

1 cup evaporated skim milk

Preheat the oven to 425°F.

Rub a shallow 3-quart baking dish with the cut sides of the garlic halves; discard the garlic. Coat the dish with cooking spray. Set aside.

Coat a small nonstick skillet with cooking spray; place over medium heat until hot. Add the onions and sauté for 5 minutes or until tender; set aside.

Arrange one-third of the potato slices in the prepared baking dish, and sprinkle with half of the salt and half of the pepper. Top with half of the sautéed onions and half of the cheeses. Repeat the layers, ending with the remaining potato slices. Set aside.

Bring the stock and milk to a boil over low heat in a small saucepan; pour over the potato mixture. Bake for 50 minutes or until tender. Let stand 5 minutes before serving.

Roesti (Fried Potatoes with Wisconsin Cheese and Onion)

MAKES 6 SERVINGS

½ cup chopped onion

2 tablespoons butter

4 raw potatoes, chopped or coarsely shredded (or use frozen diced or grated potatoes)

Salt and pepper, to taste

1 cup (4 ounces) shredded Swiss cheese

In a large nonstick skillet, sauté the onion in butter. Add the potatoes, salt, and pepper, and press evenly into the pan. Cook, covered, over medium heat until the bottom of the potatoes are golden brown, about 8 minutes. Loosen the edges of the potato mixture, and invert the potatoes onto a baking sheet; slide the potatoes back into the skillet. Cook an additional 7 minutes until the bottom is browned. Sprinkle with the cheese; cover the skillet and allow the cheese to melt. Serve immediately.

Twice-Baked Potatoes with Greens and Wisconsin Mascarpone

MAKES 4 SERVINGS

4 baking potatoes (about 12 ounces each)

1 (6-ounce) package baby spinach or arugula–baby spinach mix

2 teaspoons salt

¼ teaspoon white pepper (optional)

½ cup (4 ounces) mascarpone cheese

4 heaping teaspoons Parmesan cheese

Preheat the oven to 400°F.

Prick the potatoes with a fork or make a short, deep slit in each, and bake about 1 hour or until tender when pierced with a fork.

Meanwhile, wilt the greens: Place 2½ cups of water in a deep saucepan. Bring to a boil and add a pinch of salt. Add the greens, and boil until wilted, about 4 minutes. Remove to a fine sieve and rinse with cold water to cool. Squeeze out the water to dry the greens. Snip the greens with scissors, and resqueeze to remove moisture. Set aside on absorbent paper towels.

When the potatoes are cooked, cool slightly. Cut off a shallow slice from the top of each potato. With a sharp-tipped spoon, scoop the potato pulp into a mixing bowl. Add the salt, pepper, and mascarpone cheese. Whip with an electric mixer until smooth, or alternatively, mash by hand. You may have to add more mascarpone, depending on the dryness of the potatoes. Fold the reserved greens into the whipped potatoes.

Place the potatoes on a baking sheet. Sprinkle a heaping teaspoon of Parmesan over each. Bake for about 15 to 20 minutes.

Note: The potatoes may be stuffed ahead and refrigerated until baking time.

Squash and Wisconsin Colby Gratin

1 butternut squash (about 2 pounds)

2 tablespoons butter

3 medium leeks, trimmed and sliced (1¼ inch thick)

½ cup breadcrumbs

½ teaspoon dried thyme

¼ teaspoon pepper

1½ cups (about 6 ounces) shredded Colby cheese, divided

Salt, to taste

⅓ cup milk

Preheat the oven to 375°F.

Halve and seed the squash; place the halves cut sides down in ½ inch of boiling water in a shallow baking pan. Cover snugly with foil. Bake for 35 to 45 minutes until tender when pierced. Cool slightly.

Meanwhile, melt the butter in a large skillet. Add the leeks; cook over low heat, stirring occasionally, until wilted, 5 to 8 minutes. Add the crumbs, thyme, and pepper. Cook and stir over medium heat about 3 minutes until the crumbs are lightly browned. Remove from the heat.

With a spoon, scoop the squash from the skin in small chunks; add to the skillet; toss. Add 1 cup of the cheese and the salt. Toss to mix thoroughly. Turn into a shallow, buttered, 1½- to 2-quart baking dish. Pour the milk over the squash, and sprinkle with the remaining cheese. Cover snugly with foil. Bake for 20 minutes; remove the foil. Increase the temperature to 425°F. Bake for 10 minutes longer.

Blue Cheese and Tomato-Leek Galette

MAKES 4 TO 6 SERVINGS

2 tablespoons butter

2 large leeks, the white and about 1 inch of the green part, thinly sliced

1 teaspoon chopped fresh sage or ½ teaspoon dried sage

¼ teaspoon black pepper

2 teaspoons all-purpose flour (for the baking sheet)

1 refrigerated pie crust

3 to 4 large plum tomatoes, cut into ⅓-inch slices

1 cup (6 ounces) crumbled blue cheese

1 egg, lightly beaten

In a medium skillet, heat the butter over medium heat; cook the leeks for 5 minutes or until tender. Cool slightly; stir in the sage and pepper.

Preheat the oven to 425°F.

On a floured baking sheet, roll the pie crust into a 14-inch circle. Spread the leek mixture over the top; arrange the tomatoes on top of the leeks. Sprinkle with the cheese; fold over the edges of the dough, pinching to make a border. Brush the egg over the outside dough. Bake for 10 minutes. Reduce the oven temperature to 375°F. Bake for 15 minutes or until golden brown.

Mediterranean Grilled Mozzarella Skewers

CHEF JAMES CAMPBELL

MAKES 6 SERVINGS

1 cup extra-virgin olive oil

2 tablespoons Spanish sherry vinegar

1 tablespoon fresh lemon juice

1 tablespoon chopped fresh oregano

1 teaspoon crushed red pepper flakes

2 teaspoons minced garlic

12 fresh mozzarella ciliegine (cherry-sized) balls (⅓ ounce each)

12 seedless red grapes

12 pitted kalamata olives

12 cherry tomatoes

12 large caperberries

6 (8-inch) to 12 (6-inch) skewers

In a large bowl, mix the oil, vinegar, lemon juice, oregano, pepper flakes, and garlic. Add the remaining ingredients; toss well to coat. Refrigerate for 2 hours to marinate.

Heat a gas or charcoal grill to medium.

For 8-inch skewers, thread 1 mozzarella ball, 1 grape, 1 olive, 1 tomato, and 1 caperberry on each skewer; repeat so you have two of each item on each skewer. For 6-inch skewers, thread 1 of each item, in the same order.

Grill the skewers on all sides for 5 to 7 minutes or until the cheese is soft and the skewers are thoroughly heated. Serve the skewers as a tapa or side to grilled meat.

Savory Stuffed Zucchini

MAKES 4 SERVINGS

2 medium zucchini, halved lengthwise

½ cup chopped onion

1 teaspoon finely minced garlic

½ cup (2 ounces) shredded Monterey Jack cheese

½ cup (2 ounces) shredded medium Cheddar cheese

½ cup cornbread stuffing mix

1 egg, lightly beaten

1 teaspoon chopped fresh parsley

Salt and pepper, to taste

⅓ cup (scant 1 ounce) grated Asiago cheese

Scoop the pulp from the zucchini, leaving a shell about ¼ inch thick. Chop the pulp in a glass mixing bowl. Add the onion and garlic to the pulp. Microwave on high for 4 minutes. Pour off any liquid. Stir in the Monterey Jack and Cheddar cheeses, stuffing mix, egg, chopped parsley, and seasonings.

Arrange the zucchini shells in a 12-inch round glass baking dish. Fill each shell with the stuffing mixture. Sprinkle with Asiago cheese. Cover with plastic wrap. Microwave on high for 6 to 8 minutes, turning the dish once during the cooking time.

Roasted Fall Vegetables with
Wisconsin Swiss Cheese Vinaigrette

MAKES 4 SERVINGS

VEGETABLES

1 small butternut squash, peeled, seeded, quartered lengthwise, and cut into 1/2-inch pieces

2 carrots, cut diagonally into 1/2-inch pieces

1 potato, peeled, quartered lengthwise, and cut into 1/2-inch pieces

2 medium portobello mushrooms (about 1/2 pound), stems removed, caps cut into 1/2-inch pieces

2 onions, cut into 1/2-inch pieces

2 tablespoons olive oil

Salt and pepper, to taste

WISCONSIN SWISS CHEESE VINAIGRETTE

1 cup (about 4 ounces) coarsely grated Swiss cheese

3 tablespoons extra-virgin olive oil

1 tablespoon white wine vinegar

3 tablespoons water

1/4 teaspoon Tabasco sauce

For the vegetables, preheat the oven to 475°F.

Toss the squash, carrot, potatoes, mushrooms, and onions with the olive oil, and salt and pepper. Divide the vegetables between two baking sheets and spread in an even layer. Roast the vegetables on the top and bottom shelves of the oven for 10 to 15 minutes or until the vegetables are browned and just done. Stir the vegetables once while they are roasting.

For the cheese vinaigrette, in a blender, blend together all of the ingredients, until the vinaigrette is smooth. Serve the roasted vegetables with the vinaigrette on the side.

Vegetable Medley Italiano

MAKES 8 SERVINGS

3 cups broccoli florets

2 medium zucchini, cut into ¼-inch slices

1 medium red pepper, cut into strips

1 medium onion, cut into strips

1 garlic clove, crushed

1½ teaspoons chopped fresh basil or ½ teaspoon dried basil

3 tablespoons butter, divided

20 Ritz™ crackers, crushed (about 1 cup)

1 cup (4 ounces) shredded mozzarella or other favorite cheese

Preheat the oven to 350°F.

In a large skillet, over medium heat, cook the broccoli, zucchini, pepper, onion, garlic, and basil in 1 tablespoon of the butter until crisp-tender, stirring occasionally. Spoon the mixture into a 2-quart casserole dish.

Melt the remaining butter. In a medium bowl, combine the crackers, cheese, and melted butter. Sprinkle evenly over the vegetable mixture. Bake, uncovered, for 20 to 25 minutes or until the vegetables are hot and the cheese melts.

Asiago and Asparagus Risotto

MAKES 6 SERVINGS

1 pound fresh asparagus or 1 (10-ounce) package frozen cut asparagus

2 cups water

1 teaspoon salt

1 tablespoon butter

1 cup chopped onion

1 teaspoon minced garlic

1 cup uncooked long-grain rice

¼ cup chopped fresh parsley

½ cup (about 2 ounces) grated Asiago cheese

Wash the asparagus, cut off the tough ends, and cut into 2-inch pieces. Combine the asparagus, water, and salt in a 3-quart covered casserole. Cover and microwave on high power for 8 to 10 minutes. Let stand 5 minutes. Remove the asparagus with a slotted spoon; reserve the liquid. Set aside.

In a glass mixing bowl, combine the butter, onions, and garlic. Cover and microwave on high for 3 minutes. Add the rice and the reserved asparagus liquid. Cover and microwave on high for 10 minutes. Stir. Microwave on medium for an additional 10 minutes. Let stand, covered, for 10 minutes. Add the asparagus, parsley, and cheese to the rice. Blend lightly. Serve immediately.

Asiago and Corn Risotto

MAKES 6 SERVINGS

2 (15-ounce) cans vegetable or chicken stock

1 cup (8 ounces) carrot juice

2 tablespoons olive oil

1 onion, coarsely chopped

1 tablespoon chopped garlic

1 cup Arborio or short-grained rice

1 (16-ounce) package frozen corn, thawed, drained

¼ cup chopped fresh Italian parsley

2 teaspoons chopped fresh thyme or rosemary, or 1 teaspoon dried thyme or rosemary

½ cup (about 2 ounces) grated Parmesan cheese

½ cup (about 2 ounces) grated Romano cheese

½ teaspoon pepper

1 teaspoon chopped chives

1 cup (4 ounces) shaved Asiago cheese

In a 2-quart saucepan, heat the stock and carrot juice until simmering. In a Dutch oven, heat the olive oil; add the onion, garlic, and rice. Cook over medium heat, adding 1 cup of the simmering stock mixture. Stir the rice constantly; gradually add the remaining stock mixture. Cook for 25 to 30 minutes, allowing the liquid to be absorbed. Add the corn, parsley, and herbs; stir in the Parmesan and Romano cheeses. Before serving, sprinkle with pepper and chives; top with the shavings of Asiago cheese.

Creamy Risotto with Wisconsin Cheeses

MAKES 4 SERVINGS

2 teaspoons vegetable oil

1 cup finely chopped mild white onion

2 garlic cloves, smashed into a paste

1½ cups Arborio rice (if you want a creamier style, try cracked Arborio)

1¾ cups vegetable stock*

Pinch of salt

Freshly ground pepper, to taste

½ cup (2 ounces) shredded fontina cheese

¼ cup (about 1 ounce) grated Parmesan cheese

3 tablespoons chopped fresh Italian parsley

White truffle oil, to taste (optional)**

 * For fuller-flavored rice, use chicken stock.

** For a pungent, earthy flavor that brings out the full flavor of the cheeses, add a few drops of white truffle oil to the risotto a few seconds before plating.

Heat a 2-quart, thick-bottomed saucepan. Add the oil, then the onion and garlic. Cook, stirring, until the onion is translucent. Add the rice and stir to coat it with the onion mixture. Add the stock, slowly, ½ cup at a time, as the rice absorbs the liquid. Continue to stir slowly. When most of the liquid is added and the rice has a firm texture and is cooked through, add a pinch of salt and fresh pepper.

Stir in the fontina cheese, then the Parmesan. If the mixture is dry, add a little more stock. Taste and reseason, as necessary. Stir in the parsley and white truffle oil, if desired. Distribute the risotto into four bowls. Sprinkle additional herbs around the plate for a colorful finish.

Wisconsin Smoked Gouda Risotto

MAKES 6 SERVINGS

RISOTTO

2 cups water

2 (16-ounce) cans fat-free, low-sodium chicken stock

1 tablespoon butter

⅓ cup chopped shallots

2 cups Arborio or other short-grain rice

½ cup dry white wine

½ teaspoon salt

1½ cups (6 ounces) shredded smoked Gouda cheese

5 cups chopped fresh spinach

MUSHROOMS

1 tablespoon olive oil

8 cups sliced assorted mushrooms

⅓ cup chopped shallots

¼ cup dry white wine

1½ teaspoons chopped fresh thyme

1½ teaspoons chopped fresh rosemary

1 garlic clove, minced

¼ teaspoon salt

¼ teaspoon pepper

¼ cup (about 2 ounces) grated fresh Parmesan cheese

Fresh rosemary sprigs (optional), for garnish

For the risotto, combine the water and the stock; set aside.

Melt the butter in a large nonstick saucepan over medium heat. Add the shallots, cover, and cook 2 minutes. Add the rice; cook 2 minutes, uncovered, stirring constantly. Stir in the wine; cook 30 seconds or until the liquid is nearly absorbed, stirring constantly. Add the salt and the stock mixture, ½ cup at a time, stirring constantly until each portion of the stock mixture is absorbed before adding the next (about 20 minutes total). Stir in the smoked Gouda and cook just until melted. Stir in the spinach; cook just until spinach is wilted.

For the mushrooms, heat the olive oil in a large nonstick skillet over medium-high heat. Add the mushrooms and sauté 5 minutes or until they begin to brown. Add the shallots, wine, thyme, rosemary, and garlic, and sauté 1 minute or until the wine is absorbed. Sprinkle with the salt and pepper.

To serve, divide the risotto evenly among six bowls; top with the mushroom mixture, and sprinkle with the Parmesan. Garnish with rosemary sprigs, if desired.

Risotto Croquettes with Smoked Ham and Wisconsin Mozzarella

CHEF TOM CATHERALL

MAKES 24 CROQUETTES

RISOTTO

3 cups chicken stock

1 cup water

2 tablespoons olive oil

1 small onion, minced

1½ cups Italian Arborio rice

½ cup tomato sauce, home-made or canned

½ cup (about 2 ounces) grated Parmesan cheese

1 egg yolk, beaten

Salt and freshly ground pepper, to taste

FILLING

2 ounces smoked ham, cut into ¼-inch dice

⅓ cup green beans or asparagus, trimmed, cut in ¼-inch lengths, blanched

4 ounces smoked mozzarella cheese, cut into ¼-inch dice

CROQUETTES

Corn oil for deep frying

3 eggs, beaten

2 cups fine dry breadcrumbs

For the risotto, bring the chicken stock and water to a boil in a saucepan on the back burner of the stove. Reduce the heat to simmer.

Heat the olive oil in a large saucepan over medium heat. Add the onion and sauté until soft, 5 to 10 minutes. Add the rice and continue to stir over medium heat, uncovered, 3 to 4 minutes, until the outside edge of each grain of rice is transparent and there is a tiny white dot in the interior of each grain. Add a ladle of stock (¼ to ½ cup); stir. When the liquid is absorbed, add another ladleful of stock, and continue to stir. Keep the grains moist at all times. Stir frequently, adding more stock a ladleful at a time. Cook 18 to 22 minutes, until the rice is tender and has no chalky center. (If necessary, add hot water if you run out of stock.) Continue cooking, stirring, until all the liquid is absorbed and the rice is very dry. Remove from the heat. Add the tomato sauce and Parmesan cheese. Mix well. Cool completely.

When the risotto has cooled, add the egg yolk, and mix well. Season with salt and pepper. For easier handling, chill at least 1 hour.

(continued on next page)

For the filling, in a small bowl, combine the ham, green beans or asparagus, and diced mozzarella.

To assemble the croquettes, work with half of the rice mixture at a time; keep the other half refrigerated. Pat 2 rounded tablespoons of rice mixture to cover the palm of one hand. Place 1 tablespoon of filling in the center. Gently close your hand to envelop the filling. Using both hands, shape the mass into an oval about the size and shape of a large egg. Place the croquettes on a baking sheet and continue until you have used all of the ingredients.

Heat 3 inches of oil to 375°F.

Dip the croquettes in the beaten eggs, and then roll in the breadcrumbs. Set on a baking sheet or waxed paper. Deep-fry the croquettes, a few at a time, until golden brown, about 45 seconds. Remove and drain. Serve hot, warm, or at room temperature.

Roasted Red Beet Risotto with Goat Cheese

MAKES 4 SERVINGS

2 medium red beets, trimmed and scrubbed

6 cups vegetable broth

1 tablespoon butter

1 tablespoon olive oil

1 small onion, grated

2 cups Arborio rice

½ cup (3 ounces) soft fresh goat cheese

¼ cup chopped fresh chives, for garnish

Preheat the oven to 350°F. Wrap each beet tightly in aluminum foil and place on a baking sheet. Transfer the beets to the oven and roast until the beets are very tender, about 1 hour. Let the beets cool in the foil before handling.

When the beets are cool enough to handle, peel them and cut them into ½-inch cubes. Transfer the beets to a blender and pureé, adding water by tablespoonfuls if necessary to achieve a smooth consistency. Transfer the pureé to the refrigerator.

In a heavy, 4-quart saucepan, bring the vegetable broth to a simmer; cover the broth and keep at a bare simmer over medium-low heat.

In a large, heavy saucepan, melt the butter with the olive oil over medium heat. Add the onion and cook until softened and translucent, about 3 minutes. Add the rice and cook, stirring, 1 minute. Stir in 1 cup of the hot broth, simmering briskly and stirring constantly, until the broth is absorbed. Continue simmering and adding broth ½ cup at a time, stirring constantly and allowing each addition of broth to be absorbed by the rice before adding more broth, until the rice is just tender (not mushy) and creamy looking, 18 to 22 minutes.

Stir in the beet pureé. Remove the risotto from the heat and stir in the cheese until it is melted and combined. Add salt to taste, if necessary. Divide the risotto among bowls, and garnish with the chives. Serve immediately.

Wisconsin Parmesan Crisps

MAKES 12 TO 20 CRISPS

SKILLET METHOD
(MAKES ABOUT 20 CRISPS)

Olive oil

½ pound (about 2 cups) grated
    Parmesan or aged Asiago
    Cheese

OVEN METHOD
(MAKES 12 CRISPS)

1 cup (about 3 ounces) grated
    Parmesan or aged Asiago
    Cheese

2 teaspoons all-purpose flour

For the skillet, brush the bottom of a heavy, nonstick 10- to 12-inch skillet with a film of olive oil. Heat on medium until hot, not smoking. Sprinkle about 2 tablespoons of the grated cheese over the skillet bottom, forming a 4-inch round. Repeat until the skillet is filled, but not crowded, with the crisps.

Fry until the cheese melts and the edges of the rounds are crisp. If the crisps puff up, press down with a spatula to keep flat. After the cheese spreads, bubbles, and firms, flip over with a spatula and cook the second side until golden and crisp. Drain on a wire rack lined with paper towels, and blot lightly to remove any excess oil. Cool to room temperature.

To form a "basket" with the crisps, shape the hot rounds (make larger, if preferred) around the bottom of a cup. Cool and fill with a salad of micro greens.

For the oven, place the rack in the middle of the oven and preheat the oven to 350°F. Line a lightly greased baking sheet with parchment paper.

Mix the Parmesan and flour together. Using a tablespoon, place mounds of the mixture on the prepared baking sheet, about 4 inches apart. Flatten the mounds into 3-inch circles. Bake the crisps for 8 to 10 minutes, or until golden. Cool the crisps until completely cool on the baking sheet. Remove with a spatula. Repeat the process until all of the cheese is used.

Crisps can be prepared 2 days ahead. Store in an airtight container, separating the crisps with waxed paper.

Creamy Cornmeal Pudding

MAKES 4 SERVINGS

2 cups milk

½ cup yellow cornmeal

4 tablespoons cream cheese

1½ tablespoons heavy cream

2 tablespoons grated Asiago cheese

½ cup chopped pecans, lightly toasted

Salt, to taste

Bring the milk to a boil, stirring as it heats. Mix the cornmeal into the milk, stirring constantly to prevent it from lumping. Cook the mixture for 15 minutes or until done, stirring often. Blend in the cream cheese and heavy cream.

To serve, sprinkle the pudding with the grated Asiago. Top with the toasted pecans. Add salt.

Caesar Salad with a Twist

MAKES 6 SERVINGS

2 boneless, skinless chicken breasts

1 cup prepared Caesar salad dressing, divided

4 cups torn romaine lettuce

2 ounces dry rotini pasta, cooked

1½ cups (6 ounces) julienned Gouda cheese

¾ cups croutons

Prepare the grill according to the manufacturer's directions, Marinate the chicken breasts in ½ cup of the salad dressing for 30 minutes. Grill the chicken for 15 to 20 minutes over medium heat, turning once, until cooked.

While the chicken is grilling, combine the salad greens, cooked pasta, cheese, croutons, and remaining salad dressing. Arrange on a serving platter. Cut the chicken into strips; place on the pasta salad.

Catalan Endive-Avocado Salad with Wisconsin Blue Cheese

MAKES 6 SERVINGS

DRESSING

¼ cup half-and-half

2 tablespoons mayonnaise

¾ tablespoon tarragon vinegar

1½ teaspoons grainy mustard

½ teaspoon dried tarragon

SALAD

2 heads Belgian endive

1½ large avocados, thinly sliced

3 cups loosely packed, peeled and coarsely shredded carrots

12 ounces blue cheese

½ cup chopped walnuts, toasted

For the dressing, in a small bowl, stir together the half-and-half, mayonnaise, tarragon vinegar, mustard, and dried tarragon. Put the dressing into a squirt bottle.

For the salad, trim the endive heads and separate the leaves. Arrange the leaves in a circle on salad plates, dividing them among six plates. Top each endive leaf with a thin slice of avocado. Toss 2 tablespoons of the dressing with the coarsely shredded carrots. Spoon ½ cup of the carrot mixture onto the middle of each plate. Crumble the blue cheese and sprinkle about ¼ cup over each salad. Sprinkle with the walnuts. Drizzle the salads with the remaining salad dressing.

Grilled Boston Lettuce with Blue Cheese–Bacon Dressing

1 cup heavy cream

1 cup (6 ounces) crumbled blue cheese, divided

¼ cup sour cream

1 teaspoon white wine vinegar

¼ teaspoon salt

¼ teaspoon pepper

4 slices applewood smoked bacon, cooked and crumbled into medium pieces

4 heads Boston lettuce, rinsed and dried

¼ cup extra-virgin olive oil

Salt and pepper, to taste

3 medium tomatoes, sliced, for garnish

Chopped fresh parsley, for garnish

Preheat a gas or charcoal grill to medium heat.

In a small saucepan over medium heat, bring the cream to a boil, stirring frequently. Stir in ¾ cup of the blue cheese, immediately reduce the heat, and simmer for 5 minutes, stirring frequently. Stir in the sour cream, vinegar, salt, pepper, and bacon. Keep warm.

Cut each head of lettuce in half through the core, leaving the core intact. Brush all sides with the olive oil. Grill each half over medium heat for 45 seconds on each side.

Place each lettuce half on a serving plate; sprinkle with salt and pepper. Garnish with the tomato slices; sprinkle with the chopped parsley.

Add the remaining ¼ cup blue cheese to the dressing; mix well. Ladle the warm dressing over the lettuce.

Gruyère Fritters with Frisée and Pears

CHEF GOVIND ARMSTRONG

MAKES 8 SERVINGS

FRITTERS

¼ pound (1 stick) unsalted butter

1½ cups all-purpose flour

1½ cups whole milk

1 egg

1¼ cups (5 ounces) grated Gruyère cheese

Oil, for frying

VINAIGRETTE

1 tablespoon diced shallot

1 tablespoon champagne vinegar

1 teaspoon honey

3 tablespoons olive oil

Salt and pepper, to taste

FRISÉE AND PEARS

2 ripe medium Anjou pears

3 heads extra yellow baby frisée, washed, removed from root (about 4 cups)

For the fritters, melt the butter in a medium saucepot over low heat. Stir in the flour and milk. Whisk until smooth. Whisk in the egg. Pour into a large bowl. Stir in the cheese until smooth. Chill thoroughly, 30 to 60 minutes, while making the vinaigrette.

With small teaspoons, using the chilled batter, make fritters on a baking sheet. When all are formed, heat 3 inches of oil to 365° to 375°F. Fry the fritters until crisp and golden, about 45 seconds. Drain on paper towels.

For the vinaigrette, in a small bowl, whisk together the shallot, vinegar, and honey. Whisk in the oil. Season with salt and pepper. Set aside.

To serve, cut the pears in quarters; core. For each serving, slice a quartered pear and fan out on a plate. Brush with a little vinaigrette. Toss the frisée with the remaining vinaigrette. Place beside the pear. Arrange the fritters around the greens and pear.

Insalata Bianca Appetitosa
with Wisconsin Fresh Mozzarella

CHEF ROBERTO DONNA

MAKES 4 SERVINGS

1 fennel bulb

1 celery heart

1 heart of romaine

9 ounces fresh mozzarella cheese

½ cup extra-virgin olive oil

Juice of 1 lemon (¼ cup)

1 tablespoon mascarpone cheese

1 teaspoon Dijon mustard

¼ teaspoon salt

Pinch of ground white pepper

Thoroughly wash and dry the fennel, celery, and romaine. Cut the fennel into thin slices, about 2 cups. Cut the celery into thin juliennes, about ½ cup. Reserve 4 well-shaped romaine leaves, and then cut the remaining romaine into thin juliennes, about 3 cups. Cut the mozzarella cheese into thin strips. Place all into a large mixing bowl.

Place the olive oil, lemon juice, mascarpone cheese, mustard, salt, and pepper in a blender container. Blend until thick and smooth, about 5 seconds. Pour over the salad; toss to coat. Divide the salad, arranging on serving plates, using the reserved lettuce leaves for garnish.

Organic Sweet Greens Salad with Wisconsin Pepato

CHEF GOOSE SORENSEN

MAKES 4 SERVINGS

2 teaspoons butter

1 cup shelled green pistachios

Pinch of salt

¼ cup sweet Riesling wine

2 tablespoons champagne vinegar

1 tablespoon lemon juice

1 shallot, chopped

1 garlic clove, minced

2 tablespoons chopped fresh tarragon

½ cup olive oil

Salt and pepper, to taste

1 (5-ounce) package organic mixed baby greens, cleaned and sorted

12 cherry tomatoes, halved

6 ounces pepato cheese

Melt the butter in a small sauté pan over medium heat; add the pistachios. Sauté the nuts until slightly brown, 2 to 3 minutes. Dry the nuts on paper towels; sprinkle with a pinch of salt.

In a blender beaker, combine the wine, vinegar, lemon juice, shallot, garlic, and tarragon. Blend on high for 30 seconds. Slowly add the olive oil and blend for at least 1 minute and 30 seconds, until the dressing becomes emulsified. Add salt and pepper. Let stand at least 1 hour.

Toss the greens in a small amount of the vinaigrette. Slowly add more until the greens are coated. Add the pistachios, and season with salt and pepper. Place the salad on four cold plates. Sprinkle the cut sides of the tomatoes with salt and pepper; distribute on the plates, around the greens. With a potato peeler or thin cheese knife, shave the pepato cheese over the top of each salad. Refrigerate any remaining vinaigrette up to 1 week.

Pear Salad

RED WINE VINAIGRETTE

2 ounces red wine vinegar

1 tablespoon minced shallot (1 small)

1 teaspoon prepared mustard

2 teaspoons honey

¼ teaspoon salt

¼ teaspoon pepper

3 ounces extra-virgin olive oil

SALAD

½ cup walnut halves

1 tablespoon olive oil

5 ounces baby lettuce, washed and dried

1 Asian or Bosc pear

1 cup (6 ounces) crumbled Gorgonzola,

Raspberries (optional), for garnish

For the vinaigrette, in a small jar, combine the vinegar, shallot, mustard, honey, salt, and pepper. Add the olive oil, and shake to incorporate. Shake again before serving.

For the salad, in a hot sauté pan, toss the olive oil and walnuts quickly to toast (about 1 minute). Separate the lettuce equally onto four chilled plates. Cut the pears into quarters and core. Thinly slice the pear and evenly distribute over the lettuce (about ¼ pear per portion). Top the lettuce evenly with the cheese and the walnuts.

Garnish each salad with raspberries, if desired. Drizzle the vinaigrette over the entire salad.

Pleasant Ridge Reserve and Warm Arugula Salad

CHEF TODD DOWNS

MAKES 6 SERVINGS

APPLE CIDER VINAIGRETTE

2 cups apple cider

2 ounces (½ cup) apple cider
vinegar

1 tablespoon Dijon mustard

1½ tablespoons shallots, briefly
sautéed and cooled

1½ tablespoons fresh chopped
chervil

⅓ cup walnut oil

⅓ cup vegetable oil

Sea salt, to taste

Freshly ground pepper, to taste

CRISPY BEETS

6 baby beets, sliced paper-thin

Oil for frying (heated to 375°F),
as needed

Sea salt, to taste

SALAD

4 cups (12 ounces) baby arugula

2 cups (6 ounces) baby spinach

1 cup dried cranberries,
plumped in port wine

3 Granny Smith apples, sliced
thinly

1 bunch green onions, roasted
and diced

1½ cups (6 ounces) grated
Pleasant Ridge Reserve
Cheese

For the vinaigrette, reduce the cider in a sauté pan over medium heat until ⅔ cup remains. Cool. Place the vinegar, mustard, shallots, and chervil in a bowl. Mix well. Drizzle the oils in slowly. After the dressing has emulsified, add the cider. Season and reserve.

For the crispy beets, fry the sliced beets in oil until crisp. Drain on paper towels and salt lightly.

For the salad, combine the salad ingredients with half of the vinaigrette in a large metal mixing bowl. Place the bowl over a medium flame. Quickly toss the salad to wilt the greens slightly. Transfer to six plates. Top with the crispy beets. Drizzle the remaining vinaigrette around the salad.

Spiced Wisconsin Blue Cheese Salad

MAKES 2 SERVINGS

1 small yellow onion, cut up

1 cup best-quality mayonnaise

⅓ cup vegetable oil

¼ cup ketchup

2 tablespoons sugar

2 tablespoons vinegar

1 teaspoon prepared mustard

½ teaspoon salt

½ teaspoon paprika

¼ teaspoon celery seed

Pinch of cracked pepper

1 cup crumbled blue cheese

Iceberg lettuce wedges

Additional blue cheese crumbles (optional), for garnish

Place all of the ingredients except the blue cheese and lettuce in a blender or small food processor. Blend until quite smooth. Pour into a bowl and gently fold in the blue cheese. Cover tightly and chill.

Just before serving, place the lettuce wedges on salad plates. Pour about ¼ cup of the dressing horizontally over the center of the wedge. Garnish with additional cheese, if desired. Serve immediately, and pass more dressing.

Warm Goat Cheese Salad

MAKES 4 SERVINGS

1 (8-ounce) log soft fresh goat cheese, cut into 8 pieces

1 cup extra-virgin olive oil

6 sprigs fresh herbs, coarsely chopped (choose from thyme, oregano, and rosemary)

1 cup dry breadcrumbs

2 tablespoons balsamic vinegar

1 shallot, minced

1 teaspoon Dijon mustard

Salt and pepper, to taste

1 (6-ounce) bag mixed baby greens

1 medium head radicchio, thinly sliced

Place the goat cheese rounds in a glass baking dish; pour the oil over the cheese and sprinkle with the chopped herbs. Marinate the cheese at least 1 hour and up to 3 days (cover with plastic wrap and refrigerate).

Preheat the oven to 350°F. Spray the baking sheet with nonstick spray. Remove the goat cheese rounds from the olive oil, and dip each round into breadcrumbs, pressing gently to adhere. Place the coated goat cheese rounds on a prepared baking sheet. Bake the goat cheese until heated through, about 10 minutes.

Meanwhile, discard the herbs from the olive oil marinade. Measure $\frac{1}{4}$ cup of the herbed olive oil and pour into a glass measuring cup (discard the remaining olive oil marinade, or save for another use). Add the vinegar, shallot, and mustard, and whisk to blend. Season the dressing with salt and pepper.

In a large mixing bowl, combine the mixed baby greens and radicchio. Drizzle some of the dressing over the lettuces and toss well to blend. Divide the salad greens among four plates and top each with 2 rounds of warm goat cheese. Drizzle each serving with a little more dressing, if desired.

Watercress–Gorgonzola Salad with Spiced Walnuts

CHEFS FRANK RANDAZZO AND ANDREA CURTO-RANDAZZO

MAKES 6 SERVINGS

SPICED WALNUTS

⅓ cup walnuts (halves and pieces)

¼ teaspoon cayenne pepper

½ cup pure maple syrup

SALAD

1 cup plus 2 tablespoons balsamic vinegar, divided

1 bunch watercress, rinsed, dried and stems removed

½ head romaine lettuce, cleaned and cut into ½-inch strips

½ cup (3 ounces) crumbled Gorgonzola cheese

¼ cup dried cranberries

2 tablespoons julienned red onion

¼ cup extra-virgin olive oil

Salt, to taste

Freshly cracked pepper, to taste

For the spiced walnuts, preheat the oven to 375°F. Place the walnuts on a baking sheet and toast lightly, about 5 minutes. Remove to a bowl and toss with the cayenne pepper and maple syrup. Return the coated nuts to the baking sheet. Return to the oven for 5 minutes. Remove the walnuts to oiled wax paper to cool.

For the salad, bring 1 cup of balsamic vinegar to a boil in a small saucepan. Simmer to reduce the liquid by two-thirds, and remove from the heat. Set aside to cool.

In a large bowl, mix the remaining ingredients, including the remaining 2 tablespoons of balsamic vinegar. Divide the salad among six plates. Drizzle the reserved reduced balsamic vinegar around the plates.

Serve immediately.

Roasted Beet, Goat Cheese, and Toasted Walnut Salad

MAKES 4 SERVINGS

8 small-to-medium red beets, trimmed and scrubbed

2 tablespoons vegetable oil

3 tablespoons fresh orange juice

2 teaspoons grated orange zest

2 tablespoons balsamic vinegar

1 shallot, minced

2 tablespoons extra-virgin olive oil

Fine sea salt or kosher salt and freshly ground pepper

1 (6-ounce) bag mixed baby greens

1 bunch watercress, stemmed

½ cup (3 ounces) crumbled soft fresh goat cheese

¼ cup walnuts, toasted in a 350°F oven until fragrant and lightly browned, about 8 minutes

Preheat the oven to 350°F. Place the beets in the center of a large piece of foil. Drizzle vegetable oil over the beets and enclose in the foil. Roast the beets until tender (when they can be easily pierced with the tip of a knife), about 1 hour. Open the foil packet and allow the beets to cool slightly. When cool enough to handle, peel the beets. Cut the beets into ¼-inch-thick slices and place in a medium mixing bowl.

In a small bowl, combine the fresh orange juice, zest, vinegar, and shallot; whisk to combine. Slowly pour in the olive oil while whisking to blend. Season the vinaigrette to taste with salt and pepper. Pour half of the vinaigrette over the beets and toss gently to coat.

In a large serving bowl, combine the greens and watercress; toss with the remaining vinaigrette. Mound the beets in the center of the greens and sprinkle with the cheese and toasted walnuts.

Variation: If golden beets are available at your farmers' market, mix in a few with the red beets for beautiful color variation. Fresh orange segments would be a nice addition to the salad.

Caribbean Spinach Salad with Wisconsin Cotija

MAKES 6 SERVINGS

SALAD

1 pound baby spinach leaves

6 Roma tomatoes, quartered

½ large cucumber, peeled and thinly sliced

½ sweet red onion, cut in thin rings

1 cup peeled, diced fresh mango

1 cup (about 6 ounces) crumbled Cotija cheese

⅓ cup walnuts, broken

2 ounces pancetta, finely diced

VINAIGRETTE

Juice and grated zest of 1 lemon

¼ cup rice wine vinegar

¼ cup honey

2 tablespoons vegetable oil

½ teaspoon ancho chile powder

GARNISH

2 ounces aged Gruyère cheese

For the salad, arrange the spinach on a plate and top with the tomatoes, cucumbers, onion, and mangoes. Sprinkle with the Cotija cheese, walnuts, and diced pancetta.

For the vinaigrette, whisk together the lemon juice and zest, vinegar, honey, oil, and ancho chile powder. Drizzle over the top of the salad. Refrigerate while the garnish is prepared.

For the garnish, preheat the oven to 350°F. Shave the Gruyère into thin slices (about 2 inches square) and place them on a nonstick baking sheet. Bake for 10 minutes until the cheese is crisp. (Cheese bakes into irregular rounds or ovals.) Remove from the oven and let the cheese cool on the baking sheet.

To serve, place 2 to 3 crisps of Gruyère slightly upright onto the center of the salad.

Ginger-Berry Spinach Salad

MAKES 6 SERVINGS

¼ cup orange juice

3 tablespoons vegetable oil

1 tablespoon honey

1 teaspoon grated orange zest

¼ teaspoon garlic salt

⅛ teaspoon paprika

4 cups fresh spinach

1 pint strawberries, stemmed, halved

1 cup (6 ounces) cubed Gouda cheese

½ cup pecan or walnut halves

In a small, tight-lidded container, combine the orange juice, oil, honey, orange zest, garlic salt, and paprika; cover tightly. Shake well; set aside.

In a large salad bowl, toss the spinach, strawberries, cheese, and nuts with the dressing. Refrigerate for later, or serve immediately.

Spinach and Strawberry Salad with Wisconsin Gouda

MAKES 6 SERVINGS

1 cup sliced fresh strawberries

½ cup (4 ounces) part-skim ricotta cheese

½ teaspoon ground ginger

3 cups torn fresh spinach

3 cups torn iceberg lettuce

½ cup celery

¼ cup unsalted sunflower kernels

Combine the strawberries, ricotta cheese, and ginger in the container of an electric blender or food processor; cover and process until smooth. Chill.

Place the torn spinach, lettuce, and celery in a large bowl, tossing gently to combine. Pour the dressing mixture over the spinach mixture; sprinkle with the sunflower kernels.

Swiss and Broccoli Salad

MAKES 6 SERVINGS

1 (10-ounce) package frozen chopped broccoli

1 (10½-ounce) can beef consommé

1½ envelopes unflavored gelatin

¼ cup cold water

2 tablespoons fresh lemon juice

1 tablespoon tarragon-flavored wine vinegar

¾ cup mayonnaise

2½ cups (10 ounces) grated Swiss cheese

Cook the broccoli until crisp-tender. Drain and refrigerate.

In a small saucepan, bring the consommé to a boil. Set aside.

Combine the gelatin and cold water and stir. Add the lemon juice and vinegar and stir. Add to the hot consommé. Stir until the gelatin is completely dissolved. Chill until the mixture is of a syrupy consistency.

Once the gelatin-consommé mixture has chilled, remove from the refrigerator and beat with an electric mixer until frothy. Add the mayonnaise and beat until smooth. Fold in the Swiss cheese and broccoli. Pour into a lightly oiled 3-cup mold. Chill until firm. Unmold and garnish for serving.

Mexican-Style Asparagus Salad
with Wisconsin Queso Blanco

MAKES 4 TO 6 SERVINGS

ASPARAGUS SALAD

Pinch of salt

1 pound fresh asparagus, tough ends discarded and cut across diagonally in pieces 1 inch long

⅓ cup finely chopped fresh cilantro

⅓ cup diced white onion

1 serrano chile, chopped, or ½ jalapeño pepper, chopped, or more to taste

VINAIGRETTE

1 garlic clove, peeled and crushed

¼ teaspoon salt

¼ cup fruity olive oil

1 teaspoon dried Mexican oregano

2 tablespoon rice vinegar

1 tablespoon fresh lime juice

ASSEMBLY

1 medium tomato, seeded and chopped

1 cup (about 4 ounces) crumbled queso blanco

For the asparagus salad, bring $2\frac{1}{2}$ cups water to a boil. Add the salt and asparagus. Return to a boil. Test after 1 minute—the asparagus should be crisp-tender. Cook longer if necessary, being careful not to overcook. Rinse with cold water and drain. Place the asparagus in a bowl, and add the cilantro, onion, and chile; mix well.

For the vinaigrette, combine all of the vinaigrette ingredients and shake well in a jar with lid. Discard the garlic.

To assemble, toss the asparagus mixture with the vinaigrette, and refrigerate 2 hours or overnight. Just before serving, add the tomato and queso blanco. Stir to mix.

Mozzarella and Green Bean Salad

2 cups fresh green beans,
   cooked crisp-tender and
   drained

2 cups (8 ounces) shredded
   mozzarella cheese

1 cup cherry tomato quarters

¼ cup torn fresh basil

1 small red onion, cut into
   ⅛-inch rings

1 (2¼-ounce) can sliced black
   olives, drained

½ cup prepared Italian dressing

In a large bowl, combine all of the ingredients; mix well.

Cover and refrigerate for 1 hour to blend the flavors.

Toss before serving.

Watermelon and Avocado Salad with Ricotta Salata

MAKES 6 SERVINGS

2 tablespoons lime juice

2 tablespoons extra-virgin olive oil

1 teaspoon ground cumin

Fine sea salt or kosher salt and freshly ground pepper, to taste

1 (4-pound) seedless watermelon (rind trimmed and discarded), cut into ½-inch cubes (about 6 cups)

1 cup (4 ounces) crumbled ricotta salata

2 ripe Hass avocados, seeded, peeled, cut into ¼-inch pieces

¼ cup pumpkin seeds (pepitas)

¼ cup coarsely chopped fresh cilantro

Coarsely ground black pepper, to taste

In a small bowl, combine the first 3 ingredients and whisk together to blend. Season the dressing with salt and pepper.

In a large bowl, combine the watermelon, ricotta salata, avocado, pumpkin seeds, and cilantro. Pour the dressing over the salad and toss gently to combine. Season with freshly ground pepper, if necessary.

Note: Ricotta salata (dried, salted ricotta cheese) has a milky mildness. It is salty, so taste the salad before determining if you need to season it with additional salt.

Garbanzo Beans with Wisconsin Feta and Sun-Dried Tomatoes

MAKES 4 SERVINGS

3 cups cooked garbanzo beans (chickpeas) or canned beans, rinsed and drained

1 small cucumber, peeled, seeded, and diced

¾ cup (about 5 ounces) crumbled feta cheese

2 tablespoons sun-dried tomatoes (not oil-packed), coarsely chopped

2 teaspoons chopped fresh thyme or 1 teaspoon dried

2 tablespoons balsamic vinegar

1 teaspoon extra-virgin olive oil

In a large bowl, combine all of the ingredients, tossing well. Cover and refrigerate for several hours, or until ready to serve.

Feta and White Bean Salad

¼ cup lemon juice

¼ teaspoon pepper

¼ cup olive oil

5¼ cups cooked, drained white beans, or 3 (16-ounce) cans, drained

¾ cup thinly sliced green onion

1 pound (2 large) tomatoes, seeded and diced

1 cup (6 ounces) crumbled feta cheese

¼ cup chopped fresh parsley

2 tablespoons chopped fresh dill or 2 teaspoons dried dill

Mix the lemon juice and pepper. Beat in the oil; reserve.

Combine the remaining ingredients. Fold in the reserved dressing. Chill to marry the flavors. Serve at cool room temperature.

Family-Style Potato Salad

MAKES 8 LARGE SERVINGS

2 pounds red boiling potatoes

¾ cup sour cream

¼ cup mayonnaise

¼ cup grainy or spicy brown mustard

½ teaspoon salt

½ teaspoon freshly ground pepper

8 ounces Muenster, brick, or Havarti cheese, diced

¼ cup chopped chives or red onion

¼ cup plus 2 tablespoons chopped fresh parsley, divided

2 hard-cooked eggs, chopped (optional)

¼ cup crumbled, crisply cooked bacon

Simmer the potatoes in salted water to cover until tender, 20 to 25 minutes, depending on the size of the potatoes. Drain; rinse with cold water to stop the cooking, and cool the potatoes. Peel, if desired, and cut into ¾-inch chunks.

In a large bowl, combine the sour cream, mayonnaise, mustard, salt, and pepper, mix well. Add the potatoes, cheese, chives, and ¼ cup of the parsley; toss well. Stir in the eggs, if desired. Cover and chill at least 2 hours or up to 8 hours before serving.

To serve, sprinkle with the bacon and the reserved 2 tablespoons of parsley

True-Blue Potato Salad

MAKES 6 SERVINGS

1¼ cups sour cream

2 tablespoons minced fresh parsley

2 tablespoons tarragon white wine vinegar*

½ teaspoon celery seed

½ teaspoon salt

⅛ teaspoon pepper

¾ cup (about 5 ounces) crumbled blue cheese

4 cups (1½ pounds) cooked red, white, and All Blue potatoes, cubed**

½ cup diced celery

½ cup sliced green onions

½ cup sliced water chestnuts

* You can substitute 2 tablespoons white wine vinegar mixed with ⅛ teaspoon dried tarragon leaves.

** The recipe can also be made with all red or yellow potatoes.

Combine the sour cream, parsley, vinegar, and seasonings; mix well. Stir in the blue cheese.

Combine the potatoes, celery, green onions, and water chestnuts in a bowl. Add the sour cream mixture and toss lightly.

Feta Potato Salad

SALAD

1 pound new red potatoes, cooked, quartered

½ cup sliced ripe or Greek olives

1 cup (6 ounces) crumbled peppercorn feta cheese

1 (14-ounce) can artichoke hearts, quartered

DRESSING

¼ cup olive oil

1 tablespoon lemon juice

1 tablespoon pepper

1 tablespoon chopped chives

1 teaspoon Dijon mustard

1 garlic clove, minced

Salt, to taste

For the salad, in a large bowl, combine the potatoes, olives, cheese, and artichoke hearts.

For the dressing, in a small jar with a tight-fitting lid, combine all of the dressing ingredients. Shake well to mix; pour over the salad ingredients. Toss gently; chill before serving.

Smoked Salmon Potato Salad with Wisconsin Fontina

1½ pounds small new potatoes, unpeeled

4 ounces smoked salmon or lox, chopped

⅔ cup (4 ounces) cubed fontina cheese

1 cup chopped cucumber

¼ cup sliced green onions

1 cup sour cream

½ cup mayonnaise

2 tablespoons chopped fresh dill or 1 teaspoon dried dill

Salt and pepper

Fresh dill sprigs (optional), for garnish

Cook the potatoes until tender; cool. Cut the potatoes in half; and place them in a large bowl. Add the remaining ingredients; mix lightly. Season to taste with salt and pepper. Chill thoroughly. Serve on lettuce-lined plates; garnish with additional fresh dill, if desired.

Variation: For a milder flavor, Havarti cheese may be substituted for the fontina cheese.

Wisconsin Seven-Layer Salad with Feta Yogurt Dressing

MAKES 8 SERVINGS

½ cup plain low-fat yogurt

½ cup buttermilk

¼ cup mayonnaise

½ cup (3 ounces) crumbled feta cheese

1 teaspoon sugar

¼ teaspoon dried dill

¼ teaspoon dried basil

⅛ teaspoon ground white pepper

1 (9-ounce) package uncooked cheese tortellini

2 cups shredded red cabbage

6 cups torn fresh spinach

2 cups (12 ounces) cubed fontina cheese

1 cup cherry tomatoes, halved

¼ cup diagonally sliced green onions

8 slices bacon, cooked and crumbled

In an electric blender or a food processor, blend the yogurt, buttermilk, mayonnaise, feta cheese, sugar, dill, basil, and pepper until smooth. Chill.

Cook the tortellini according to the package directions. Drain; rinse with cold water. In a 2½-quart bowl, layer the cabbage, spinach, tortellini, fontina cheese, tomatoes, and green onions. Pour the dressing over the salad; sprinkle with the bacon. Cover and chill for 3 to 4 hours or until serving time.

Tabbouleh and Wisconsin Cheese Salad

MAKES 4 SERVINGS

2 cups warm water

1 cup bulgur wheat

1 (10-ounce) package frozen peas, thawed

1 cup (6 ounces) crumbled feta cheese

¾ cup julienned Swiss or brick cheese

¼ cup vegetable oil

2 tablespoons lemon juice

½ teaspoon dried dill

¼ teaspoon salt

Lettuce leaves

1 medium tomato, cut into thin wedges

Pour the warm water over the bulgur in a medium mixing bowl. Let the bulgur stand for 1 hour. Drain the bulgur well, pressing out excess water.

Stir in the thawed peas and the cheeses. For the dressing, in a screw-top jar, combine the vegetable oil, lemon juice, dill, and salt; cover and shake well. Pour the dressing over the bulgur mixture; toss gently. Cover and chill in the refrigerator for at least 1 hour.

To pack for a picnic, spoon the salad into a lettuce-lined, airtight container; top with the tomato wedges.

Couscous and Asparagus with Wisconsin Queso Blanco

1 (10-ounce) package couscous

10 spears large asparagus, washed, trimmed, and cut diagonally into 1-inch pieces

½ cup prepared fat-free Italian dressing

2 tablespoons Dijon mustard

1 cup canned chickpeas, rinsed and drained

1½ cups (9 ounces) crumbled queso blanco or feta cheese

3 green onions, thinly sliced

Romaine lettuce leaves

Prepare the couscous according to the package directions, omitting the butter. Fluff the prepared couscous lightly with a fork; cool, uncovered, for 10 minutes.

Meanwhile, place the asparagus on a microwave-safe plate; sprinkle with 1 tablespoon of water. Cover loosely with plastic wrap. Microwave on high for 2 minutes; set aside.

In a small bowl, whisk together the dressing and mustard. In a large bowl, combine the couscous, asparagus, dressing, chickpeas, cheese, and green onions; toss well. Cover; chill at least 2 hours before serving on a bed of lettuce.

Summer Farro Salad with Ricotta Salata

MAKES 4 TO 6 SERVINGS

2 cups farro or spelt*

½ teaspoon sea salt or kosher salt

4 cups loosely packed arugula

2 cups cherry tomatoes, quartered

¾ cup (3 ounces) crumbled ricotta salata **

2½ tablespoons red wine vinegar

1 large garlic clove, pressed or finely minced

6 tablespoons olive oil

Sea salt or kosher salt and freshly ground pepper, to taste (optional)

* Similar to wheat berries (which can be substituted in this recipe), farro cooks quickly and has a delicious light and nutty flavor—not to mention an extraordinary nutritional content. Farro is available at some specialty and Italian markets and from Anson Mills. Wheat berries are sold at natural foods stores and some supermarkets.

** If you can't find ricotta salata, try crumbled feta instead.

Bring 6 cups of water to a boil in a medium saucepan. Stir in the farro and salt, and return to a boil. Reduce the heat to medium, and cover partially. Simmer until the farro is tender but firm to the bite, about 25 minutes. Drain in a colander and rinse under cool running water; drain well.

In a large bowl, combine the farro with the arugula, tomatoes, and cheese. In a small bowl, combine the vinegar and garlic; gradually whisk in the olive oil. Season with salt and pepper if needed. Pour the vinaigrette over the farro salad and toss to combine. Add more salt and pepper, if necessary.

Crisp Asiago Chips with Fregola Sardo

CHEF GOVIND ARMSTRONG

MAKES 8 SERVINGS

ASIAGO CHIPS

2 cups (8 ounces) finely grated Asiago cheese

SALAD

1 pound Fregola Sardo (Italian couscous) pasta

1 tablespoon salt

2 tablespoons plus 1 cup olive oil

3 ounces piquillo peppers, julienned (½ cup from a 6-ounce can)

1 medium seedless cucumber, diced (1½ cups)

1 medium red onion, diced (1 cup)

½ cup chopped fresh Italian parsley

2 teaspoons chopped fresh oregano

1 teaspoon chopped fresh thyme

6 tablespoons diced shallots

4 tablespoons Dijon mustard

4 tablespoons sherry vinegar

2 tablespoons red wine vinegar

Salt and pepper, to taste

8 cups baby arugula (4 to 5 ounces)

For the Asiago chips, preheat the oven to 300°F. On a nonstick baking sheet, place quarter-sized thin layers of the cheese (about 1½ teaspoons each). Bake 10 to 12 minutes or until browned and crisp, rotating the pan for even baking. Remove and place on a paper towel–lined wire rack to cool.

For the salad, bring 3 quarts of water to a boil in a large pot. Add the Fregola Sardo pasta and salt. Bring to a boil again. Cook 5 to 7 minutes, or until al dente. Drain and rinse with cold water. Place in a large bowl. Toss with 2 tablespoons of the olive oil. Add the peppers, cucumber, onion, parsley, oregano, and thyme. Toss; set aside.

In a medium bowl, whisk the shallots, mustard, and vinegars. Slowly whisk in the remaining 1 cup of olive oil. Season with salt and pepper. In a medium bowl, toss ¼ cup of the vinaigrette with the arugula. Toss the remaining vinaigrette with the pasta salad.

To serve, spoon the pasta salad onto a large platter, making a well in the center. Arrange the arugula in the center of the pasta. Garnish with Asiago chips.

Antipasto Salad

½ pound rotini, uncooked

1 (10¾-ounce) can cream of celery soup

½ cup mayonnaise

3 tablespoons wine vinegar

2 tablespoons grated onion

1 tablespoon chopped fresh basil or 2 teaspoons dried basil, crushed

1 cup (6 ounces) cubed provolone cheese

1½ cups (8 ounces) salami, cut into 1 x ¼-inch strips (optional)

½ medium green bell pepper, cut into matchstick strips

½ medium red bell pepper, cut into matchstick strips

¼ cup sliced ripe olives

Leaf lettuce

Cook the rotini according to the package directions; drain.

In a small bowl, stir together the soup, mayonnaise, vinegar, onion, and basil. Set aside.

In a large bowl, combine the rotini, cheese, salami, peppers, and olives. Add the soup mixture; toss to coat well. Cover and refrigerate until serving time, at least 4 hours.

To serve, arrange the lettuce on a serving platter. Toss the rotini mixture and arrange over the lettuce.

Grilled Vegetable and Pasta Salad

MAKES 12 SERVINGS

4 Italian baby eggplants, sliced ½ inch thick

2 zucchini, sliced ¼ inch thick

2 yellow squash, sliced ¼ inch thick

½ pound mushrooms, halved

⅔ cup olive oil

½ cup balsamic vinegar

4 garlic cloves, minced

1 pound penne pasta, cooked and drained

1 cup sliced black olives

1½ cups (9 ounces) cubed mozzarella cheese

1½ cups (about 6 ounces) grated Asiago or Parmesan cheese

1 (7-ounce) jar roasted red peppers, drained and diced

¼ cup chopped fresh parsley

½ teaspoon salt

¼ teaspoon black pepper

Preheat the broiler.

Place the vegetables and mushrooms on a baking sheet. In a bowl, combine the olive oil, vinegar, and garlic. Brush the vegetables and mushrooms with the vinegar-oil dressing; reserve the remaining dressing. Grill or broil the vegetables on both sides, about 8 to 10 minutes.

In a large bowl, gently combine the grilled vegetables, pasta, olives, cheeses, and red peppers. Stir in the remaining dressing, the parsley, and the salt and pepper. Serve warm or at room temperature.

Marinara Pasta Salad with Fresh Wisconsin Mozzarella

MAKES 8 SERVINGS

3 cups rotini pasta

1¼ cups (about 12 ounces) refrigerated marinara sauce

¼ cup red wine vinegar

¼ to ½ teaspoon hot pepper sauce

¼ teaspoon salt

2 balls (8 ounces each) fresh mozzarella cheese, cubed

1 medium zucchini, cut in half lengthwise, sliced

1 cup marinated olives, halved and pitted

½ green bell pepper, cut into small strips

½ red bell pepper, cut into small strips

Cook the pasta according to the package directions. Drain; run under cold water to chill.

Combine the marinara sauce, vinegar, pepper sauce, and salt. Pour over the combined remaining ingredients; mix lightly. Serve immediately or refrigerate.

Variation: Omit the marinara sauce, vinegar, pepper sauce, and salt. Toss the ingredients with ½ cup prepared oil and vinegar salad dressing.

Orecchiette, Asparagus, and Summer Squash Salad

MAKES 4 SERVINGS

1½ teaspoons olive oil

2 garlic cloves, minced

12 slender asparagus spears, cut diagonally into 1-inch pieces

1½ cups cubed yellow squash (½-inch cubes)

¾ cup thinly sliced fennel

1 cup packed arugula leaves, coarsely chopped

12 ounces orecchiette pasta, cooked, drained, rinsed, and cooled

1¼ cups fontina cheese, cut into ¼-inch cubes

⅓ cup nonfat Italian dressing

¼ teaspoon salt

⅛ teaspoon red pepper flakes, or to taste

2 tablespoons chopped fennel fronds

In a nonstick skillet, heat the oil over medium-high heat. Add the garlic, asparagus, squash, and fennel; cook for 3 minutes, or until the vegetables are crisp-tender, stirring occasionally. Stir in the arugula; remove from the heat.

In a large serving bowl, combine the pasta, vegetables, cheese, dressing, salt, and red pepper flakes; toss well. Sprinkle with the fennel fronds; serve.

Apple and Brown Rice Salad with Wisconsin Blue Cheese

MAKES 6 SERVINGS

1¼ cups whole-grain brown rice

2½ cups water

¼ cup white wine vinegar

½ teaspoon salt

¼ teaspoon pepper

¼ cup olive oil

1 cup (6 ounces) crumbled
   blue cheese, divided

1½ cups diced green apple
   (1 medium)

¾ cup diced red onion

1 cup celery, thinly sliced
   (3 ribs)

½ cup raisins

Combine the rice and water in a medium saucepan and stir lightly. Bring to a rolling boil. Cover tightly and reduce the heat. Simmer for 35 minutes or until the water is absorbed. Cool slightly.

Meanwhile, in a large bowl mix the vinegar, salt, pepper, and olive oil. Add the rice. Stir in ¾ cup of the blue cheese, the apple, the onion, the celery, and the raisins. Cool. Refrigerate two hours or more to allow the flavors to blend. Garnish with the remaining ¼ cup of blue cheese. Serve at cool room temperature.

Heartland Wild Rice Salad

⅔ cup wild rice, uncooked

4 ounces roast pork, cut into bite-size pieces

¼ pound fresh mushroom slices

¼ cup chopped green onions

¼ cup chopped fresh parsley

1 teaspoon fresh rosemary or ½ teaspoon dried rosemary

1 cup Muenster cheese, cut into matchstick strips

1 tablespoon balsamic vinegar

2 tablespoons olive oil

Plain yogurt (optional), for garnish

Cook the rice according to the package directions. Cool. Add the remaining ingredients, except the yogurt, to the cooked rice; mix lightly. Chill. Serve topped with a dollop of yogurt, if desired.

Variation: For an added twist, mix in two cheeses. Use a combination of Muenster with aged provolone, fontina, Gouda, or Havarti.

Wisconsin Blue Cheese Turkey Salad

MAKES 4 SERVINGS

DRESSING

½ cup olive oil

½ cup chopped onion

¼ cup white wine vinegar

¼ cup honey

1 tablespoon hot pepper sauce

SALAD

8 cups torn assorted salad greens

2 cups chopped cooked turkey or 8 ounces sliced turkey

1 cup (6 ounces) crumbled blue cheese

1 cup pecan halves

For the dressing, in a blender or food processor, combine the oil, onion, vinegar, honey, and hot pepper sauce; purée.

For the salad, toss the greens lightly with some of the dressing, to coat. Arrange the greens on a platter. Top with the turkey, blue cheese, and pecans; drizzle with additional dressing.

Variation: Gorgonzola cheese can be substituted for the blue cheese.

Prosciutto-Wrapped Figs with Wisconsin Blue Cheese

MICHAEL SYMON

MAKES 6 SERVINGS

18 fresh figs, cut in half

1 cup (6 ounces) blue cheese, softened

18 slices prosciutto ham, cut $1/16$ inch thick by 2 inches wide

Juice of 1 lemon

$1/3$ cup extra-virgin olive oil

$1\frac{1}{2}$ cups arugula

$1/2$ cup slivered almonds, toasted

Preheat the oven to 500°F.

Scoop a small amount out of the center of each fig half and fill equally with the blue cheese. Put the halves back together and wrap each fig with prosciutto. Bake until the prosciutto begins to crisp, about 4 minutes. Remove from the oven and set aside.

Whisk together the lemon juice and olive oil and toss with the arugula. Place three warm figs on each plate. Place $1/4$ cup of arugula in the center. Sprinkle with the almonds and serve.

Fusilli Chicken Salad with Wisconsin Fontina

MAKES 6 SERVINGS

½ cup balsamic or red wine vinegar

⅔ cup olive oil

1 teaspoon chopped fresh tarragon

½ teaspoon salt

½ teaspoon pepper

1 pound boneless, skinless chicken breasts

½ pound fusilli or rotini, cooked according to package directions

¾ cup julienned roasted red peppers

¾ cup thinly sliced green onions

1½ cups julienned fontina cheese

½ cup (about 2 ounces) grated Parmesan cheese

Whisk together the vinegar, olive oil, tarragon, salt, and pepper. Reserve 1 cup. Pour the remaining dressing into a plastic zippered bag, add the chicken, and marinate for 30 minutes or more.

Grill or broil the chicken for 15 to 20 minutes, turning once, until fully cooked. Slice thinly when cool enough to handle.

In a large bowl, toss together the pasta, peppers, onions, cheeses, reserved dressing, and chicken.

Feta and Shrimp Cool Summer Salad

MARINADE

½ cup olive oil

½ cup fresh lime juice

1 garlic clove, minced

1 tablespoon chopped fresh cilantro

1 serrano pepper, minced

1 teaspoon pepper

½ teaspoon salt

SALAD

1 pound medium raw shrimp, peeled and deveined

1 cup sliced bell peppers (red, yellow, orange, and/or green)

½ cup sliced jicama

3 cups mixed salad greens

1½ cups (about 9 ounces) crumbled feta cheese

For the marinade, whisk together the marinade ingredients. Pour ½ cup of marinade over the shrimp in a glass bowl; cover and refrigerate 30 minutes or more.

For the salad, in another glass bowl, combine the peppers and jicama slices, and toss with the remaining marinade; cover and refrigerate 30 minutes or more.

Sauté the shrimp with the marinade in a skillet over medium-high heat, 3 to 5 minutes or until fully cooked.

To serve, toss the salad, marinated vegetables, and shrimp together. Top with the feta cheese.

Note: Instead of sautéing the shrimp, you can grill or broil it.

Crab Salad with Wisconsin Swiss Cheese

MAKES 4 SERVINGS

1 (6-ounce) package frozen crabmeat or 1 (6-ounce) can crabmeat, drained

½ cup (2 ounces) shredded Swiss cheese

¼ cup chopped onion

¼ cup finely chopped celery

¼ cup finely chopped green pepper

2 hard-cooked eggs

¼ cup mayonnaise

¼ cup French dressing or seafood cocktail sauce

Salt, to taste

Drain approximately half of the liquid from the defrosted crab. Combine the crab and remaining liquid with all of the other ingredients; mix well. Chill several hours. Serve as a sandwich filling or as a salad on a bed of lettuce.

MAIN DISHES

Wisconsin Cheddar and Mushroom Meatloaf ...299

Beef Tortillas with Frijoles Borrachos and Wisconsin Jalapeño Jack ...300

Steak with Gorgonzola Thyme Crust ...302

Cold Sliced Sirloin with Shaved Pecorino ...304

Rolled Steak with Wisconsin Mozzarella and Pepperoni ...305

Veal Stuffed with Shiitake Mushrooms and Wisconsin Provolone ...306

Roasted Lamb Loin with Mushrooms and Wisconsin Smoked Butterkäse and Gorgonzola ...307

Lamb Chops with Gremolata Goat Cheese Crumbles ...308

German Stuffed Pork Chops ...309

Skillet-Seared Pork Tenderloin with Wisconsin Cheddar Sauce ...310

Pork Loin with Prunes, Apple, and Wisconsin Muenster ...311

Pork Porterhouse with Wisconsin Queso Blanco and Corn Salsa ...313

Pork Scaloppine with Pecorino, Prosciutto, and Sage ...315

Pork Tenderloin with Wisconsin Parmesan Potatoes and Greens ...317

Gruyère, Smoked Bacon, and Potato Tart ...318

Goat Cheese Tart with Pancetta and Wild Mushrooms ...319

Swiss, Ham, and Onion Pie ...320

Italian Sausage–Stuffed Peppers with Wisconsin Cheeses and Orzo ...321

Parmesan and Sausage Polenta with Arugula Salad ...323

Sauerkraut and Sausage over Mashed Potatoes ...324

Sausage and Sweet Pepper Tart with Wisconsin Mozzarella ...325

Swiss Cheese and Sausage Tart ...326

Barbecue Chicken Quesadillas ...328

Chicken and Broccoli Crêpes ...329

Chicken Roulades with Wisconsin Provolone and Peppers ...331

Chicken Souvlaki with Wisconsin Feta ...332

Chicken Stuffed with Wisconsin Fontina Cheese and Ham ...335

Wisconsin Cheddar and Mushroom Meatloaf

MAKES 8 SERVINGS

2 tablespoons butter

1 cup sliced mushrooms

1 cup finely diced onion

1 cup diced red pepper

1 garlic clove, minced

1¼ pounds ground beef

1¼ cups Italian-style breadcrumbs

½ cup (about 2 ounces)
grated Parmesan cheese

½ cup plain yogurt

1 egg, beaten

¼ cup ketchup

2 teaspoons Worcestershire
sauce

1⅓ cups (8 ounces) cubed
Cheddar cheese

1 teaspoon salt

1 teaspoon pepper

Preheat the oven to 350°F.

In a nonstick skillet, melt the butter and cook the mushrooms, onion, red pepper, and garlic over medium heat until softened, 5 to 6 minutes.

In a large bowl, combine the mushroom mixture with the remaining ingredients; mix thoroughly.

Place in a 9 x 5-inch loaf pan and bake for 50 to 60 minutes. Drain the fat. Let the meatloaf stand for 5 minutes before slicing.

Beef Tortillas with Frijoles Borrachos and Wisconsin Jalapeño Jack

CHEF BEN BERRYHILL

MAKES 12 SERVINGS

FRIJOLES BORRACHOS (DRUNKEN BEANS)

6 slices smoked bacon

6 green jalapeño peppers, stemmed and seeded

3 medium yellow onions, peeled

3 carrots, trimmed and peeled

3 stalks celery, trimmed

18 garlic cloves

6 cups dried pinto beans

6 quarts water

3 ancho chiles, slit lengthwise, stemmed and seeded

1 bunch fresh cilantro, 12 sprigs reserved for garnish

9 Roma tomatoes, chopped

12 ounces dark Mexican beer

BEEF

12 beef tenderloin medallions, 6 ounces each

6 tablespoons olive oil

Salt, to taste

TORTILLAS

12 thick corn tortillas

12 slices jalapeño Jack cheese, ¼ inch thick

1½ cups (about 6 ounces) grated Cotija cheese

For the beans, finely mince the bacon. Roughly chop the jalapeños, onions, carrots, celery, and garlic. Place the vegetables in a food processor and chop until very fine.

In a medium stock pot, sauté the bacon until it begins to brown. Add the chopped vegetable mixture to the pot and sauté until the vegetables begin to become transparent. Add the pinto beans and stir to incorporate the vegetables. Add the water and bring to a simmer. Lightly toast the ancho chiles over an open flame or under the broiler. Chop the ancho chiles, cilantro, and tomatoes. Add these ingredients and the beer to the beans. Continue to slowly simmer, stirring occasionally, until the beans are tender, about 2 hours.

For the beef, rub the medallions with olive oil and salt. Grill, preferably over mesquite, to desired doneness.

For the tortillas, lightly toast the corn tortillas over an open flame. They will become pliable as they warm. Place one tortilla on each serving plate. Spoon some hot beans over the tortilla and top the beans with sliced jalapeño Jack cheese. Slice the tenderloin medallion and fan over the beans and cheese. Sprinkle the Cotija cheese over the plate and garnish with the remaining cilantro sprigs. Repeat with the remaining servings. Serve immediately.

Steak with Gorgonzola Thyme Crust

MAKES 2 SERVINGS

2 teaspoons Worcestershire sauce

2 (6-ounce) beef tenderloins or small rib-eye steaks, cut ¾ inch thick

1 large or 2 small garlic cloves, minced

¼ teaspoon freshly ground pepper

2 teaspoons chopped fresh thyme or ½ teaspoon dried

½ cup (3 ounces) crumbled Gorgonzola cheese

Preheat the broiler. Spoon the Worcestershire sauce over both sides of the steaks; let stand for 5 minutes. Sprinkle the garlic and pepper over the steaks. Place the steaks on the rack of the broiler pan. Broil 3 to 4 inches from the heat source for 3 to 4 minutes per side for a medium-rare steak. Remove the pan from the broiler. Sprinkle the thyme, then the cheese, over the steaks. Return the steaks to the oven and broil for 2 minutes or until the cheese is golden brown.

Cold Sliced Sirloin with Shaved Pecorino

MAKES 6 SERVINGS

SIRLOIN

1 (3-pound) beef sirloin steak (about 2 inches thick)

Fine sea salt or kosher salt and freshly ground pepper

1 tablespoon butter

¼ cup olive oil

SALSA VERDE

2 tablespoons red wine vinegar

1 tablespoon chopped capers

1 tablespoon chopped fresh parsley

¼ cup extra-virgin olive oil

Salt and pepper, to taste

ASSEMBLY

1 (5-ounce) bag baby arugula

1 (2-ounce) piece Pecorino Romano cheese, shaved into thin slices using a vegetable peeler

For the sirloin, season the beef on all sides with salt and pepper. In a large, heavy skillet, melt the butter with the oil over medium-high heat. Add the beef to the pan and cook, turning occasionally, about 20 minutes for medium rare. Let the beef cool at room temperature for up to 1 hour; then wrap in plastic and chill in the refrigerator. When ready to serve, thinly slice the beef and shingle the slices on a serving platter.

For the salsa verde, in a small bowl, combine the red wine vinegar, capers, and parsley. Gradually add the olive oil, whisking to blend. Season the salsa verde with salt and pepper.

To assemble and serve, sprinkle the arugula over the beef and then add the pecorino slices. Drizzle with the salsa verde and serve.

Tip: Chilling the beef makes it easier to get neat, thin slices. A vegetable peeler makes quick work of shaving thin strips of cheese.

Rolled Steak with Wisconsin Mozzarella and Pepperoni

1 pound round steak, cut or pounded to ¼ inch thickness

3 ounces large pepperoni, thinly sliced

6 ounces sliced mozzarella cheese

1 (14-ounce) jar spaghetti sauce, divided

½ cup (2 ounces) shredded Parmesan cheese

Pasta of choice

Preheat the oven to 400°F.

Layer the steak with pepperoni and mozzarella slices. Starting at the wide end, roll up the steak; tie it with kitchen twine or secure it with wooden picks. Bake for 15 to 20 minutes, or until browned. Pour 1 cup of the spaghetti sauce over the steak; continue baking for 10 to 15 minutes, or until the steak reaches desired doneness. Cut the steak diagonally into ½-inch slices. Warm the remaining spaghetti sauce in a saucepan over medium heat and serve with the steak. Sprinkle with Parmesan cheese and serve with pasta.

Veal Stuffed with Shiitake Mushrooms and Wisconsin Provolone

MAKES 2 SERVINGS

STUFFED VEAL

8 ounces veal leg (4 medallions), pounded thin

Salt and pepper, to taste

½ teaspoon minced garlic

½ teaspoon minced shallots

Olive oil, for sautéing

2 oven-roasted or sun-dried Roma tomatoes, finely julienned

¼ cup chopped fresh spinach

¼ cup chopped, stemmed shiitake mushrooms

2 tablespoons balsamic vinegar

2 tablespoons port wine

¼ cup (1 ounce) grated aged provolone cheese

¼ cup breadcrumbs from a crusty Italian loaf

Additional vinegar, wine, or stock (optional)

SAUCE

1 tablespoon minced garlic

3 tablespoons white wine

¼ cup heavy cream

2 tablespoons grated aged provolone cheese

For the stuffed veal, prepare the grill according to the manufacturer's directions. Season the veal with salt and pepper. Set aside.

Sauté the garlic and shallots in a small amount of olive oil. When opaque, add the tomatoes, spinach, and mushrooms. Add the vinegar and wine. Remove the mixture to a bowl and cool slightly but not completely. Add the cheese until slightly melted. Add the breadcrumbs. Add more vinegar, wine, or stock to moisten, if necessary.

Place 2 to 3 tablespoons of stuffing on each veal medallion, and roll. Skewer the meat with toothpicks to keep them from unwrapping. Grill until the veal is just done.

For the sauce, mix all the sauce ingredients in a small bowl. Pour some of the sauce on each plate and over the veal to serve.

Roasted Lamb Loin with Mushrooms and Wisconsin Smoked Butterkäse and Gorgonzola

CHEF FRANCIS ROY

MAKES 6 SERVINGS

LAMB

6 (6-ounce) lamb tenderloins

1 pound smoked butterkäse cheese, cut into strips

2 to 3 tablespoons ground cumin

Salt and freshly ground black pepper

2 tablespoons olive oil

⅓ cup pear liqueur

¾ cup cream

¾ cup (about 5 ounces) crumbled Gorgonzola cheese

MUSHROOMS

12 tablespoons (1½ sticks) unsalted butter

¼ cup olive oil

2 Idaho potatoes, peeled and diced

1 pound oyster mushrooms

1 pound shiitake mushrooms

¾ cup (about 5 ounces) crumbled Gorgonzola cheese

Chives, Belgian endive, red bell pepper, for garnish

For the lamb, two hours before cooking, stud the lamb with butterkäse strips using a zucchini corer or the tip of a potato peeler (or make small slits with a knife and insert the cheese into the slits). Rub the lamb with cumin, salt, and pepper. Refrigerate until ready to cook.

Preheat the oven to 400°F. In a large pan over medium-high heat, add the olive oil. Brown the lamb tenderloins. Place the pan in the oven and roast for 7 to 8 minutes or to desired doneness. Remove the pan from the oven. Remove the lamb to a plate and keep warm. Deglaze the pan with pear liqueur. Add the cream and Gorgonzola. Reduce the mixture to a sauce consistency.

For the mushrooms, in a large sauté pan over medium heat, add the butter and olive oil. Sauté the diced potatoes. Add the mushrooms. Cook for 5 to 6 minutes. Stir in the Gorgonzola. Reduce the heat.

To serve, slice the lamb on the diagonal. Pour the sauce over the bottom of the plate. Fan the lamb and mushrooms over the sauce. Garnish with chives, endive, and red pepper.

Lamb Chops with Gremolata Goat Cheese Crumbles

MAKES 4 SERVINGS

½ cup (3 ounces) crumbled soft fresh goat cheese

¼ up pitted green olives, minced

2 tablespoons finely chopped fresh oregano

2 teaspoons finely grated lemon zest

8 (¾- to 1-inch-thick) lamb rib or loin chops

Fine sea salt or kosher salt and freshly ground pepper, to taste

2 tablespoons vegetable oil

Lemon wedges (optional), for serving

Fresh oregano sprigs (optional), for garnish

In a medium mixing bowl, combine the goat cheese, olives, oregano, and lemon zest and toss with a fork to combine.

Sprinkle the lamb chops on both sides with salt and pepper. In a large skillet, heat 1 tablespoon of the oil over medium-high heat. Working in batches, add the lamb chops and cook to the desired doneness, 3 to 5 minutes per side for medium-rare. (Place the first batch of cooked lamb on a platter and tent with foil while cooking the remaining lamb.)

To serve, arrange the lamb chops on a large platter (or divide among plates) and sprinkle the goat cheese mixture over the chops. Serve the lamb chops with lemon wedges and garnish with oregano sprigs, if desired.

German Stuffed Pork Chops

1½ cups (9 ounces) cubed Cheddar cheese

¾ cup soft breadcrumbs

½ cup diced dried apricots

¼ teaspoon celery seeds

1 (6-ounce) can apple juice

4 (¾-inch-thick) loin pork chops with pocket cut

2 tablespoons butter

1 cup chopped celery

1 cup thinly sliced carrots

Preheat the oven to 325°F.

In a mixing bowl mix together the cheese, crumbs, apricots, celery seeds, and ¼ cup of the apple juice. Stuff the pockets of the chops; set aside the remaining stuffing.

In a large skillet melt the butter; slowly brown the chops in the melted butter.

Place the celery and carrots in the bottom of a buttered 1½-quart casserole with cover; arrange the browned chops over the vegetables. Top each chop with one-fourth of the remaining stuffing. Pour ½ cup of apple juice over all. Cover. Bake for 45 minutes; remove the cover and bake an additional 15 to 20 minutes.

Skillet-Seared Pork Tenderloin
with Wisconsin Cheddar Sauce

PORK

2¼ pounds whole pork tenderloins, trimmed of silver skin

½ teaspoon salt

1 teaspoon fresh ground black
pepper

2 tablespoons butter

CHEDDAR SAUCE

½ cup finely diced onions

⅓ cup mustard seeds

1 cup heavy cream

1½ cups (6 ounces) shredded
sharp Cheddar cheese

For the pork, season the pork with salt and pepper. Heat the skillet over medium-high heat and melt the butter in the pan. Carefully add the pork and brown well on each side, cooking to desired doneness.* Remove the pork and allow to rest.

For the sauce, drain the butter from the pan and add the onion; cook until slightly brown. Stir in the mustard seeds and cook for 1 minute. Add the cream and stir until the mixture boils. Reduce the heat to low and simmer for 5 minutes. Stir in the cheese just until melted and smooth. Remove from the heat.

To serve, slice the pork into 1-inch-thick slices. Place on individual serving plates or arrange on a large platter. Serve with the sauce.

* Pork may be served medium, but should reach an internal temperature of 165°F.

Pork Loin with Prunes, Apple, and Wisconsin Muenster

MAKES 8 SERVINGS

2 tablespoons vegetable oil

1½ chopped sweet onions

2 garlic cloves, minced

1 cup (4 ounces) shredded Muenster cheese

1 cup diced apple

1 cup diced prunes

½ cup dry breadcrumbs

½ cup chopped walnuts, toasted

2 tablespoons chopped fresh sage or 1 tablespoon dried sage

Salt and pepper, to taste

3 pounds boneless pork loin, split

¼ cup water

Fresh sage leaves (optional)

In a skillet over medium-high heat, heat the oil. Add the onions; cook 2 minutes, stirring constantly. Add the garlic; cook 1 minute, stirring constantly. Remove from the heat and cool completely.

In a large bowl, combine the onion mixture, cheese, apples, prunes, breadcrumbs, walnuts, sage, salt, and pepper; mix well. Cover and refrigerate until chilled.

Preheat the oven to 400°F.

To stuff the pork, lay the loin out flat; spread the stuffing over the surface of the meat. Roll up the loin, jelly-roll style, enclosing the stuffing. Tie the loin securely with string and place it in a roasting pan. Roast, uncovered, for 15 minutes. Remove the pan from the oven.

Reduce the oven to 325°F; add ¼ cup of water to the bottom of the roasting pan. Cover and roast 1½ to 2 hours, until the pork is thoroughly cooked and tender. Remove from the oven; let stand, covered, for 15 minutes before slicing.

To serve, cut into ½-inch-thick slices. Garnish with fresh sage leaves.

Pork Porterhouse with Wisconsin Queso Blanco and Corn Salsa

CHEF GOOSE SORENSEN

MAKES 4 SERVINGS

SALSA

2 ears fresh corn

½ red bell pepper, finely diced

½ yellow bell pepper, finely diced

½ red onion, finely diced

1 green onion, sliced

1 Roma tomato, finely diced

¼ cup chopped chipotle chiles in adobo sauce (from can)

½ cup chopped fresh cilantro

Juice of 1½ limes

2 tablespoons champagne vinegar

¼ teaspoon toasted cumin

Pinch of cayenne

GRATIN

3 poblano chiles

1½ cups heavy cream

Pinch of salt

2 pounds potatoes, such as red or Yukon Gold

3 cups (18 ounces) finely crumbled queso blanco cheese

¼ cup minced garlic

Salt

White pepper

½ cup dry breadcrumbs

For the salsa, roast corn on a grill or in a 450°F oven for about 15 minutes or until soft. Cut off the cob. Place the corn in a large bowl. Add the bell peppers, onions, tomatoes, chipotle chiles, cilantro, lime juice, vinegar, cumin, and a pinch of cayenne. Let the salsa stand at room temperature at least 1 hour. Adjust the seasoning and heat level as desired.

For the gratin, preheat the oven to 375°F. Roast and peel the poblano chiles. Place the cream in a large bowl; add a pinch of salt. Slice the potatoes lengthwise, as thin as you can, still keeping the potatoes intact. Place the potatoes in the bowl with the cream.

Grease an 8-inch square casserole dish. Place a layer of potatoes in the bottom of the dish, keeping an even pattern and barely overlapping the slices. Sprinkle a very thin layer of cheese, garlic, and salt and pepper. For the next layer, place the slices in the other direction, making a crosshatch pattern. Sprinkle with the cheese, garlic, salt, and pepper. After 3 layers, add a layer of poblano chiles, adding cheese between both sides so the layers stick together. Repeat with the potatoes, cheese, garlic, salt, and pepper. Top generously with the remaining cheese. Cover with foil. Bake about 1 hour or until a toothpick can be easily inserted.

(continued on next page)

PORK

½ cup cumin

¼ cup paprika

¼ cup chili powder

1 tablespoon coriander

1 teaspoon cayenne pepper

1 teaspoon freshly ground
    pepper

4 large pork porterhouse chops

Salt, to taste

Fresh cilanto sprigs (optional),
    for garnish

When the potatoes are soft, turn the oven to 425°F. Sprinkle the potatoes with breadcrumbs. Bake, uncovered, until toasted. Let cool. (The potatoes can be made ahead, cooled, cut in portions, and reheated on a small baking sheet at 450°F.)

For the pork, prepare the grill according to the manufacturer's directions, until very hot.

Place the spices in a small sauté pan. Sauté on low heat until they start to smoke. Purée the heated spices in a spice grinder or coffee grinder. Sprinkle the chops with salt; let stand 5 minutes. Rub with the spice mixture and let stand another 5 minutes. Place the chops on the grill and cook to the desired temperature. (Chops this big might require some time in an oven to finish cooking without overbrowning.) The total cooking time will be about 20 minutes.

To complete the recipe, cut the gratin in squares or triangles and place them on plates. Lean a chop against the gratin. Spoon salsa on top of the pork, letting some of the juice run onto the plate. Garnish with a sprig of cilantro, if desired.

Pork Scaloppine with Pecorino, Prosciutto, and Sage

MAKES 4 SERVINGS

4 pork leg cutlets (about 1 pound total), pounded to ¼-inch thickness

Fine sea salt or kosher salt and freshly ground pepper

All-purpose flour, for dredging

6 tablespoons butter, divided

½ cup (2 ounces) finely grated Pecorino Romano cheese

8 thin slices prosciutto

⅔ cup Marsala*

2 teaspoons minced fresh sage

* White wine can be substituted for the Marsala.

Preheat the oven to 375°F. Sprinkle the pork on both sides with salt and pepper. Dredge the pork in flour, coating both sides, and shake off any excess.

In a large skillet, melt 4 tablespoons of the butter over medium-high heat. Add the pork and sauté until brown, turning once, about 5 minutes. Transfer the pork to a rimmed baking sheet (reserve the skillet). Sprinkle 2 tablespoons of the grated cheese over each pork cutlet. Cover the cheese with 2 prosciutto slices, folding them over crosswise and overlapping slightly to fit neatly atop the cutlet. Transfer the pork to the oven and bake until the chicken is cooked through, about 5 minutes.

Meanwhile, add the Marsala, minced sage, and the remaining 2 tablespoons of butter to the reserved skillet. Bring the mixture to a boil and continue to cook until the sauce is reduced to ⅓ cup, scraping up any browned bits, about 4 minutes.

To serve, place the pork on a serving platter or individual plates and drizzle with the sauce.

Pork Tenderloin with
Wisconsin Parmesan Potatoes and Greens

CHEF SETH BIXBY DAUGHERTY

MAKES 6 SERVINGS

POTATOES

1 onion, thinly sliced

1 tablespoon olive oil

6 Yukon gold potatoes, peeled, thinly sliced

5 dried plums (prunes), diced

1¼ cups (about 5 ounces) grated SarVecchio Parmesan cheese

½ cup heavy cream

Salt and pepper, to taste

PORK

2 (12- to 14-ounce) pork tenderloins

Vegetable oil

Salt and pepper, to taste

PAN JUS

1 cup apple cider

½ cup maple syrup

GREENS

4 shallots, thinly sliced

4 tablespoons olive oil

1 pound cleaned fresh mustard greens

Salt and pepper, to taste

For the potatoes, heat the oven to 350°F. Cook the onion in the olive oil until soft. In an 8 x 8-inch baking dish, layer one-third of the potatoes. Top with a thin layer of onion, prunes, cheese, and cream. Season with salt and pepper. Repeat twice, forming three layers. Bake about 1¼ hours, until golden brown and tender. Cover loosely with foil after 45 minutes if browning too quickly.

For the pork, heat the oven to 375°F. Brush the pork with oil and season with salt and pepper. Bake for 45 minutes. Let stand for 5 to 10 minutes, until the pork reaches a 160°F internal temperature. Cover to keep warm.

For the pan jus, mix the cider and syrup in a small saucepan. Bring to a boil and simmer over low heat until syrupy and reduced by half, 15 to 20 minutes.

For the greens, in a large sauté pan, cook the shallots in 4 tablespoons of olive oil over very low heat until soft, about 15 minutes. Add the greens. Cook until wilted, about 10 minutes. Season with salt and pepper.

To serve, place a bed of greens on each plate. Place a portion of potatoes over the greens. Slice and fan a portion of the pork on top of the greens. Drizzle pan jus around the outer edges of the greens.

Gruyère, Smoked Bacon, and Potato Tart

MAKES 4 SERVINGS

2 strips excellent-quality smoked bacon

2 russet potatoes (8 ounces each)

1½ cups (6 ounces) shredded Gruyère cheese

4 baked tart shells (about 4 inches wide)

Salt and pepper, to taste

1½ cups port wine

Julienne the bacon strips, sauté to cook through, and drain. Preheat the oven to 400°F.

Peel the potatoes and partially cook in boiling water about 15 minutes. When cool enough to handle, slice the potatoes thinly. Spread a little cheese over a tart shell bottom. Scatter a few pieces of the julienned bacon on top of the cheese. Fan a few potato slices over the bacon, and sprinkle with salt and pepper. Repeat the layers. Top with additional cheese. Sprinkle with salt and pepper. Repeat with the remaining three tarts. Place the tarts on a baking sheet and bake for 6 to 8 minutes, or until the potatoes are tender and the cheese melts.

Heat the port wine in a heavy saucepan over medium heat, to simmer. Simmer until the liquid is reduced to a syrup consistency. Remove from the heat and drizzle over each tart.

Goat Cheese Tart with Pancetta and Wild Mushrooms

MAKES 4 TO 6 SERVINGS

1 (9-inch) prepared pie dough, thawed if frozen (not pie shells)

2 tablespoons olive oil, divided

4 ounces thinly sliced pancetta, chopped

2 garlic cloves, minced or pressed

8 ounces fresh wild mushrooms (such as chanterelles or stemmed shiitakes), sliced*

Fine sea salt or kosher salt and freshly ground pepper

1 cup whipping cream

1 large egg

4 ounces soft fresh goat cheese, at room temperature

1 tablespoon minced fresh thyme

* If fresh wild mushrooms are not available, use any combination of cultivated mushrooms (such as cremini) that you like.

Preheat the oven to 375°F.

Roll out the dough on a lightly floured surface into an 11-inch round. Transfer the dough to a 9-inch-diameter tart pan with a removable bottom, pressing onto the bottom and up the sides of the pan. Trim the excess dough, leaving a ½-inch overhang. Fold the overhang in and press against the side of the pan. Pierce the bottom and sides with a fork. Line the tart shell with aluminum foil and fill with pie weights or dried beans. Bake the shell on the middle rack of the oven until the dough is pale golden around the edges, about 20 minutes. Lift the foil and weights out of the tart shell and continue to cook the shell until golden, about 10 minutes. Let the shell cool in the pan on a baking rack.

In a small skillet, heat 1 tablespoon of the olive oil over medium-high heat. Add the pancetta and cook until crisp, stirring frequently, about 6 minutes. Using a slotted spoon, transfer the pancetta to paper towels to drain.

In a large skillet, heat the remaining 1 tablespoon of olive oil over medium-high heat. Add the garlic and cook, stirring, 30 seconds. Add the mushrooms, and sauté until tender, about 5 minutes. Sprinkle the mushrooms with salt and pepper to taste, and allow to cool.

In a medium mixing bowl, whisk together the cream and egg. Stir in the pancetta. In a small bowl, mash together the goat cheese and thyme. Spread the goat cheese over the bottom of the crust. Add the mushrooms and the cream mixture. Bake until the filling is set, about 20 minutes.

Swiss, Ham, and Onion Pie

MAKES 8 SERVINGS

3 eggs

1 cup half-and-half

¼ teaspoon salt

¼ teaspoon white pepper

1¼ cups diced ham

1 cup diced white onion

1½ cups (6 ounces) shredded Swiss cheese

1 (9-inch) unbaked deep-dish frozen pie crust

2 tablespoons sliced green onions

Combine the eggs and half-and-half and bring to room temperature.

Preheat the oven to 350°F.

Whisk in the salt and pepper until well blended. Stir in the ham, onion, and cheese. Pour into the unbaked pie crust; sprinkle the top with the green onions. Bake for 40 to 45 minutes, or until the top is light golden brown and the center is set. Let the pie stand for 10 minutes before cutting; serve warm.

Italian Sausage–Stuffed Peppers with Wisconsin Cheeses and Orzo

MAKES 6 SERVINGS

4 cups water

1 tablespoon salt

1 cup orzo*

12 ounces fresh Italian sausage, either hot or mild

1 cup chopped roasted red peppers, drained

1 cup (4 ounces) shredded mozzarella cheese

1 cup (4 ounces) shredded provolone cheese

6 large fresh whole red peppers, tops sliced off and seeded

½ cup fresh breadcrumbs

4 tablespoons homemade or prepared refrigerated basil pesto

* Orzo is a dried pasta, shaped like short-grain rice.

Preheat the oven to 400°F.

Bring the water to a boil in a large, deep pot. Add the salt and orzo. Boil for 9 minutes. Drain in a wire sieve and rinse with cold water. Drain again. Set aside.

Remove the sausage from the casings, if necessary, and break up into small pieces. Sauté over medium-high heat until browned and barely cooked through. Add the chopped red peppers. Remove from the heat and stir in the orzo and cheeses until the cheese melts. Cool.

Coat a 10 x 10-inch baking pan with cooking spray. Stuff the sausage-orzo mixture into the whole peppers and place the peppers upright in the pan. Mix the breadcrumbs and the pesto and spread evenly over the tops of the stuffed peppers. Cover with foil and bake for 45 minutes. Remove the foil and bake an additional 15 minutes or until the surface is lightly browned.

Serve immediately.

Parmesan and Sausage Polenta with Arugula Salad

CHEF TORY MILLER

MAKES 6 SERVINGS

POLENTA

1 cup boiling water

1 cup golden raisins

2 tablespoons olive oil, plus some for greasing pan

¾ pound bulk sweet sausage

¼ pound pancetta, diced

1 small onion, minced

2 cups polenta

½ cup (about 2 ounces) grated SarVecchio Parmesan cheese, plus extra for sprinkling*

1 tablespoon julienned fresh sage

3 egg yolks

Salt and pepper, to taste

4 cups boiling water or stock

1 cup extra-virgin olive oil, divided

VINAIGRETTE

2 tablespoons balsamic vinegar

1 tablespoon honey

½ tablespoon Dijon mustard

1 small shallot, minced

6 cups arugula

* Grated Parmesan may be substituted for the SarVecchio cheese

For the polenta, heat the oven to 375°F. Grease a 12 x 9-inch baking dish with olive oil. Pour 1 cup of boiling water over the raisins, to plump. Heat 2 tablespoons of olive oil in a medium sauté pan over medium-high heat. Add the sausage and pancetta; stir until cooked but not browned and crisp. Add the onion; reduce the heat, and sweat until the onion is translucent. Set aside.

In large bowl, combine the polenta, cheese, sage, and egg yolks. Whisk in the salt, pepper, and boiling water or stock. Drain the raisins and add to the polenta with about three-fourths of the sausage-and-onion mixture. Stir until smooth and slightly thick. Pour the mixture into the prepared baking dish; top with the remaining sausage mixture. Drizzle with a little olive oil; reserve the remaining olive oil for the vinaigrette.

Bake for about 45 minutes or until the sausage is browned and crisp, and the polenta is set. Remove from the oven and let stand 10 minutes.

For the vinaigrette, in a small bowl, whisk together the vinegar, honey, mustard, and shallot. Gradually whisk in the reserved olive oil to taste.

To serve, cut the polenta into 6 squares. Place one square on each plate. Place a 1-cup mound of arugula beside the polenta; drizzle with the vinaigrette. Pass extra grated cheese to sprinkle on top.

Sauerkraut and Sausage over Mashed Potatoes

MAKES 6 SERVINGS

MASHED POTATOES

2½ pounds russet potatoes, cut into large chunks

2 cups (8 ounces) shredded medium Cheddar cheese

1 cup milk

½ teaspoon salt

½ teaspoon coarse ground pepper

½ cup chopped fresh Italian parsley

SAUERKRAUT AND SAUSAGE

2 medium sweet onions, cut into wedges

5 peeled carrots, cut into ½-inch pieces

1 (32-ounce) jar sauerkraut, drained

2 cups apple juice

1 tablespoon caraway seeds

1 teaspoon coarse ground pepper

2 pounds smoked Ukraine or Polish sausage (2 rings or 8 links, 5 inches each)

8 (1-ounce) slices caraway Havarti or caraway Jack cheese

½ cup chopped fresh Italian parsley

For the mashed potatoes, in a 3-quart saucepan, boil the potatoes until tender, 20 to 30 minutes. Drain the potatoes; add the Cheddar cheese. Mash the potatoes until smooth. Stir in the milk, salt, pepper, and parsley. Spoon the potatoes into a 2-quart rectangular or oval casserole. Cover and refrigerate overnight.

For the sauerkraut and sausage, preheat the oven to 350°F. In a Dutch oven, combine the onions, carrots, sauerkraut, apple juice, caraway seeds, and pepper. Top with the sausage. Cover and bake for 1 hour.

Bake the mashed potatoes in the same oven for 1 hour, to heat. Place the Havarti cheese over the sausages; continue baking until the cheese is melted. Stir in the parsley.

To serve, spoon the mashed potatoes onto individual plates; top with sauerkraut and portions of sausage.

Sausage and Sweet Pepper Tart with Wisconsin Mozzarella

MAKES 6 SERVINGS

1 (9-inch) refrigerated pie crust

8 ounces spicy Italian sausage (remove the casings, if present)

1 (4-ounce) jar roasted red peppers, drained and rinsed, cut into strips

½ small red onion, peeled and sliced thinly

Pinch of dried basil

Pinch of dried oregano

Freshly ground pepper

1 cup (about 4 ounces) grated mozzarella or provolone cheese

½ cup (about 2 ounces) grated Parmesan or Asiago cheese

3 eggs

⅓ cup whole milk

Preheat the oven to 425°F.

Prick the bottom of the crust with a fork 20 times, and place in the oven for 7 minutes. Remove from the oven and pierce any bubbles that formed. Return to the oven and bake until the crust is golden brown, about 11 minutes. Remove from the oven and cool slightly.

Heat a large sauté pan over medium heat, and add the sausage, crumbling well and allowing the meat to cook through. Add the roasted red peppers, onions, herbs, and pepper, and cook the onions through, stirring occasionally, about 10 minutes. Spoon the sausage mixture into the tart shell with a slotted spoon, allowing the drippings to drain. Cover the mixture with the grated cheeses.

Combine the eggs and milk in a bowl with a whisk. Pour the eggs over the sausage mixture. Place the tart in the oven until the egg mixture is set, about 27 minutes. Remove from the oven and allow to cool before serving.

Swiss Cheese and Sausage Tart

1¼ cups all-purpose flour

1 teaspoon baking powder

½ teaspoon salt

¼ pound (1 stick) butter, chilled, cut into ½-inch cubes

¾ cup sour cream

8 ounces Italian sausage

1 tablespoon butter

1 cup sliced onion

1 cup sliced mixed red, yellow, and green peppers

1 cup sliced portobella mushrooms

½ teaspoon salt

½ teaspoon pepper

4½ cups (18 ounces) shredded Swiss cheese

Combine the flour, baking powder, and salt; mix well. Cut in the butter until the mixture is the consistency of coarse meal. Add the sour cream and toss together until the dough forms a ball. Flatten the dough into a disk; wrap in plastic wrap and refrigerate 2 hours.

Preheat the oven to 400°F.

Roll out the dough and gently press into a 10-inch tart or pie pan. Prick the bottom with a fork and bake for 30 minutes or until the crust is golden. Meanwhile, in a large nonstick skillet, cook the sausage until no longer pink, stirring frequently and breaking apart. Using a slotted spoon, remove the sausage to a plate and set aside. Add the butter to the skillet and melt over medium-high heat. Add the onions and peppers and cook, stirring frequently, until soft and beginning to brown, about 10 to 15 minutes. Add the mushrooms, salt, and pepper, and cook, stirring frequently, until the mushrooms are tender and the onions are brown.

Distribute the sausage evenly over the tart shell. Gently toss the cheese with the warm vegetables and spread evenly over the sausage layer. Bake for 15 to 20 minutes or until the cheese is melted.

Barbecue Chicken Quesadillas

MAKES 10 QUESADILLAS

2 cups diced cooked chicken breast

1 cup barbecue sauce

3 cups (12 ounces) shredded queso quesadilla cheese

¾ cup sliced green onions

1 tablespoon chili powder

¾ teaspoon ground cumin

½ teaspoon granulated sugar

10 (9-inch) flour tortillas

2 cups salsa

2 cups guacamole

1 cup sour cream

20 fresh cilantro sprigs

Combine the chicken, barbecue sauce, cheese, green onions, and seasonings. Spread the chicken mixture over half of each tortilla, spreading to the edge. Fold the plain half over the filling; press down firmly. Cook the filled tortillas in a dry skillet until crisp and lightly browned, turning once. For each portion, cut the quesadilla into six wedges. Place on a serving plate, with the points toward the center. Serve with salsa, guacamole, sour cream, and the cilantro sprigs.

Chicken and Broccoli Crêpes

MAKES 10 CRÊPES

½ cup half-and-half

½ cup all-purpose flour

½ teaspoon garlic salt

1¼ cups chicken stock

1 cup (4 ounces) shredded Cheddar cheese

½ cup (2 ounces) shredded Monterey Jack cheese

½ cup dairy sour cream

2 tablespoons diced pimiento

1 tablespoon dried parsley flakes

1 teaspoon paprika

1 (4-ounce) can sliced mushrooms, drained

2 tablespoons butter

10 (4-inch) crêpes*

2 (10-ounce) packages frozen broccoli spears, cooked and drained

2 cups chopped cooked chicken

1 cup dairy sour cream

1 cup (4 ounces) shredded Cheddar cheese

* These can be purchased frozen, or use your favorite crêpe batter recipe.

Preheat the oven to 350°F.

Combine the half-and-half, flour, and garlic salt, and beat until smooth. Blend in the chicken stock. Stir in the cheeses, sour cream, pimiento, parsley, and paprika. Cook the sauce over low to medium heat until the mixture thickens, stirring constantly. Set aside.

In a small saucepan, sauté the mushrooms in butter. On each crêpe place some of the cooked broccoli, chicken, and mushrooms, and spoon 1 to 2 tablespoons of sauce over each. Fold the crêpes and place them in a large, shallow baking dish. Pour the remaining sauce over the crêpes. Top with sour cream and cheese. Cover and bake for 20 to 30 minutes.

Chicken Roulades with Wisconsin Provolone and Peppers

MAKES 4 SERVINGS

1½ teaspoons dried oregano, divided

1 cup (4 ounces) shredded Provolone cheese, divided

4 boneless, skinless chicken breast halves

1 tablespoon vegetable or olive oil

½ cup yellow onion, chopped

1 cup chopped roasted red peppers, drained

Salt and pepper, to taste

4 strips bacon, fried crisp, drained and crumbled

Preheat the oven to 375°F. Butter a baking pan that can accommodate the roulades in one layer (at least 8 inches square).

Mix ½ teaspoon of the oregano and 2 tablespoons of the provolone cheese in a small bowl. Set aside.

Place one piece of chicken between two sheets of wax paper. Pound until thin, about ¼ inch thick. (Or ask the butcher to do this step for you.) Repeat with the remaining chicken breasts. Refrigerate.

Heat the oil in a medium skillet. Add the onion and sauté until soft, 7 to 10 minutes. Add the roasted red peppers and the remaining 1 teaspoon of oregano. Heat through. Remove from the heat and cool. Stir in the remaining cheese.

Remove the chicken from the refrigerator. Lay each piece flat. Season with salt and pepper. Spread a generous ¼ cup of the pepper filling over each chicken piece, leaving the edges bare. Roll each piece, jelly roll–style. Place the chicken seam side down in a baking dish. Bake for 30 minutes.

Remove the chicken from the oven and sprinkle with the reserved cheese-oregano mixture and the bacon crumbles. Return to the oven for 5 minutes, until the cheese melts and the juice from the chicken runs clear.

Chicken Souvlaki with Wisconsin Feta

MAKES 6 SERVINGS

SOUVLAKI

1 pound boneless, skinless chicken breasts, cut into ½-inch cubes

½ cup minced sweet onions

2 teaspoons ground cumin

1 teaspoon cinnamon

½ teaspoon cayenne pepper

½ teaspoon salt

2 tablespoons olive oil

6 flat breads (6- to 7-inch pita, naan, or tortillas)

1 cup (4 ounces) pepato or Asiago cheese, grated

½ cup diced black olives

½ cup diced tomatoes

1 cup (6 ounces) crumbled feta cheese

YOGURT SAUCE

1 cup plain yogurt

1 tablespoon minced mint

½ cup diced cucumber

For the souvlaki, Preheat the oven to 400°F.

In a large bowl, combine the chicken, onion, spices, and salt. Heat the oil in a large skillet; add the chicken mixture and cook over medium-high heat until fully cooked, about 5 to 8 minutes.

To assemble, sprinkle the tops of the flat bread rounds with the pepato or Asiago cheese; bake until the cheese is melted, about 5 minutes. Remove the bread from the oven and top with the chicken, olives, and tomatoes. Sprinkle with feta cheese and return to the oven for 5 minutes, or until toasted.

For the yogurt sauce, combine the yogurt, mint, and cucumbers; mix well. Serve with the toasted bread.

Chicken Stuffed with Wisconsin Fontina Cheese and Ham

CHEF TODD DOWNS

MAKES 6 SERVINGS

BOURBON-PEACH RELISH

1 tablespoon unsalted butter

1 (16-ounce package) frozen peaches, diced and dried (about 3 cups)

½ cup bourbon

½ cup firmly packed light brown sugar

1 serrano chile, seeded and minced

½ cup diced roasted red peppers

2 teaspoons rice wine vinegar

½ cup unsalted peanuts, toasted

COMPOUND BUTTER

¼ pound (1 stick) unsalted butter, softened

1 tablespoon chopped fresh rosemary

1 garlic clove, minced

2 teaspoons Tabasco sauce

Freshly ground pepper, to taste

CHICKEN

6 slices Black Forest or Bavarian ham

4 cups baby spinach, sautéed and blotted dry

6 slices fontina cheese

6 bone-in chicken breasts, with rib bones only removed (skin on)

Chopped fresh rosemary or peanuts (optional), for garnish

For the relish, heat a large sauté pan over medium heat. Add the butter and cook until it foams. Add the peaches and sauté, about 30 seconds. Add the bourbon and continue to cook 2 to 3 minutes. Add the brown sugar and cook just until it dissolves and the bourbon evaporates, 3 to 5 minutes. Transfer the mixture to a medium bowl and cool. Add the remaining relish ingredients. Toss well and reserve.

For the compound butter, in the bowl of an electric mixer, combine all of the ingredients and mix well. Reserve at room temperature.

For the chicken, Preheat the oven to 400°F. Make 6 stacks, layering the ham slices, spinach, and cheese. Stuff each chicken piece, placing one stack between the skin and meat of each piece. Rub the tops of the chicken pieces with the compound butter, and place them on the baking sheet. Bake, skin side up, for 20 to 25 minutes or until the internal temperature reaches 160°F.

To serve, place 1 breast on each of six serving plates. Top each with a portion of the relish. Sprinkle the chopped rosemary or peanuts around the chicken, for garnish, if desired.

Enchilada con Queso

1 cup prepared red taco sauce

1½ tablespoons water

12 (6-inch) corn tortillas

12 slices tomato (optional)

3 cups (12 ounces) shredded pepper Jack cheese

1 cup diced cooked chicken

1 cup finely chopped zucchini

½ cup sliced black olives, drained

3 cups (12 ounces) shredded Colby cheese

Dairy sour cream, guacamole, and additional ripe olives (optional), for garnish

Preheat the oven to 425°F.

Mix the taco sauce and the water. Dip or brush each tortilla to coat well on both sides with the sauce mixture. Place a tomato slice on each tortilla.

Mix the pepper Jack cheese with the chicken, zucchini, and olives. Place ¼ cup of the mixture onto each tortilla. Roll up the tortillas and place, seam side down, on a baking sheet lined with silicone. Sprinkle ¼ cup of Colby cheese over each enchilada.

Bake for 10 to 12 minutes, until the cheese melts and the filling is hot.

Garnish with dairy sour cream, guacamole, and additional ripe olives, if desired.

Festive Chicken Fajitas

MAKES 6 SERVINGS

½ cup fresh orange juice

1½ teaspoons grated orange zest

2 garlic cloves, minced

¾ teaspoon cumin seeds

¾ teaspoon salt

2½ teaspoons dried oregano

2 pounds boneless, skinless chicken breasts, cut in ½-inch strips

2 teaspoons butter

1 large onion, thinly sliced

2 bell peppers (1 yellow and 1 red), cut in ½-inch strips

2 cups (8 ounces) crumbled queso blanco cheese, divided

1 tablespoon chopped fresh cilantro

12 medium tortillas, warmed

Shredded lettuce, salsa, guacamole, and sour cream, for serving

In a large bowl, combine the orange juice, zest, garlic, cumin, salt, and oregano. Add the chicken; stir to combine. Cover and refrigerate for 1 hour to marinate.

In a large skillet, heat the butter over medium-high heat. Add the onion; cook for 2 minutes. Add the peppers; cook 2 minutes longer. Using a slotted spoon, transfer the chicken to the skillet, discarding any remaining marinade. Cook for 8 to 10 minutes, or until the chicken is cooked through, stirring frequently. Transfer the chicken to a warmed, large serving platter. Sprinkle ½ cup of cheese and the cilantro over the top.

Roll the chicken in warmed tortillas. Serve with the remaining cheese, shredded lettuce, salsa, guacamole, and/or sour cream.

Middle Eastern Chicken with Tomato and Wisconsin Feta Relish

MAKES 2 SERVINGS

2 boneless, skinless chicken breast halves

4 teaspoons red wine vinegar

1½ teaspoons Dijon mustard

1 teaspoon ground cumin

½ teaspoon ground coriander

¼ teaspoon ground red pepper

1 large tomato, seeded and diced

3 green onions, sliced

3 tablespoons chopped fresh mint

¼ cup crumbled feta cheese

1 tablespoon olive oil, divided

Put each breast half between 2 sheets of plastic wrap. Flatten to a uniform thickness of ¼ inch; set aside. Mix the vinegar, mustard, and seasonings in a small dish. Combine the tomatoes, green onions, mint, cheese, 1½ teaspoons of the oil, and 1½ teaspoons of the vinegar mixture in a small bowl; set aside. Brush the remaining vinegar/mustard mixture onto both sides of the chicken. Set aside.

Place a large skillet over high heat. When hot, add the remaining 1½ teaspoons of oil and heat about 30 seconds. Add the chicken breasts. Cook, turning once, until they are cooked through, about 3 minutes total. Transfer the chicken to two dinner plates.

Add the tomato mixture to the skillet, cook, and stir about 20 seconds and divide between the chicken breasts. Serve at once.

Havarti Curried Chicken Cornbread

MAKES 8 SERVINGS

1 to 2 tablespoons vegetable oil

¾ pound boneless, skinless chicken breasts, diced

¾ cup thinly sliced green onions, including greens

1 tablespoon finely grated fresh ginger

1 tablespoon finely minced garlic

Salt and pepper, to taste

¾ cup cornbread mix

2 eggs

1 cup milk or buttermilk

2 to 3 tablespoons curry powder

¼ cup unsweetened shredded coconut

½ cup toasted sliced almonds

2 cups (8 ounces) shredded Havarti cheese

Mango chutney

Preheat the oven to 400°F.

Heat the oil in a skillet over medium heat. Sauté the chicken, green onions, ginger, and garlic for 5 to 7 minutes. Stir often. Remove the pan from the heat. Season to taste. Set aside.

In a large bowl, combine the cornbread mix, eggs, and buttermilk. Stir in the curry, coconut, and almonds. Add the chicken mixture and the cheese. Pour into a well-buttered 10-inch cast-iron skillet or cake pan. Bake for 25 minutes, until lightly browned. Cool the cornbread 10 minutes before cutting into serving pieces. Top with a dollop of chutney.

Gorgonzola Chicken

6 boneless, skinless chicken breast halves

¼ teaspoon salt

⅛ teaspoon pepper

2 tablespoons butter

1 tablespoon olive oil

½ cup chicken stock

¼ whipping cream

¼ cup (about 2 ounces) creamy Gorgonzola cheese

½ cup chopped walnuts (optional)

2 tablespoons chopped fresh basil

Cooked wild rice

Pound the chicken to ¼ inch thickness. Season the chicken with salt and pepper. Melt the butter with olive oil over medium-high heat in a large skillet. Add the chicken and cook 2 minutes. Turn and cook 2 to 3 minutes more or until the chicken is white throughout. Remove to a platter and cover.

Add the stock to the pan and cook over high heat for 1 minute. Reduce the heat to low and gradually add the cream, stirring constantly. Blend in the cheese and stir until the cheese is melted and the sauce is smooth. Continue cooking until the sauce is of the desired consistency. Pour the sauce over the chicken and garnish with the walnuts and basil. Serve with wild rice.

Old-Fashioned Chicken Pot Pie

MAKES 8 SERVINGS

FILLING

1 (10¾-ounce) can cream of chicken soup

½ cup milk

½ cup chopped onion

1 (3-ounce) package cream cheese, softened and cubed

¼ cup (about 1 ounce) freshly grated Parmesan cheese

¼ cup chopped celery

¼ cup shredded carrot

3 cups cubed cooked chicken

1 (10-ounce) package frozen cut broccoli, cooked and drained

PASTRY

1 cup packaged complete buttermilk pancake mix

1 cup (4 ounces) shredded sharp Cheddar cheese

1 egg, lightly beaten

½ cup milk

1 tablespoon cooking oil

¼ cup sliced almonds

Preheat the oven to 375°F.

For the filling, in a large saucepan, combine the soup, milk, onions, cheeses, celery, and carrot. Cook and stir until the mixture is hot and the cream cheese is melted. Stir in the chicken and broccoli and heat through. Pour into an ungreased 2-quart casserole.

For the pastry, in a medium mixing bowl, combine the pancake mix and the shredded Cheddar cheese. In a small mixing bowl, stir together the egg, the milk, and the oil. Add to the pancake mix; stir until well combined. Spoon the pastry mixture over the hot chicken mixture. Sprinkle with the nuts. Bake for 20 to 25 minutes or until the topping is golden brown and the chicken mixture is bubbly around the edges.

Pepper Jack and Smoked Turkey Enchiladas

MAKES 8 SERVINGS

1 (15-ounce) can enchilada sauce

1 (14.5-ounce) can diced tomatoes with mild green chilies

1 tablespoon fresh lime juice

8 (7-inch) flour tortillas

10 ounces deli smoked turkey breast, chopped

1 (15-ounce) can black beans, rinsed, drained

2 cups (8 ounces) coarsely grated pepper Jack cheese, divided

2 cups (8 ounces) coarsely grated Monterey Jack cheese, divided

Combine the enchilada sauce, tomatoes, and lime juice in a medium microwave-safe glass bowl. Microwave on high for 3 minutes or until hot. Set aside.

Warm the tortillas according to the package instructions. Brush one side only of each warm tortilla with the hot sauce, reserving the rest of the sauce for topping. Set aside.

Combine the turkey, beans, and 1 3/4 cups of each of the cheeses in a large bowl. Spoon the mixture evenly into the center of each tortilla. Roll up tightly and place in a sprayed microwave-safe, large oval casserole dish or a 12 x 9-inch microwave-safe baking pan. Spoon the remaining sauce over the tortillas; sprinkle the top with the remaining cheeses. Microwave on high until the enchiladas are hot throughout, about 3 minutes. Serve immediately.

Tip: Serve the enchiladas with a side of butter lettuce salad with orange or pink grapefruit sections and citrus-flavored vinaigrettes.

Prosciutto-Stuffed Chicken with Wisconsin Asiago and Potato Salad

CHEF CORY SCHREIBER

MAKES 6 SERVINGS

STUFFED CHICKEN BREASTS

6 (6- to 7-ounce) boneless, skinless chicken breasts

Salt and freshly ground pepper, to taste

2 ounces Asiago cheese, thinly sliced

6 ounces proscuitto, thinly sliced

Olive oil, for sautéing

POTATO-ARUGULA SALAD

6 Yellow Finn (or other thin-skinned) potatoes, cut into sixths

2 fennel bulbs, cored, trimmed, and cut into ¼-inch slices

1 red onion, cut into ¼-inch slices

½ cup olive oil, divided

Salt and pepper, to taste

2 tablespoons red wine vinegar

½ teaspoon ground cinnamon

⅛ teaspoon ground cloves

2 tablespoons finely chopped dried cherries

1 bunch arugula or watercress

6 ounces fresh, tart cherries, stemmed and pitted

2 ounces aged Asiago cheese, shaved

For the stuffed chicken breasts, preheat the oven to 350°F.

Pound the chicken breasts, skin side down, to ¼ inch thickness. Season with salt and pepper. Top each with a slice of Asiago cheese and a slice of proscuitto. Fold the chicken breasts in half. Secure with wooden picks to enclose the filling.

Brown in hot oil, skin side down, over medium-high heat. Transfer to a baking pan, skin side up. Bake for 15 minutes or until done. Remove the pan from the oven, and remove the wooden picks. Set aside. Raise the oven temperature to 375°F.

For the potato-arugula salad, in a baking dish, toss the potatoes, fennel, and onion with ¼ cup of the oil to coat. Season with salt and pepper. Roast for 45 minutes, or until tender.

Meanwhile, whisk together the remaining ¼ cup of olive oil, the vinegar, the cinnamon, and the cloves, and add salt and pepper to taste. Stir in the dried cherries. Let stand for 30 minutes to blend the flavors.

To assemble, toss the hot potato mixture with the arugula, fresh cherries, and salad dressing. Place the salad on serving plates. Place the chicken breasts next to the salad. Top all with the shaved cheese.

Provolone and Shiitake Smothered Chicken Breasts

MAKES 6 SERVINGS

¼ cup all-purpose flour

1 teaspoon pepper

½ teaspoon salt

4 tablespoons (½ stick) butter, divided

2 tablespoons olive oil

6 boneless, skinless chicken breast halves

¼ cup chopped shallot (1 large)

5 ounces fresh shiitake mushrooms, stems discarded, chopped

½ teaspoon dried thyme, crumbled

2 cups (8 ounces) shredded provolone cheese

Stir together the flour, pepper, and salt; set aside.

Simultaneously, heat two skillets, one large and one 10-inch: In the large skillet, heat 2 tablespoons of the butter and the olive over high heat. Dredge the chicken breasts in the flour mixture and cook approximately 4 minutes per side, until golden and fully cooked. In the 10-inch skillet, heat the remaining 2 tablespoons of butter over medium-high heat, and sauté the shallot for 2 to 3 minutes, stirring occasionally. Add the mushrooms and cook until tender, about 5 minutes. Add the thyme and cheese, and stir to combine. As the cheese begins to melt, remove the skillet from the heat, but continue to stir until the cheese has fully melted. Pour over the chicken breasts and serve immediately.

Queso Jalapeño Deep-Dish Enchilada Suiza

MAKES 4 SERVINGS

TOMATILLO SAUCE

12 fresh tomatillos

2 to 3 garlic cloves

DEEP-DISH ENCHILADA SUIZA

3/4 cup vegetable oil

12 corn tortillas

2 (6-ounce) boneless, skinless chicken breasts, poached and shredded

½ cup chopped onion

½ cup chopped zucchini

½ cup chopped bell pepper

1 large, diced tomato, divided

4 cups (16 ounces) shredded hot pepper cheese, or jalapeño Jack cheese, divided

For the tomatillo sauce, husk and rinse the tomatillos. Cover with water and boil until tender, reserving the water. Place the tomatillos in a food processor and purée, adding a little water as needed. Add the garlic and purée until the sauce reaches a gravylike consistency.

For the enchilada suiza, in a large skillet, heat the oil over medium heat, but do not allow it to smoke. Using kitchen tongs, carefully place the tortillas, one at a time, in the skillet for 5 to 7 seconds until soft and pliable. Gently shake off any excess oil and stack the tortillas on paper towels.

Preheat the oven to 400°F.

In a mixing bowl, combine the chicken, onion, zucchini, bell pepper, half of the tomato, and half of the cheese. In a baking pan, place four tortillas end to end, overlapping the edges. Spread half of the chicken mixture evenly over the tortillas; cover with four more tortillas. Repeat the layering process with the remaining chicken mixture and tortillas. Sprinkle the tortillas with half of the remaining cheese; arrange the tomatoes on top. Cover with the remaining cheese. Bake for 5 minutes, or until the cheese is golden brown. Serve with the tomatillo sauce.

Salmon with Wisconsin Parmesan–Horseradish Crust and Dijon Cream

MAKES 6 SERVINGS

SALMON

1½ cups Italian-seasoned dry breadcrumbs

1 cup (about 4 ounces) grated Parmesan cheese

½ cup prepared horseradish

2 tablespoons olive oil

2 teaspoons dry Cajun seasoning mixture

6 (8-ounce) salmon fillets

DIJON CREAM

1½ cups heavy cream

1½ tablespoons Dijon mustard

Salt and ground white pepper

For the salmon, preheat the oven to 400°F. In a bowl, combine the breadcrumbs, cheese, horseradish, oil, and seasoning; mix well. Pat ½ cup of the seasoned crumb mixture on top of each salmon fillet to completely cover. Oven roast the crusted fillets for 15 to 18 minutes or until cooked through. While the salmon is cooking, prepare the Dijon cream.

For the Dijon cream, in a heavy-gauge saucepan, cook the cream over low heat until it is reduced to approximately ¾ cup. Stir in the mustard and season with salt and white pepper. Serve each fillet with 2 tablespoons of dijon cream.

Pignoli-Crusted Snapper with Wisconsin Artisan Cheese

MAKES 4 SERVINGS

COATING

1½ cups toasted pignoli (pine nuts)

⅓ cup all-purpose flour

1 teaspoon dried rosemary, crushed

Kosher salt, to taste

Freshly ground white pepper, to taste

½ cup (about 2 ounces) freshly grated Parmesan cheese

FILLETS

4 (6-ounce) red snapper fillets*

2 eggs, whisked with 2 tablespoons milk or buttermilk

1⅓ cups (8 ounces) Italian-style Gorgonzola cheese, softened

White pepper, to taste

2 tablespoons heavy cream

2 tablespoons fresh basil, cut in chiffonade (very fine slices)

4 tablespoons mild olive oil, divided

¼ cup finely chopped green onion tops

Lemon slices, for garnish

* If red snapper is unavailable, substitute small brook trout, salmon trout, or sea bass fillets, cleaned and ready to cook.

For the coating, combine the pignoli, flour, rosemary, salt, and pepper in a food processor and pulse until the mixture is the texture of fine breadcrumbs but is not pasty. Mix with the Parmesan and spread on a sheet of wax paper.

For the fillets, dry the fillets, dip them in the egg-milk mixture, and then coat them in the pignoli-Parmesan mixture. Gently press the coating on to ensure that it adheres to the fish. If time permits, chill on a rack for 30 to 45 minutes.

Combine the Gorgonzola cheese, white pepper, cream, and basil, set aside.

Preheat the oven to 350°F. Heat 2 tablespoons of the oil in a wide, heavy skillet to medium high; add 2 of the fillets. When a crust forms and the fish moves easily, turn and brown briefly. Remove, add the remaining 2 tablespoons of oil, and repeat with the last two fillets. Return all of the fillets to the skillet and finish cooking them in the oven until the fillets are opaque when pierced with a knife tip, or until they reach a desired doneness. Remove from the oven and serve each fillet on a large dollop of Gorgonzola cheese–basil cream. Garnish the fillets with the green onion tops and lemon. Serve hot.

Cool 'n' Creamy Tuna Cheesecake

MAKES 6 SERVINGS

2 tablespoons butter

¼ cup minced green pepper

¼ cup minced onion

1 teaspoon dried dill

1 teaspoon seasoned salt

¼ teaspoon pepper

2 (8-ounce) packages cream cheese, at room temperature

¼ cup sour cream

2 eggs

1 (6½-ounce) can chunk-style tuna in oil (drained)

1 (4½-ounce) can chopped black olives

1 cup (4 ounces) shredded sharp Cheddar cheese

Sour cream, for garnish

Preheat the oven to 350°F. Cover the sides and bottom of an 8-inch springform pan with baking spray. Set aside.

Melt the butter in a medium saucepan over very low heat; add the green pepper and onion and sauté for 5 minutes. Remove from the heat.

In a large mixing bowl, combine the dill, seasoned salt, pepper, cream cheese, and sour cream. Beat with an electric mixer for 1 minute until well blended. Add the eggs, one at a time, beating until the mixture is smooth. Stir in the tuna and black olives. Using a spatula, fold in the shredded Cheddar cheese. Pour the creamy batter into the springform pan.

Place the pan onto a baking sheet and bake for 1 hour. Remove from the oven and cool for 1 hour. Run a knife between the cheesecake and the pan to loosen; release the sides. Place the cheesecake in the refrigerator to cool completely.

When ready to serve, cut the cheesecake into six wedges. Garnish with small dollops of sour cream. Complement your summer supper entrée with crusty bread and a fresh fruit mixture, such as melon balls, grapes, berries, bananas, or whatever is in season.

Arepas with Wisconsin Jalapeño Jack and Grilled Shrimp

CHEF TREY FOSHEE

MAKES 6 SERVINGS

SHRIMP

1 tablespoon smoked Spanish paprika

1 tablespoon minced garlic

1 teaspoon cumin

1 teaspoon salt

½ teaspoon black pepper

¼ cup olive oil

20 extra-large (16 to 20 count) shrimp, peeled and deveined

AREPAS

1⅛ cups fresh corn kernels

¾ cup semolina

3 ounces jalapeño Jack cheese, grated

2 tablespoons sugar

1 teaspoon salt

1 teaspoon baking powder

1½ jalapeño peppers, cored and minced

¼ cup milk

2 tablespoons olive oil, divided

20 fresh cilantro sprigs, for garnish

For the shrimp, combine the paprika, garlic, cumin, salt, pepper, and olive oil in a medium bowl. Stir in the shrimp. Refrigerate for 30 minutes to marinate.

For the arepas, process the corn in a food processor until fine. Transfer to a bowl and mix in the semolina, cheese, sugar, salt, baking powder, and jalapeños. Mix the milk with 1 teaspoon of hot water and stir into the corn mixture. Divide the dough into 10 to 12 balls of equal size; flatten into 2-inch-diameter cakes. Heat 1 tablespoon of olive oil in a large nonstick sauté pan. Fry half of the arepas until brown on one side, about 1 minute. Turn and brown the other side. Remove from the pan and keep warm. Repeat with the remaining tablespoon of olive oil and arepas.

To complete the recipe, grill the shrimp until just done, 2 to 3 minutes. Place a shrimp on top of each arepa; garnish with cilantro.

Cool Shrimp Tacos

1½ cups sour cream

1 (1-ounce) package taco seasoning mix, divided

1 cup diced seedless cucumber

3 green onions, thinly sliced (¼ cup)

2 avocados, peeled and diced

1 tablespoon lemon juice

1 pound medium shrimp, shelled, deveined, and cooked

Butter lettuce leaves, torn

2 cups (8 ounces) shredded Colby Jack cheese

1 cup chunky salsa

12 flour tortillas

In a large bowl, combine the sour cream and 2 tablespoons of the taco seasoning mix; mix well. Stir in the cucumber, onion, avocado, and lemon juice.

In a small bowl, toss the shrimp and the remaining taco seasoning mix together.

Serve family style with individual bowls for the sour cream mixture, shrimp, lettuce, cheese, and salsa. Top each tortilla with the sour cream mixture and shrimp, and garnish with lettuce, cheese, and salsa as desired.

Greek Shrimp with Feta and Tomatoes

MAKES 6 TO 8 SERVINGS

¼ cup olive oil

3 medium onions, chopped

1 (28-ounce) can peeled diced tomatoes in juice

½ cup dry white wine

3 tablespoons chopped fresh parsley

3 tablespoons chopped fresh dill, divided

1 tablespoon dried oregano

5 garlic cloves, minced or pressed

1 teaspoon crushed red pepper flakes

½ cup halved pitted kalamata or other Greek brine-cured olives

Fine sea salt or kosher salt and freshly ground pepper, to taste

2 pounds uncooked large shrimp, peeled with tails left intact

2 cups (8 ounces) crumbled feta cheese

Preheat the oven to 400°F. In a large saucepan, heat the olive oil over medium heat. Add the onions and cook, stirring, until golden, about 10 minutes. Add the tomatoes with their juices, the wine, the parsley, 2 tablespoons of the dill, the oregano, the garlic, and the red pepper flakes. Increase the heat to high and bring to a boil. Reduce the heat and simmer, covered, to thicken the sauce, about 25 minutes. Stir in the kalamata olives. Season the sauce with salt and pepper.

Arrange the shrimp in the bottom of a large baking dish. Pour the sauce over the shrimp and sprinkle with the cheese. Transfer the dish to the oven and bake until the shrimp are cooked through, about 10 minutes. Sprinkle with the remaining tablespoon of chopped fresh dill.

Three-Bean Chili with Wisconsin Colby

1 large onion, chopped (about 2 cups)

2 large green bell peppers, cut into ½-inch squares

1 tablespoon finely chopped garlic (approximately 3 cloves)

2 tablespoons vegetable oil

1 (15.5-ounce) can black beans, drained

1 (15.5-ounce) can pinto beans, drained

1 (15.5-ounce) can black-eyed peas, drained

1 (14.5-ounce) can diced tomatoes with juice

1 (14-ounce) can vegetable stock

1 cup dry red wine (or water)

3 tablespoons cornmeal

1 tablespoon chili powder, or to taste

1 teaspoon dried oregano

1 teaspoon ground cumin

Salt and pepper, to taste

1 bay leaf

¼ teaspoon hot pepper sauce, or to taste

2 cups (8 ounces) shredded Colby cheese, divided

In a Dutch oven, sauté the onion, bell peppers, and garlic in oil on medium heat for about 5 minutes or until soft.

Stir in the remaining ingredients, except the cheese. Simmer uncovered on low heat, stirring occasionally, about 1 hour or until thick. Remove from the heat. Remove and discard the bay leaf.

Stir in half of the cheese until melted. Serve with the remaining cheese sprinkled on top.

Wisconsin Four-Cheese Chiles Rellenos

CHEF KEVIN TUBB

MAKES 12 SERVINGS

12 (5-inch-long) poblano chiles

2 cups (12 ounces) crumbled feta cheese

2 cups (8 ounces) shredded white Cheddar cheese

2 cups (8 ounces) shredded Monterey Jack cheese

1 (8-ounce) package cream cheese

1 tablespoon fresh lime juice

4 green onions, thinly sliced

1 tablespoon pepper

Vegetable oil, as needed

8 eggs, separated

1½ cups all-purpose flour

Roast the whole chiles over an open flame, turning frequently, until blackened and blistered all over. Put the roasted chiles into an ice-water bath to cool; peel off the skin under running water. Cut a slit in the side of each chile to make a pocket. Set aside.

Mix the cheeses, lime juice, green onions, and pepper together until well blended. Carefully stuff each chile with the cheese mixture. Set aside.

In a 10-inch skillet, heat ¾ inch of oil to 325°F. While the oil is heating, beat the egg whites in a large bowl until stiff. Add the yolks and mix just until blended, 5 to 10 seconds more. Roll the stuffed chiles in flour, coating completely. Coat the chiles with the egg mixture and fry, 3 to 4 at a time, until both sides are golden brown. Remove onto paper towels. Repeat the process until all of the chiles are fried. Chiles can be reheated in the microwave for 1 to 2 minutes before serving with your favorite salsa.

Baked Polenta with Wisconsin Asiago and Mushroom Sauce

MAKES 6 SERVINGS

POLENTA

6 cups water

1 teaspoon salt

1½ cups polenta-style (coarse) cornmeal

2 cups (8 ounces) shredded Asiago cheese, divided

SAUCE

1 (7-ounce) jar roasted red peppers, drained

1 pound medium mushrooms, sliced

2 tablespoons olive oil

1 (16-ounce) jar fresh-style spaghetti sauce

1 cup water

1 teaspoon dried rosemary, crushed

¼ cup chopped fresh parsley

For the polenta, preheat the oven to 350°F.

Bring the water to a boil; add the salt. Add the cornmeal slowly, stirring constantly. Cook, continuing to stir, until the polenta begins to thicken, about 5 minutes. Stir in half of the cheese. Pour into a buttered 8 x 8-inch baking pan. Bake until firm, about 35 minutes.* Cool for 25 minutes. Sprinkle the top with the remaining cheese. While the polenta bakes, make the sauce.

For the sauce, purée the peppers in a food processor or blender; reserve. Over high heat, brown the mushrooms in oil. Remove the mushrooms from the pan, and reserve. In the same pan, place the reserved pepper sauce, spaghetti sauce, water, and rosemary. Simmer over medium heat until the sauce thickens, about 10 minutes. Stir in the reserved mushrooms and the parsley.

To serve, cut the polenta into pieces. Serve topped with the sauce.

* This recipe may be prepared ahead to this point. Once the polenta has cooled, store tightly wrapped in the refrigerator for up to 3 days or in the freezer for up to 6 weeks. Return to room temperature before proceeding with the recipe.

Broccoli and Wisconsin Cheese Pie

MAKES 6 SERVINGS

1 (10-ounce) package frozen chopped broccoli

6 eggs, slightly beaten

1 (3-ounce) package cream cheese, softened

½ cup (2 ounces) shredded Cheddar cheese

½ cup finely diced cooked ham

2 tablespoons diced onion

½ teaspoon salt

⅛ teaspoon pepper

1 unbaked 9-inch pie crust

⅓ cup (about 1½ ounces) grated Parmesan cheese

Preheat the oven to 425°F.

Cook the broccoli according to the package directions. Drain well. Combine the eggs and the cheeses in a mixing bowl. Beat until smooth. Stir in the cooked broccoli, ham, onion, salt, and pepper. Turn into the pie crust. Sprinkle the top with grated Parmesan cheese. Bake for 30 minutes. Allow to stand 10 minutes before slicing.

Feta Spanokopitas

MAKES 6 SERVINGS

1 tablespoon olive oil

1 medium onion, chopped

1 medium red bell pepper, chopped

1 teaspoon red pepper flakes

1 (10-ounce) package fresh spinach

1 tablespoon coarsely chopped garlic

2 cups (12 ounces) crumbled feta cheese

1 cup (8 ounces) ricotta cheese

1 egg, slightly beaten

¾ cup chopped pistachios, divided

6 sheets phyllo pastry, thawed

2 tablespoons melted butter

In a skillet, heat the oil over medium-high heat; add the onion, red bell pepper, and red pepper flakes. Sauté, stirring occasionally, until the vegetables are browned. Add the spinach and garlic; sauté until the spinach begins to wilt, 2 to 3 minutes. Remove from the heat.

In a bowl, combine the cheeses, the egg, $\frac{1}{2}$ cup of the pistachios, and the spinach mixture. Set aside.

Divide the phyllo into two stacks of 3 sheets each. Cut each stack into 3 equal strips. Cover the strips of unused phyllo with a damp towel while working with the pastry. Place about $\frac{1}{2}$ cup of the spinach mixture on one strip, 2 inches from the bottom. Fold the corner of the pastry over the filling to start forming a triangle. Fold from one corner to the opposite side, as you would a flag, for the entire strip.

Preheat the oven to 400°F and repeat with the remaining strips. Place the pastries on a baking sheet; brush with melted butter. Sprinkle with the remaining finely chopped pistachios. Bake for 25 to 30 minutes or until the pastry is lightly browned.

Feta-Zucchini Phyllo Pie

MAKES 10 TO 12 SERVINGS

3 tablespoons olive oil

2 large onions, chopped

2 large zucchini (1½ pounds), chopped

2 cups packed (about 9 ounces) grated sheep's milk Gouda cheese

1½ cups (8 ounces) crumbled feta cheese

½ cup (3 ounces) grated myzithra cheese*

¼ cup chopped fresh parsley

3 tablespoons chopped fresh oregano

Salt and pepper, to taste

1½ cups whipping cream

3 large eggs

½ cup melted butter or olive oil

16 sheets phyllo dough, thawed if frozen

* If myzithra, a Greek grating cheese, is not available, substitute Pecorino Romano or ricotta salata.

In a large, heavy skillet, heat the olive oil over medium heat. Add the onions and cook, stirring, until golden, about 10 minutes. Add the zucchini and cook until just tender, about 5 minutes. Add all of the cheeses and stir just until melted. Remove the mixture from the heat; stir in the parsley and oregano, and season with salt and pepper. In a medium bowl, whisk together the cream and the eggs; stir into the cheese mixture.

Preheat the oven to 350°F. Brush a 13 x 9-inch glass baking dish with some of the melted butter. Place one phyllo sheet in the bottom of the dish. Brush the phyllo sheet with melted butter. Top with another phyllo sheet and brush with butter. Repeat with 6 more phyllo sheets. Pour the cheese mixture over the phyllo crust in the baking dish, spreading evenly. Cover the filling with 1 phyllo sheet; brush the phyllo with melted butter. Repeat with the remaining phyllo sheets, brushing each with melted butter.

Transfer the pie to the oven and bake until the filling is cooked and the phyllo crust is golden, about 45 minutes. Let the pie cool in the pan on a rack for at least 15 minutes before serving.

Goat Cheese Strata with Oven-Dried Tomatoes

MAKES 8 SERVINGS

OVEN-DRIED TOMATOES

¼ cup olive oil, plus additional for greasing baking sheet

1 pound plum tomatoes, cored, halved crosswise, seeded

Fine sea salt or kosher salt and freshly ground pepper, to taste

STRATA

2 cups milk

¼ cup olive oil

1 loaf artisanal (country-style) bread, crust removed, cut into 1-inch cubes (about 8 cups)

1½ cups whipping cream

5 large eggs

2 garlic cloves, minced or pressed

2 teaspoons salt

1 teaspoon freshly ground pepper

1 (11-ounce) log soft fresh goat cheese, crumbled

2 tablespoons chopped fresh oregano

1 tablespoon chopped fresh thyme

1½ teaspoons dried mixed Italian herbs (Italian seasoning)

3 (6½-ounce) jars marinated artichoke hearts, drained and halved lengthwise

1 cup (6 ounces) coarsely grated Edam cheese

1½ cups (6 ounces) freshly grated Pecorino Romano cheese

For the tomatoes, preheat the oven to 300°F. Line a baking sheet with foil. Brush the foil with olive oil (about 1 tablespoon). Place the tomatoes, cut side up, on the prepared baking sheet. Drizzle ¼ cup of olive oil over the tomatoes, and season with salt and pepper. Bake the tomatoes until they are shriveled but are still soft, about 2 hours. Let the tomatoes cool on the baking sheet.

For the strata, increase the oven to 350°F. Grease a 13 x 9-inch glass baking dish with butter. In a large mixing bowl, whisk together the milk and oil. Add the bread cubes and let them sit to allow the liquids to absorb, about 10 minutes.

In another large mixing bowl, whisk together the cream, eggs, garlic, salt, and pepper. Stir in the goat cheese. In a separate small bowl, stir together the chopped fresh herbs.

Arrange half of the bread mixture in the bottom of the buttered baking dish. Arrange half of the tomatoes, cut side up, over the bread. Add half of the artichokes, herbs, and cheeses over the bread. Pour half of the cream–goat cheese mixture over all. Repeat with the remaining ingredients.

Transfer the strata to the oven and bake until the filling sets and browns around the edges and the cheeses are melted.

Torta Rustica

MAKES 6 SERVINGS

2 prepared refrigerated pie crusts

1 egg, lightly beaten

2 cups (16 ounces) ricotta cheese

1 cup (4 ounces) shredded pepato cheese (or 1 cup shredded Asiago cheese and 1 teaspoon black peppercorns, coarsely ground)

½ cup (about 2 ounces) grated Parmesan cheese

3 eggs

1 teaspoon dried basil

1 (10-ounce) package frozen chopped spinach, thawed and squeezed dry

¼ cup seasoned breadcrumbs

¼ cup coarsely chopped sun-dried tomatoes, drained

Preheat the oven to 425°F.

Place 1 pie crust in a 9-inch pie pan. Brush ½ of the beaten egg over the crust; set aside. Reserve the other crust for the top of the torta.

In a large bowl, combine the cheeses, eggs, and basil until well blended. Stir in the spinach, breadcrumbs, and tomatoes until thoroughly combined. Scrape the mixture into the prepared pie crust; smooth the top to make the filling even. Place the reserved pie crust over the top; brush with the remaining beaten egg. Bake for 15 minutes. Reduce the heat to 375°F and bake for 20 minutes or until golden brown. Cool on a wire rack for 30 minutes before slicing. Serve warm or at room temperature.

Wild Mushroom Pie with Smoked Baby Swiss Crust

CHEFS MARY AND GREG SONNIER

MAKES 8 SERVINGS

CRUST

6 tablespoons solid vegetable shortening

¼ pound (1 stick) unsalted butter

2½ cups all-purpose flour

½ teaspoon ground cayenne pepper

½ teaspoon salt

1 teaspoon sugar

4 ounces (1 cup) grated smoked baby Swiss cheese

7 tablespoons ice-cold water

FILLING

3 quarts salted water

6 cups chopped fresh greens, turnip, Swiss chard, or spinach

8 ounces sliced mushrooms, such as chanterelles, oyster, shiitake, or cremini

1 tablespoon olive oil

4 tablespoons (½ stick) butter

1½ cups chopped onions

½ cup all-purpose flour

1 cup warm milk

1 cup warm half-and-half

1½ teaspoons salt

½ teaspoon freshly ground pepper

½ teaspoon cayenne

¼ teaspoon freshly grated nutmeg

For the crust, flatten the shortening into a disk on a piece of plastic wrap; wrap and freeze. Cut the unsalted butter into small cubes; wrap and freeze for ½ hour.

Place the flour, cayenne, salt, and sugar in a food processor and pulse 2 times for 1 to 2 seconds each time. Scatter the frozen butter cubes over the flour and pulse about 8 times. Break up the frozen shortening over the flour mixture and pulse 6 times. Add the cheese and pulse 3 times. Pour the cold water over the pastry mixture and pulse 6 to 8 times, just until the dough comes together.

Place the pastry on a floured surface, pressing to form a ball. Divide and shape the dough into 2 disks, one slightly larger than the other. Wrap in plastic wrap and refrigerate for at least 1 hour and up to 3 days.

For the filling, bring 3 quarts of salted water to a boil. Boil the greens for 3 minutes. Drain and plunge the greens into ice water. Drain well, squeezing all of the water out of the greens. Set aside.

In a 5-quart Dutch oven, sauté the mushrooms in the olive oil over high heat until softened, 2 to 3 minutes. Remove from the pot; set aside.

Add the butter and onions to the pot. Sauté 4 to 5 minutes or until the onions are translucent. Sprinkle the flour over the onions. Stir and cook 2 minutes.

½ cup grated Swiss cheese

2 tablespoons lemon juice

TO COMPLETE THE RECIPE

1 egg yolk

1 tablespoon cream

Slowly stir in the warm milk and half-and-half. Cook until bubbly and thick, stirring constantly. Stir in the salt, pepper, cayenne, and nutmeg. Remove from the heat. Stir in the greens and mushrooms. Add the cheese and lemon juice and stir. Cool 30 minutes.

To complete the pie, heat the oven to 350°F. On a floured surface, roll out the larger disk to an 11-inch circle. Press into a 9-inch pie plate. Roll the other disk to a 9½-inch circle. Pour the filling into the prepared pie crust. Top with the smaller crust. Trim the edges and crimp.

Mix the egg yolk and the cream. Brush over the top pie crust. Cut 5 slits in the top crust. Place the pie on the baking sheet. Bake for 30 minutes. Reduce the oven temperature to 325°F. Bake for 40 to 50 minutes longer, until the pie is golden brown. Allow the pie to rest at least 20 minutes before cutting.

Cheesy Mushroom au Gratin

MAKES 12 SERVINGS

6 tablespoons (¾ stick) butter, divided

½ cup all-purpose flour

6 cups (1½ quarts) milk, heated

1 cup (4 ounces) shredded Colby cheese

1 cup (4 ounces) shredded Muenster cheese

1½ teaspoons salt

1½ teaspoons red pepper sauce

½ teaspoon ground nutmeg

3 pounds fresh white mushrooms, sliced

2¼ pounds fresh shiitake mushrooms, sliced

1 cup green onions, sliced

1 tablespoon dried fines herbes*

24 slices assorted breads (such as rustic white, whole wheat, and sourdough), toasted

¾ cup (about 3 ounces) grated Asiago cheese

Asparagus spears, for serving

* The classic recipe for fines herbes is a blend of equal quantities of very finely minced parsley, chervil, tarragon, and chives.

Preheat the oven to 400°F.

In a large skillet, heat 4 tablespoons of the butter; whisk in the flour to create a roux. Cook on low heat for 3 to 4 minutes. Slowly whisk in the hot milk, stirring well between additions. Bring the sauce to a boil; then reduce to a simmer. Cook 5 to 6 minutes, stirring occasionally. Add the Colby and Muenster cheeses and stir well until melted. Season with the salt, red pepper sauce, and nutmeg; set aside.

In a large skillet, heat the remaining 2 tablespoons of butter; add the mushrooms, green onions, and fines herbes. Cook on high heat until the mushrooms are golden brown, about 10 to 12 minutes. Stir into the cheese sauce.

Place 2 slices of toasted bread in each of 12 shallow, lightly buttered ramekins or oven-to-table dishes; top each serving with ½ cup of mushroom sauce, and sprinkle with 1 tablespoon of the Asiago. Bake for 8 to 10 minutes, or until brown and bubbly.

To serve, top with the asparagus spears and the remaining shredded Asiago cheese.

Colby Rarebit

MAKES 12 SERVINGS

2 ounces (½ stick) butter

¾ cup all-purpose flour

3 cups chicken stock (hot)

3 cups light cream or milk

2 egg yolks

2 tablespoons dry mustard

¼ teaspoon cayenne
   (red pepper)

2 tablespoons Worcestershire
   sauce

3 tablespoons dry sherry

1 pound (4 cups) grated Colby
   cheese

Toast points and sliced tomatoes, for serving

On medium heat, melt the butter in a heavy-gauge stainless soup pot; whisk in the flour to create a paste. Let the mixture cook for 5 to 6 minutes. Slowly whisk in the hot stock and cream to create a smooth sauce. Cook for 5 to 6 minutes more.

Combine the egg yolks, mustard, cayenne, Worcestershire sauce, and sherry; mix well. Add the egg mixture to the sauce and mix well. Add the cheese and stir to melt. Season the rarebit and serve over toast points and sliced tomatoes.

Note: English muffins and bacon are also tasty with this rarebit.

Five-Minute Two-Cheese Sauce

MAKES 1½ TO 2 CUPS

1 tablespoon butter

1 tablespoon all-purpose flour

Pinch of white pepper

¾ cup milk

WISCONSIN CHEESE COMBINATIONS (PICK ONE PAIR)

½ cup (2 ounces) shredded Monterey Jack cheese

½ cup (2 ounces) shredded Asiago cheese

½ cup (2 ounces) shredded sharp Cheddar cheese

½ cup (2 ounces) shredded baby Swiss cheese

¾ cup (3 ounces) shredded Muenster cheese

½ cup (3 ounces) crumbled blue cheese

½ cup (2 ounces) shredded fontina cheese

½ cup (2 ounces) shredded Edam cheese

½ cup (2 ounces) shredded Gruyère cheese

¼ cup (1 ounce) shredded Gouda cheese

½ cup (2 ounces) shredded brick cheese

¼ cup (about 1 ounce) grated Romano cheese

Place the butter in a 4-cup measuring cup or bowl; microwave on high for 30 seconds or until melted. Blend in the flour and pepper; microwave 20 seconds. Blend in the milk; microwave for 2 to 3 minutes or until just boiling and thickened, stirring every minute. Gradually add the two cheeses, stirring until melted. If necessary, microwave for 30 seconds to completely melt the cheese. Serve as a sauce for meats such as steaks and chicken breasts, or serve as a topping for cooked vegetables or open-faced sandwiches.

Note: This recipe may be doubled. Increase the cooking time to 5 to 6 minutes.

Gorgonzola Ale Sauce

5 pounds onion, diced

¾ cup olive oil

1½ cups amber ale

Salt and pepper, to taste

2 teaspoons dried thyme

Zest from 2 lemons, finely chopped

¼ cup minced chives

¼ cup minced red bell pepper

6 cups (24 ounces) crumbled Gorgonzola

Caramelize the onion in oil over low heat until reduced by half and golden brown. Stir in the ale, and season with salt, pepper and thyme; cook over low heat until reduced by one-third. Stir in the lemon zest; reserve.

Heat ⅓ cup of the onion mixture until it boils.

Add 1 teaspoon each of the chives and the bell pepper; cook 1 minute. Remove from the heat and stir in the cheese; serve immediately over grilled steak or chicken.

PASTA AND PIZZA

Mediterranean Macaroni and Cheese

MAKES 4 SERVINGS

3 cups (12 ounces) elbow
macaroni

¼ cup finely diced white onion

3 tablespoons butter

3 tablespoons all-purpose flour

2 cups milk, warmed

½ teaspoon ground white
pepper

1 tablespoon prepared mustard

1½ cups (6 ounces) shredded
fontina cheese

1½ cups (6 ounces) shredded
provolone cheese

2 ounces prosciutto, diced

1 tablespoon minced fresh
Italian parsley

Cook the macaroni according to the package instructions, or until al dente. Drain, rinse, and set aside.

In a large saucepan, sauté the onion in butter for 2 minutes, until transparent. Blend in the flour, stirring well to incorporate, and cook for an additional minute. Whisk the milk into the butter and flour mixture. Bring to a simmer and cook until the sauce thickens. Preheat the oven to 375°F. Reduce the stove temperature to low heat and add the pepper and mustard to the sauce. Stir in 2½ cups of the cheeses until blended into the sauce. Add the cooked macaroni and prosciutto to the cheese sauce, and mix well. Place the macaroni mixture in a buttered, ovenproof, 9 x 9-inch dish. Top with the remaining ½ cup of cheese. Bake for 30 minutes or until the top is golden brown. Sprinkle the surface with parsley prior to serving.

Five-Cheese Macaroni

1½ cups (12 ounces) small-curd cottage cheese

1 cup (8 ounces) sour cream

1 egg

¼ cup all-purpose flour

½ teaspoon salt

¼ teaspoon white pepper

½ teaspoon dry mustard

2 cups (8 ounces) shredded sharp Cheddar cheese

2 cups (8 ounces) shredded Colby cheese

8 ounces elbow macaroni, cooked, drained

⅓ cup (1 ounce) grated Parmesan cheese

⅓ cup (1 ounce) grated Romano cheese

½ teaspoon paprika

2 tablespoons chopped fresh parsley

Preheat the oven to 325°F.

Blend the cottage cheese in a food processor or blender until smooth. In a large mixing bowl, combine the cottage cheese, sour cream, egg, flour, salt, white pepper, and dry mustard. Stir in the Cheddar and Colby cheeses. Add the cooked macaroni and stir gently until well combined. Spoon into a greased 3-quart glass baking dish. Top with grated Parmesan and Romano cheese and sprinkle with paprika. Bake for 40 to 45 minutes until browned and bubbly. Sprinkle with parsley to serve.

Miami Macaroni and Cheese

CHEFS FRANK RANDAZZO AND ANDREA CURTO-RANDAZZO

MAKES 12 SERVINGS

2 cups diced pancetta (¼ inch)

¾ loaf baguette (dry)

½ pound (2 sticks) unsalted
butter, to taste

1½ pounds rotelli pasta

3 pints (6 cups) heavy cream

2 cups (about 8 ounces) finely
grated Parmesan cheese

12 ounces fontina cheese, cut
into ¼-inch cubes and chilled

Salt and pepper, to taste

Preheat the oven to 375°F. On a baking sheet with sides, cook the pancetta for 6 to 8 minutes or until just crispy. Drain and set aside.

Crush and crumble the baguette (you may use a food processor), until semi-fine, to make breadcrumbs. In a large sauté pan, melt the butter over medium heat. Add the breadcrumbs, and toast (tossing), until golden brown. Set aside.

Cook the pasta until al dente; cool, and set aside in a large mixing bowl.

In a hot saucepan add the cream and bring to a boil. Simmer and reduce by one-third. Slowly whisk in 1¼ cups of the Parmesan and the pancetta. Continue reducing slightly until the consistency is thick and creamy.

In the large mixing bowl with the pasta, add the cream mixture along with the fontina cheese. Toss quickly and season with salt and pepper. Pour the mixture into lightly buttered individual (5- to 6-ounce) casserole dishes. Top with the breadcrumbs and remaining Parmesan cheese. Bake for 12 to 15 minutes. Remove and serve hot.

Note: You may also use one large casserole dish for this recipe.

Cacio e Pepe

1 pound spaghetti

1 cup (4 ounces) finely grated Pecorino Romano cheese

1 tablespoon whole peppercorns, coarsely crushed*

* To crush the peppercorns use a mortar and pestle or enclose the peppercorns in a resealable plastic bag and crush using a rolling pin or the flat side of a chef's knife.

Cook the pasta in a large pot of salted boiling water until al dente, 8 to 10 minutes, stirring occasionally to prevent pasta noodles from sticking together. Drain the pasta in a colander, shaking to remove excess water.

Transfer the pasta to a large mixing (or serving) bowl. Add the cheese and crushed peppercorns. Using a pasta fork or tongs, mix thoroughly until the cheese adheres to the spaghetti strands and the cheese and pepper are combined with the pasta. Serve immediately.

Tip: Use an aged imported pecorino from Italy; then grate the cheese and crush the peppercorns just before cooking. After draining the pasta, let it sit for just a minute to cool ever so slightly before tossing it with the cheese. Instead of melting, the cheese will cling to each strand of pasta, giving the dish a satisfying texture.

Orecchiette with Wisconsin Cheese

MAKES 4 SERVINGS

½ pound asparagus, trimmed of tough ends

2 shallots, diced

1 garlic clove, diced

2 tablespoons extra-virgin olive oil

2 large ripe yellow tomatoes, peeled and chopped, or substitute 3 to 4 plum tomatoes

½ cup Italian white wine (for example, Orvieto)*

½ cup chicken stock, canned or homemade

½ cup fresh basil, cut in chiffonade (very fine slices)

½ pound orecchiette (little ears) pasta, cooked al dente according to package directions

½ cup (2 ounces) shredded mozzarella cheese

½ cup (2 ounces) shredded provolone cheese

2 tablespoons grated Parmesan cheese

* If you don't wish to use wine, substitute additional chicken stock.

Preheat the oven to 375°F.

Place the asparagus in a shallow dish or pan and cover with boiling water. Cover and let sit for 3 to 5 minutes. Drain and cool. Cut into 3- to 4-inch-long pieces. Set aside.

In a large sauté pan or deep skillet, sauté the shallots and garlic in olive oil until translucent. Add the tomatoes and sauté until they are soft and give up their juices. Add the wine and chicken stock. Boil over high heat until reduced by about one-fourth. Add the asparagus pieces and boil about 2 minutes. Add the basil, and mix. Add the freshly cooked pasta, and stir to coat. Add the cheeses and toss to melt. Bake for 20 minutes. Serve immediately.

Variation: You may substitute smoked provolone for the provolone.

Penne Pasta in Gorgonzola Cream Sauce

2 tablespoons butter

1 small onion, finely chopped

2 garlic cloves, smashed and chopped

1 cup vegetable or chicken stock

1 pound penne pasta, cooked al dente

1 cup heavy cream

1 cup (6 ounces) crumbled Gorgonzola cheese

Juice of ½ lemon

¼ teaspoon freshly cracked black pepper

2 tablespoons coarsely chopped fresh Italian parsley

Warm a 10-inch noncorrosive sauté pan over medium-high heat until hot. Add the butter and melt until lightly brown. Add the onion and garlic; cook until translucent. Add the stock and cook until three-fourths reduced. Add the penne. Toss and cook for 3 to 4 minutes. Add the cream and the cheese. Bring to a boil; cook 2 minutes. Add the lemon juice to thin the texture slightly. Season with the pepper and sprinkle with the parsley. Serve with warm, crusty bread and a spinach salad.

Rigatoni with Four Cheeses

CHEF NANCY LAZARA

MAKES 6 SERVINGS

3 cups milk

1 tablespoon chopped carrot

1 tablespoon chopped celery

1 tablespoon chopped onion

1 tablespoon chopped fresh parsley

¼ teaspoon black peppercorns

¼ teaspoon hot pepper sauce

½ bay leaf

Pinch of nutmeg

4 tablespoons (½ stick) butter

¼ cup all-purpose flour

½ cup (about 2 ounces) grated Parmesan cheese

¼ cup (1 ounce) grated Romano cheese

12 ounces rigatoni, cooked, drained

1½ cups (6 ounces) shredded Cheddar cheese

1½ cups (6 ounces) shredded mozzarella cheese

¼ teaspoon chili powder

In a 2-quart saucepan, combine the milk, carrots, celery, onions, parsley, peppercorns, hot pepper sauce, bay leaf, and nutmeg. Bring to a boil. Reduce the heat and simmer 10 minutes. Strain; set aside.

Preheat the oven to 350°F.

Melt the butter in a 2-quart saucepan over low heat. Blend in the flour. Gradually add the reserved milk; cook, stirring constantly, until thickened. Remove from the heat; add the Parmesan and Romano cheeses, stirring until blended. Pour over the pasta; toss well. Combine the Cheddar and mozzarella cheeses. In a buttered 2-quart casserole, layer half of the pasta mixture, the cheese mixture, and the remaining pasta mixture. Sprinkle with chili powder. Bake for 25 minutes or until hot.

Pepato Cheese and Artichoke Bake

MAKES 6 TO 8 SERVINGS

3 tablespoons butter

1 cup sliced fresh mushrooms

½ cup chopped leeks (white part only)

1 teaspoon garlic, minced

2 cups (1 pint) heavy cream

2 cups (8 ounces) shredded Gouda cheese

1 cup (4 ounces) shredded pepato cheese

1 tablespoon prepared mustard

½ teaspoon salt

½ teaspoon pepper

1 (14-ounce) can artichoke hearts, drained, chopped

4 tablespoons chopped chives, divided

1 (16-ounce) package elbow macaroni, cooked, drained

½ cup breadcrumbs

Preheat the oven to 350°F.

Melt the butter in a large saucepan, until sizzling. Add the mushrooms, leeks, and garlic, and sauté over medium heat approximately 5 minutes, or until the mushrooms are tender. Add the cream, stir, and bring to a simmer. Reduce the heat to low; add the cheeses, stirring constantly, just until melted. Stir in the mustard, salt, pepper, artichokes, and 3 tablespoons of the chives. Cook, stirring occasionally, for 3 minutes.

Gently stir in the cooked macaroni, mixing well. Spoon into a buttered 3-quart, ovenproof baking dish. Sprinkle with breadcrumbs, and bake for 20 to 25 minutes or until browned. Sprinkle with the remaining 1 tablespoon of chives before serving.

Pasta with Beans, Greens, and Wisconsin Gorgonzola

12 ounces mostaccioli (or other wide tube pasta)

1½ cups coarsely chopped, tightly packed fresh kale or Swiss chard leaves

1 cup pinto beans, cooked or canned, drained

1 cup reduced-sodium chicken stock

1 cup (6 ounces) crumbled Gorgonzola cheese

In a large pot, bring 4 quarts of water to a boil; add the pasta. Partially cover and cook for 8 minutes. Stir in the kale or chard; cook 1 minute longer. Drain; return the pasta mixture to the pot. Stir in the remaining ingredients, except the cheese. Transfer the mixture to a large, shallow serving platter. Place the cheese over the top; serve warm or at room temperature.

Wisconsin Cheese and Broccoli Penne

3 cups (8 ounces) penne pasta

2 cups broccoli florets

1 tablespoons olive oil

½ teaspoon salt

½ teaspoons pepper

1 cup (8 ounces) ricotta cheese

2 cups (8 ounces) shredded mozzarella cheese

1 cup pitted, sliced kalamata or ripe olives

1 (16-ounce) jar spicy tomato pasta sauce

Preheat the oven to 375°F.

In a 4-quart Dutch oven, cook the pasta according to the package directions; add the broccoli during the last 5 minutes of cooking. Rinse, drain, and place the pasta and broccoli back in the pan. Add the remaining ingredients, except the pasta sauce; mix well.

In a 3-quart casserole, pour the pasta sauce; top with the pasta mixture. Bake for 15 to 20 minutes or until heated. Broil for 8 to 10 minutes, or until the cheese is golden brown.

Southwest Pasta with Roasted Corn and Goat Cheese

MAKES 4 SERVINGS

2 tablespoons raw green pumpkin seeds (pepitas)

4 tablespoons olive oil, divided

¾ cup fresh corn kernels

1 medium zucchini, cut into ¼-inch dice (about 1 cup)

10 ounces campanelle pasta*

2 garlic cloves, pressed or minced

½ teaspoon chipotle powder

2 tablespoons chopped fresh oregano

2 tablespoons lime juice

1 teaspoon lime zest

Fine sea salt or kosher salt

¼ cup (2 ounces) crumbled soft fresh goat cheese

* If you can't find campanelle (a trumpet-shaped pasta), use any small pasta that can catch the corn and pumpkin seeds, such as penne, fusilli, or farfalle. Chipotle powder (from smoked, dried jalapeños) can be found in the spice section of many supermarkets. Pepitas (green pumpkin seeds) are available at health food stores and some supermarkets (in the Mexican foods section).

Toast the pumpkin seeds in a small skillet over medium heat until fragrant and browned, shaking the pan occasionally for even cooking, about 3 minutes. Transfer the toasted pumpkin seeds to a small bowl and reserve.

In a medium skillet, heat 1 tablespoon of the olive oil over high heat. Add the corn kernels and cook until light brown, stirring frequently, about 5 minutes. Transfer the corn to a bowl to cool. Reduce the heat to medium high and add 1 tablespoon of the olive oil to the same skillet. Add the zucchini and cook, stirring frequently, until the squash is just tender, about 5 minutes.

Cook the pasta in a large pot of boiling water until al dente, 8 to 10 minutes. While the pasta is cooking, combine the garlic and chipotle in a medium mixing bowl. Add the oregano, lime juice, the remaining 2 tablespoons of olive oil, and the lime zest to the bowl. Season to taste with salt. Add the cheese, corn, and squash, and toss the ingredients gently to combine. Drain the pasta, reserving ½ cup of the pasta cooking water. Transfer the pasta to a large mixing (or serving) bowl. Add the topping and toss thoroughly until the cheese melts and coats the pasta, adding the pasta cooking water by tablespoonfuls to loosen the sauce, if necessary. Season to taste with salt and pepper. Sprinkle with toasted pumpkin seeds and serve.

Linguine with Wisconsin Pepato and Roasted Peppers

MAKES 4 SERVINGS

8 ounces linguine, cooked, drained

2 tablespoons olive oil, divided

3 bell peppers (1 red, 1 yellow, and 1 orange), cut into 1½-inch pieces

1 Anaheim or poblano pepper, seeded and chopped

1 tablespoon coarsely chopped garlic

¼ teaspoon salt

2 cups (8 ounces) shredded pepato cheese*

1 cup (3 ounces) grated Romano cheese

¼ cup chopped fresh Italian parsley

* You may substitute 2 cups (6 ounces) grated Romano cheese plus 1 tablespoon of cracked pepper for the pepato cheese.

Toss the cooked linguine with 1 tablespoon of the olive oil. Set aside.

In a skillet, heat the remaining 1 tablespoon of olive oil; add all of the peppers. Cook over medium-high heat for 6 to 8 minutes, or until blackened on the edges. Reduce the heat to medium; add the garlic and salt. Cook for 2 to 3 minutes, or until the garlic is browned; add the cheeses. Toss with the linguine and the parsley.

Penne and Potatoes with Wisconsin Pepato

MAKES 4 SERVINGS

12 ounces penne or other tube pasta

8 ounces new red potatoes, cut into 1-inch cubes

½ cup coarsely chopped fresh arugula leaves

¾ cup prepared fat-free Italian dressing

1 cup (4 ounces) shredded pepato cheese*

* Substitute 4 ounces of grated Romano cheese and ½ teaspoon coarsely ground black pepper for the pepato cheese, if desired.

In a large pot, bring 4 quarts of water to a boil. Add the pasta, partially cover, and cook for 5 minutes. Stir in the potatoes and cook 4 minutes longer. Drain the pasta and potatoes, reserving ⅓ cup of the cooking water. Transfer the pasta-potato mixture to a large serving bowl. Add the reserved water, arugula, dressing, and shredded cheese; toss to combine. Serve hot, or at room temperature.

Orecchiette with Tomatoes, Garden Herbs, and Ricotta Salata

MAKES 4 SERVINGS

8 ounces orecchiette pasta

3 medium tomatoes, peeled, seeded, coarsely chopped

½ cup chopped green onions

3 tablespoons extra-virgin olive oil

2 garlic cloves, minced or pressed

Fine sea salt or kosher salt and freshly ground pepper

⅔ cup chopped fresh mixed herbs (such as oregano, basil, chives, Italian parsley)

⅔ cup (3 ounces) crumbled ricotta salata

In a large pot of boiling water, cook the pasta until it is al dente, about 10 minutes.

Meanwhile, in a large bowl, combine the tomatoes, green onions, olive oil, and garlic. Season the mixture to taste with salt and pepper (add salt sparingly, as the cheese will add more saltiness to the dish). When the pasta is cooked, drain the pasta and add it to the bowl with the tomatoes. Add the herbs and cheese to the bowl, and stir to blend.

Peppery Mascarpone Pasta Sauce with Bacon

3 tablespoons olive oil

1 garlic clove, crushed

⅓ cup diced onion

6 slices thick-cut peppered bacon, cut in thin 1-inch-long strips

2 cups tomato purée

1 cup water

Salt and pepper, to taste

1 (8-ounce) container mascarpone cheese

1 tablespoon julienned fresh basil

On low heat, heat the oil in a large sauté pan. Add the garlic and sauté until aromatic, but not brown. Remove the garlic. Add the onion and cook over low heat until tender, about 10 minutes. Do not brown. Stir in the bacon. Raise the heat and cook until the bacon cooks through but does not crisp. Add the tomato purée and water. Season with the salt and pepper. Simmer about 20 to 30 minutes or until the sauce thickens and reduces a little. Remove from the heat. Add the cheese and basil, and stir well. Makes enough for 1 pound of pasta.

Tip: This sauce is very good with fettuccine or bucatini (long, hollow pasta).

Chicken Tetrazzini with Wisconsin Parmesan

MAKES 8 SERVINGS

8 ounces uncooked spaghetti, broken in half

3 tablespoon butter, divided

¼ cup all-purpose flour

1 teaspoon salt

½ teaspoon paprika

½ teaspoon celery salt

⅛ teaspoon pepper

2 cups milk

1 cup chicken stock

3 cups chopped cooked chicken

1 (4-ounce) can mushrooms, drained

¼ cup pimiento strips

¾ cup (about 3 ounces) grated Parmesan cheese, divided

In a large saucepan cook the spaghetti according to the package directions; drain. Stir in 1 tablespoon of the butter until the butter is melted; set aside.

Preheat the oven to broil.

In a 3-quart saucepan, melt the remaining 2 tablespoons of butter; stir in the flour, salt, paprika, celery salt, and pepper. Remove from the heat. Gradually stir in the milk and chicken stock. Cook over medium heat, stirring constantly, until thickened. Add the chicken, mushrooms, pimiento, spaghetti, and ¼ cup of the Parmesan cheese; heat thoroughly. Place the chicken mixture on an ovenproof platter or shallow casserole; sprinkle the remaining ½ cup of Parmesan cheese over the top. Broil about 3 inches from the heat until lightly browned.

Pasta with Chicken, Tomato, and Wisconsin Romano

MAKES 8 SERVINGS

- 1 pound spaghetti, thin spaghetti, or linguine, uncooked
- 2 ripe tomatoes, cored
- 2 teaspoons vegetable oil
- 1 large onion, finely diced
- 4 large garlic cloves, finely chopped
- 1 pound boneless, skinless chicken breasts, cut into strips
- 1 teaspoon dried basil
- 12 to 16 coarsely chopped medium California ripe olives
- 1 green bell pepper, julienned
- 1 (15½-ounce) can low-sodium chicken stock
- 1 cup (4 ounces) grated Romano cheese, or more, to taste

Prepare the pasta according to the package directions. While the pasta is cooking, cut the tomatoes in half crosswise and scoop out the seeds. Chop the tomatoes coarsely.

Heat the oil in a large skillet over medium heat. Add the onions and garlic, and cook until the onion is lightly browned and tender, about 6 minutes. Add the chicken and basil; cook until the chicken is lightly browned, about 8 minutes. Stir in the olives, green pepper, and tomatoes, and cook until the tomatoes begin to give off liquid, about 2 minutes. Add the chicken stock to the skillet, heat to boiling, and boil until half of the liquid is evaporated, about 4 minutes.

When the pasta is done, drain it well and add it to the sauce mixture. Toss until the pasta is evenly mixed with the sauce. Transfer to a serving dish, top with the cheese, and serve.

Shrimp, Artichoke, and Olive Pasta with Wisconsin Asiago

1 pound large shrimp, shelled and deveined

¼ cup olive oil, divided

1½ cups diced onions

3 garlic cloves, minced

1 (16-ounce) can crushed tomatoes

1 (15-ounce) can quartered artichoke hearts

⅓ cup dry white wine

1 cup black olives, quartered

1 pound rotelle pasta, cooked and drained

1½ cups (about 6 ounces) grated Asiago or Parmesan cheese

¼ cup chopped fresh parsley

¼ cup julienned fresh basil or 1 tablespoon dried basil

Salt and pepper, to taste

In a large skillet over medium heat, cook the shrimp in 2 tablespoons of oil for 3 to 4 minutes, stirring often. Remove the shrimp from the skillet; set aside. In the same skillet, cook the onion and garlic in the remaining oil for 3 minutes. Add the tomatoes, artichoke hearts, and wine; heat to a boil. Reduce the heat to low; simmer for 5 minutes. Add the cooked shrimp and the olives; heat through.

In a large bowl, gently combine the pasta, shrimp-artichoke mixture, cheese, parsley, basil, salt, and pepper. Serve hot or at room temperature.

Shrimp and Olive Pasta with Wisconsin Parmesan

MAKES 10 SERVINGS

1 pound large raw shrimp, shelled and deveined

¼ cup olive oil, divided

1½ cups diced onions

3 garlic cloves, minced

1 (16-ounce) can diced tomatoes with juice

1 cup diced fresh asparagus

⅓ cup dry white wine

1 cup black olives, halved

1 pound rotini pasta, cooked and drained

1½ cups (about 6 ounces) grated Parmesan cheese

¼ cup chopped fresh parsley

¼ cup julienned fresh basil

1 teaspoon salt

½ teaspoon pepper

In a large skillet over medium heat, cook the shrimp in 2 tablespoons of oil for about 3 minutes or until opaque, stirring often. Remove the shrimp from the skillet; set aside.

In the same skillet, cook the onion and garlic in the remaining oil for 3 minutes. Add the tomatoes, asparagus, and wine; heat to a boil. Reduce the heat to low and simmer for 5 minutes. Add the cooked shrimp and the olives; heat through.

In a large bowl, gently combine the pasta, shrimp-vegetable mixture, cheese, parsley, basil, salt, and pepper. Serve immediately.

Pork Shoulder Ravioli with Wisconsin Gran Canaria

CHEF TORY MILLER

MAKES 70 RAVIOLI

PORK

1 (2- to 2½-pound) boneless pork shoulder

4 tablespoons olive oil, plus extra for drizzling

1 onion, diced

4 garlic cloves, minced

2 tablespoons tomato paste

1 teaspoon red pepper flakes

1 teaspoon dried oregano

1 teaspoon dried basil

1 cup Zinfandel wine

4 cups tomato purée

1 tablespoon sugar

Salt and pepper, to taste

PASTA

1 package fresh pasta sheets

2 cups (8 ounces) shredded Carr Valley Gran Canaria cheese

4 ounces fresh basil

For the pork, brown the meat on all sides in 4 tablespoons of the olive oil over medium-high heat. Remove the meat from the pan and add the onion. Reduce the heat to medium-low and sweat the onion for 3 minutes. Stir in the garlic and tomato paste; cook for 2 minutes. Add the red pepper flakes, oregano, and basil, and stir for about 15 seconds. Add the wine; simmer and stir about 4 minutes, until thick and the liquid is reduced. Stir in the tomato purée and sugar; return the meat to the sauce. Cover and simmer on very low heat for 3 hours or until the meat is tender and pulls apart. Remove the meat from the sauce, remove the visible fat, season, and shred the meat with two forks. Stir in enough of the tomato sauce to moisten the meat. Reserve the remaining sauce.

For the pasta, preheat the oven to 400°F. Bring a large kettle of water to a boil. Cut the pasta into 3-inch squares. Cook the squares, a few at a time, in boiling water for about 45 seconds. Placce the pasta squares flat on a work surface. Place a scant tablespoon of the pork mixture in the middle of each square. Fold the pasta over the pork. Place on a greased baking sheet. Repeat with all of the pasta squares. Top each ravioli with a teaspoon of cheese.

To complete the recipe, bake the ravioli for 10 to 12 minutes or until the cheese is brown. Drizzle with extra olive oil and sprinkle with basil. Serve with the reserved sauce.

Ricotta Spinach Rolls

MAKES 4 SERVNIGS

SAUCE

1 medium onion, finely chopped

2 garlic cloves, minced

1 tablespoon butter

3 cups tomato sauce (no salt added)

1 teaspoon dried oregano

½ teaspoon dried thyme

½ teaspoon dried basil

¼ teaspoon dried marjoram

FILLING

1 (10-ounce) package frozen chopped spinach

1 cup (8 ounces) part-skim ricotta cheese

2 tablespoons grated Parmesan cheese

¼ teaspoon nutmeg

Pinch of pepper

8 lasagna noodles, cooked and drained

For the sauce, sauté the onion and garlic in butter over medium heat until tender. Add the tomato sauce and seasonings. Simmer 30 minutes.

Preheat the oven to 350°F.

For the filling, cook the spinach according to the package directions. Drain and squeeze out the excess water. Blend together the spinach, cheeses, nutmeg, and pepper until thoroughly mixed. Spread the mixture evenly along the entire length of each lasagna noodle. Roll each one and place on its side in a buttered shallow baking dish. Cover with sauce. Bake for 20 to 30 minutes or until heated through.

Pumpkin Ravioli with Wisconsin Cheese

CHEF TONY MANTUANO

MAKES 10 SERVINGS

FILLING

2 cups solid-pack pumpkin
(not pie filling)

$\frac{1}{8}$ teaspoon nutmeg

$\frac{1}{4}$ cup assorted dried fruit,
chopped

1 cup crushed Amaretti cookies,
divided*

$\frac{1}{2}$ cup breadcrumbs

$\frac{3}{4}$ cup grated Parmesan cheese

$\frac{1}{2}$ teaspoon salt

1 teaspoon Dijon mustard

Pinch of pepper

SAUCE

$\frac{1}{4}$ pound (1 stick) butter

15 fresh sage leaves

RAVIOLI

2 packages wonton wrappers
(100 wrappers)

1 cup (about 4 ounces) grated
aged provolone cheese

* These are available in Italian delis.

For the filling, combine the filling ingredients, reserving $\frac{1}{2}$ cup of Amaretti crumbs for the topping.

For the sauce, in a sauté pan, heat the butter on high heat until the foam subsides. Remove from the heat and add the sage. Set aside and keep warm.

For the ravioli, moisten a wonton skin with water. Place another skin on top and press to seal. Place a spoonful of filling on the dough, moisten the edges, and fold the dough over to make a triangle. Cook in a large pot of rapidly boiling water for about $3\frac{1}{2}$ minutes. Remove with a slotted spoon and add to the warm sage butter. On warm plates, divide the ravioli and top with provolone and the reserved crushed Amaretti.

Potato Gnocchi with Tomatoes and Wisconsin Fresh Mozzarella

CHEF TOM CATHERALL

MAKES 8 SERVINGS

GNOCCHI*

2 pounds russet baking potatoes, peeled and quartered

2 to 2½ cups all-purpose flour

1 egg, lightly beaten

SAUCE

2 tablespoons extra-virgin olive oil

10 medium tomatoes, peeled, seeded, and diced (or 1½ cans [28 ounces each] Italian plum tomatoes, drained and chopped)

½ teaspoon dried oregano

Large pinch of red pepper flakes

2 tablespoons balsamic vinegar

1 tablespoon tomato paste

¼ cup dry red wine

1 teaspoon sugar

Salt, to taste

Freshly ground pepper, to taste

1 to 2 teaspoons red wine vinegar

6 ounces fresh mozzarella cheese, cut in ¼-inch cubes

¾ cup (3 ounces) grated Parmesan or Romano cheese

* Prepared gnocchi may be substituted for homemade

For the gnocchi, place the potatoes in a saucepan and add water just to the level of the potatoes. Salt the water. Bring to a boil and cook until very soft, 25 minutes. Drain well; let stand in the colander for 10 minutes.

Spread the flour on your work surface. With a potato ricer or food mill fit with a medium disk, rice the warm potatoes evenly over the entire top of the the flour. Toss together lightly with your fingers to distribute the potatoes and flour evenly. Make a well in the center and add the egg. Knead to form a ball. Knead 1 minute to gather up all of the bits of flour and potato on the work surface. Cover with an inverted bowl and let the dough rest for 5 minutes.

Divide the dough into 4 equal pieces. On a floured surface, roll each piece into a ½-inch-thick rope, approximately 12 inches long. Working with one rope at a time (keeping the others covered with a towel), with floured hands, cut through the dough with the curved edge of a fork, every ½ inch. On the back edge of the fork, roll each piece forward and back, making fork indentations and shell shapes.

Toss with the flour. Place on a floured baking sheet. Repeat with the remaining dough. Heat salted water in a large Dutch oven.

(continued on next page)

For the sauce, heat the olive oil in a large skillet over medium-high heat. Add the tomatoes, oregano, red pepper flakes, balsamic vinegar, tomato paste, wine, sugar, salt, and pepper. Cook for 3 to 4 minutes, until the liquid begins to evaporate and the sauce thickens slightly. Remove from the heat. Purée in a blender or food processor. Season to taste with salt, pepper, and red wine vinegar. Return to skillet.

To complete the recipe, bring salted water to a boil. Cook about half of the gnocchi until tender, 2 to 3 minutes. Remove with a slotted spoon. Repeat with the remaining gnocchi. Add the cooked gnocchi to the sauce. Heat thoroughly. Toss in the mozzarella cheese. Sprinkle with grated cheese; serve immediately.

Four-Cheese Vegetable Lasagna

1 (10-ounce) package frozen chopped spinach, thawed

2 teaspoons vegetable oil

2 cups chopped fresh broccoli

1½ cups thinly sliced carrots

1 cup sliced green onions

½ cup chopped red bell pepper

3 garlic cloves, crushed

½ cup all-purpose flour

3 cups low-fat milk

½ cup (about 2 ounces) grated Parmesan cheese, divided

Salt, to taste

¼ teaspoon pepper

1½ cups (12 ounces) part-skim ricotta cheese

1 cup (4 ounces) shredded part-skim mozzarella cheese

½ cup (2 ounces) shredded Swiss cheese

12 cooked lasagna noodles (cooked without salt or fat)

Preheat the oven to 375°F.

Press the spinach between paper towels until barely moist, and set aside.

Coat a Dutch oven with cooking spray; place over medium heat until hot. Add the broccoli, carrots, onions, bell pepper, and garlic; sauté 7 minutes. Set aside.

Place the flour in a medium saucepan. Gradually add the milk, stirring with a wire whisk until blended. Bring to a boil over medium heat, and cook for 5 minutes or until thickened, stirring constantly. Add ¼ cup of the Parmesan cheese, the salt, and the pepper; cook an additional minute, stirring constantly. Remove from the heat; stir in the spinach. Reserve ½ cup of the mixture, and set aside.

Combine the ricotta, mozzarella, and Swiss cheeses; stir well. Spread ½ cup of the spinach mixture in the bottom of a 13 x 9-inch baking dish coated with cooking spray. Arrange 4 lasagna noodles over the spinach mixture; top with half of the cheese mixture, half of the vegetable mixture, and half of the spinach mixture. Repeat the layers, ending with noodles. Spread the reserved ½ cup of spinach mixture over the noodles, and sprinkle with the remaining ¼ cup of Parmesan cheese. Cover and bake for 35 minutes. Let stand 5 minutes before serving.

Zucchini Lasagna

½ pound extra-lean ground beef

⅓ cup chopped onion

1 (15-ounce) can tomato sauce (no salt added)

½ teaspoon dried oregano

¼ teaspoon dried basil

¼ teaspoon dried thyme

⅛ teaspoon pepper

1 cup (8 ounces) low-fat cream-style cottage cheese

1 egg

4 medium zucchini

2 tablespoons all-purpose flour, divided

1½ cups (6 ounces) shredded part-skim mozzarella cheese

2 tablespoons grated Parmesan cheese

Preheat the oven to 375°F.

Brown the beef and onion in a medium saucepan over medium-high heat; drain. Return to the pan and add the tomato sauce and spices. Bring to a boil, reduce the heat, and simmer 5 to 10 minutes. Combine the cottage cheese and egg in a small bowl until thoroughly mixed. Set aside.

Slice the zucchini into ¼-inch-thick slices. Arrange half of the zucchini in the bottom of a 13 x 9-inch baking dish; sprinkle with 1 tablespoon of flour. Top with the cottage cheese mixture and half of the the beef mixture. Repeat with the remaining zucchini and flour; sprinkle with mozzarella cheese. Add the remaining beef mixture. Sprinkle with Parmesan cheese. Bake for 40 minutes. Let stand for 10 minutes before cutting.

Gruyère Linguine Tart

MAKES 8 SERVINGS

¼ pound (1 stick) butter, divided

2 garlic cloves, minced

30 very thin slices French bread

3 tablespoons all-purpose flour

1 teaspoon salt

¼ teaspoon white pepper

Pinch of nutmeg

2½ cups milk

¼ cup (about 1 ounce) grated Parmesan cheese

2 eggs, beaten

8 ounces fresh linguine, cooked, drained

1 cup (4 ounces) shredded Gruyère cheese

1 cup (4 ounces) shredded baby Swiss cheese

⅓ cup green onion slices

2 tablespoons minced fresh basil or 2 teaspoons dried basil, crushed

2 plum tomatoes

Preheat the oven to 350°F.

Melt ¼ cup of the butter in a saucepan over medium heat. Add the garlic; cook 1 minute. Brush a 10-inch plate with the butter mixture; then line the bottom and sides with the bread, allowing the bread to come 1 inch over the sides. Brush the bread with the remaining butter mixture. Bake for 5 minutes or until lightly browned. Set aside.

Melt the remaining butter in a saucepan over low heat. Blend in the flour and seasonings. Gradually add the milk and cook, stirring constantly, until thickened. Remove from the heat; add the Parmesan cheese. Stir a small amount of this sauce into the eggs; mix well, and add the remaining sauce.

Combine the Gruyère and baby Swiss cheeses and toss 1¼ cups of the combined cheeses with the linguine, green onion, and basil, in a large bowl. Pour the sauce over the linguine mixture; mix well. Pour into the crust. Cut each tomato lengthwise into eight slices; place on top of the tart. Sprinkle with the remaining ¾ cup cheese. Bake for 25 minutes. Let stand 5 minutes before serving.

Artichoke Focaccia Pizza with Wisconsin Parmesan

MAKES 6 SERVINGS

1 (14-ounce) can artichoke hearts, drained and quartered

1 red bell pepper, chopped

2 cups (8 ounces) shredded Italian cheese blend

1 cup (about 4 ounces) grated Parmesan cheese, divided

$\frac{1}{2}$ cup chopped fresh parsley

$\frac{1}{2}$ cup mayonnaise

2 teaspoons coarsely chopped garlic

1 teaspoon pepper

$\frac{1}{4}$ teaspoon cayenne pepper

1 (10-inch) focaccia bread, sliced in half horizontally

2 tablespoons olive oil

Preheat the oven to 375°F.

In a medium bowl, combine the artichokes, red pepper, cheese blend, $\frac{1}{2}$ cup of the Parmesan, the parsley, the mayonnaise, the garlic, the pepper, and the cayenne; mix well. Place the focaccia halves on a baking sheet. Sprinkle each half with 1 tablespoon of olive oil and $\frac{1}{4}$ cup of the remaining Parmesan.

Divide and spread the artichoke mixture on each focaccia half. Bake for 20 to 25 minutes or until bubbly.

Fiesta Pizza with Wisconsin Queso Blanco

MAKES 1 (12-INCH) PIZZA

1 (12-inch) prebaked thin pizza crust

1 (16-ounce) can vegetarian refried beans

¾ cup prepared salsa (medium or hot)

1 yellow or red bell pepper, julienned to make 1 cup

1 cup (4 ounces) crumbled queso blanco cheese

¼ cup sliced green onions

Preheat the oven to 450°F. Place the pizza crust on a pizza pan or large baking sheet. Spread the beans evenly on the crust; cover with the salsa. Sprinkle with the peppers, cheese, and green onions. Bake for 8 to 10 minutes, or until the cheese is melted.

Variation: Queso fresco cheese may be used in place of the queso blanco cheese.

Goat Cheese, Pesto, and Zucchini Pizza

MAKES 4 SERVINGS

Cornmeal

1 pound pizza dough, thawed if frozen

¼ cup plus 1 tablespoon pesto

1½ cups (6 ounces) shredded mozzarella cheese

2 small or 1 medium zucchini, sliced into ¼-inch rounds (about 1 cup)

Fine sea salt or kosher salt and freshly ground pepper

½ cup (3 ounces) crumbled soft fresh goat cheese

¼ cup chopped fresh basil

Set the rack in the lower third of the oven and preheat the oven to 450°F. Sprinkle some cornmeal (about 2 tablespoons) over the bottom of a large baking sheet or 12-inch round pizza pan.

Stretch the dough with your fingers into a 12-by-10-inch rectangle (or 12-inch round) and place on the prepared baking sheet.

Spread ¼ cup of pesto over the dough, leaving a border at the edges. Sprinkle the mozzarella evenly over the pesto. Arrange the zucchini rounds over the top of the mozzarella. Season the pizza with salt and pepper and sprinkle with the goat cheese. Transfer to the oven and bake until the edge of the crust is deep golden and the cheese is melted and bubbly, 15 to 20 minutes. Spoon the remaining pesto over the pizza and sprinkle with the chopped basil.

Tip: When shopping for prepared pesto, the color offers a clue to the freshness of flavor: bright green is best. Look for the refrigerated tubs instead of jars.

Gorgonzola and Caramelized Onion Pizza

MAKES 1 (12-INCH) PIZZA

1½ cups julienned onion

1 (12-inch) prebaked pizza crust

⅓ cup (3 ounces) mascarpone cheese

¾ cup (about 4 ounces) cubed Italian-style Gorgonzola cheese

¼ cup chopped pecans

Preheat the oven to 450°F.

In a sauté pan over high heat, brown the onions until caramelized; cool.

Place the pizza crust on a pizza pan or a large baking sheet. Spread the mascarpone evenly over the pizza crust. Place the cooled caramelized onions on the cheese. Sprinkle the Gorgonzola and pecans over the top. Bake for 6 to 9 minutes or until the crust is lightly browned and the cheese is hot.

Greek Pizza

MAKES 1 (12-INCH) PIZZA

1 (12-inch) prebaked pizza crust

½ cup pizza sauce

¾ cup (3 ounces) shredded aged provolone cheese

½ cup (2 ounces) shredded mozzarella cheese

20 to 25 baby spinach leaves

¼ cup julienned red onion

¾ cup (about 5 ounces) crumbled feta cheese with sun-dried tomatoes

⅓ cup sliced black olives

2 tablespoons finely diced sun-dried tomatoes

Balsamic vinegar, as needed (optional)

Preheat the oven to 475°F.

Place the pizza crust on a pizza pan or a large baking sheet. Spread the sauce on the pizza crust. Sprinkle the provolone and mozzarella on the sauce. Bake for 7 to 9 minutes or until the crust is lightly browned. Remove from the oven.

Arrange the spinach leaves over the top of the pizza. Arrange the red onion over the spinach; sprinkle the feta cheese, black olives, and sun-dried tomatoes over the top. Mist the pizza with balsamic vinegar, if desired.

Tip: You may substitute another flavored feta cheese. Homemade pizza crust may be substituted, if desired. Prebake the crust for 5 to 10 minutes; then proceed with the recipe as written. If you prefer cooked onion, place the onion over the sauce prior to baking.

Wisconsin Limburger Vegetable Pizza

1 (7-ounce) package Limburger cheese, divided

1 (12-inch) prebaked pizza crust

1 cup finely sliced new potatoes

¼ cup chopped red onion

6 stalks fresh asparagus, sliced in half, lengthwise

1 garlic clove, minced

1 tablespoon fresh thyme or 1 teaspoon dried thyme

¼ teaspoon salt

2 tablespoons olive oil

Red pepper flakes, to taste

Preheat the oven to 425°F.

Cut away ¼ inch of rind from all sides of the cheese; discard the rind. Shred the remaining cheese. Place the pizza crust on a pizza pan or large baking sheet. Sprinkle with ¾ cup of the shredded cheese; set aside.

Combine the potatoes, onion, asparagus, garlic, thyme, and salt. Sprinkle the olive oil over the mixture and toss lightly. Spread the vegetables evenly over the pizza. Sprinkle the remaining ¾ cup of shredded cheese over the vegetables. Bake for 18 to 20 minutes.

Margherite Pizza

MAKES 1 (12-INCH) PIZZA

1 (12-inch) prebaked pizza crust

3 medium Roma tomatoes, sliced ⅛ inch thick

8 ounces fresh mozzarella cheese, sliced ⅛ inch thick

12 to 14 fresh basil leaves, julienned

¼ cup pine nuts

1 tablespoon garlic-flavored olive oil (optional)

Preheat the oven to 450°F.

Place the pizza crust on a pizza pan or a large baking sheet. Arrange the tomato slices on the crust. Arrange the cheese slices on the tomatoes. Sprinkle the basil over the cheese. Sprinkle the pine nuts over the top. Drizzle garlic oil over the top, if desired. Bake for 7 to 9 minutes or until the crust is lightly browned and the cheese is melted.

Mediterranean Pizza with Fresh Mozzarella

MAKES 1 (16-INCH) PIZZA OR 2 (8-INCH) PIZZAS

1 (16-inch) prebaked pizza crust or 2 (8-inch) prebaked pizza crusts

¾ cup pesto sauce

½ cup sliced roasted red peppers

¼ cup sliced sun-dried tomatoes (packed in oil)

¼ cup sliced kalamata olives

¼ cup pine nuts

4 cups (16 ounces) shredded mozzarella cheese

4 ounces fresh mozzarella cheese, sliced

Preheat the oven to 400°F.

Place the pizza crust(s) on a pizza pan or a large baking sheet. Spread the crust(s) with pesto sauce. Top with the peppers, tomatoes, olives, and pine nuts. Sprinkle with the shredded mozzarella, and place the mozzarella slices on top. Bake 12 to 15 minutes or until the pizza has reached the desired doneness.

Pizza with Wisconsin Fontina and Artichokes

MAKES 1 (12 X 9-INCH) PIZZA

1 pound frozen white bread dough, thawed according to package directions, but chilled

2 tablespoons olive oil, divided

2 tablespoons wheat bran

1 large garlic clove, chopped finely

½ medium red onion, thinly sliced

1 (9-ounce) package frozen arti-choke hearts, thawed, or 1 (14-ounce) can, drained and sliced lengthwise

Salt and freshly ground pepper, to taste

1 cup (4 ounces) shredded fontina cheese

Preheat the oven to 450°F.

On a lightly oiled baking sheet, press the chilled dough into a 12 x 9-inch rectangle with raised edges. Brush with 1 tablespoon of olive oil. Evenly sprinkle with the bran; press lightly into the dough. Sprinkle with the garlic. Arrange the onion in one layer over the dough; top with the artichoke hearts. Drizzle with the remaining 1 tablespoon of olive oil. Lightly season with salt and pepper. Evenly sprinkle with the cheese. Do not permit the dough to rise. (The pizza may be held briefly in the refrigerator before baking.) Bake for about 15 minutes, until the crust and cheese are lightly browned.

Veggie Four-Cheese Italian-Blend Pizza

1 (12-inch) prebaked pizza crust

1 tablespoon garlic in oil

2 Roma tomatoes, sliced ⅛ inch thick

1½ cups (6 ounces) shredded four-cheese Italian blend

¼ cup julienned red onion

⅓ cup zucchini, roasted, sliced ⅛ inch thick

⅓ cup shiitake mushrooms, sliced ¼ inch thick

⅓ cup artichoke hearts, quartered

½ teaspoon chopped fresh oregano

½ teaspoon chopped fresh thyme

Preheat the oven to 450°F.

Place the pizza crust on a pizza pan or a large baking sheet. Brush the crust with the garlic in oil; arrange the sliced tomatoes over the oil. Spread 1 cup of cheese over the pizza crust. Add the vegetables and herbs, and top with the remaining cheese. Bake for 10 to 12 minutes.

White Bean Hummus and Wisconsin Asiago Pizza

MAKES 6 SMALL PIZZAS

PIZZA DOUGH

2 teaspoons sugar

1 package dry yeast

1⅔ cups warm water (105°to 115°F)

3¾ cups all-purpose flour, divided

¼ cup whole wheat flour

1 teaspoon salt

2 teaspoons olive oil

WHITE BEAN HUMMUS

1 (15-ounce) can cannellini beans or other white beans, rinsed and drained

3 tablespoons fresh lemon juice

1 tablespoon tahini (sesame seed paste)

½ teaspoon ground cumin

½ teaspoon Hungarian sweet paprika

¼ teaspoon salt

2 garlic cloves

TOPPINGS

2 tablespoons olive oil

7 cups thinly sliced onions, separated into rings

¾ cup (3 ounces) grated Asiago cheese

¾ cup (4 to 5 ounces) crumbled feta cheese

2 cups trimmed arugula

For the pizza dough, dissolve the sugar and yeast in warm water in a large bowl; let stand 5 minutes. Stir in the flours, salt, and oil to form a soft, wet dough. Turn the dough out onto a lightly floured surface, and knead until smooth and elastic (about 8 minutes).

Add enough of the remaining flour, one tablespoon at a time, to prevent the dough from sticking to your hands. Place the dough in a large bowl coated with cooking spray, turning to coat the top. Cover the dough, and let it rise in a warm place (85°F), free from drafts, for 1 hour or until doubled in bulk.

Punch the dough down, and turn out onto a lightly floured surface. Divide the dough into 6 equal portions; roll each portion of dough into a 7-inch circle. Place the pizza crusts on preheated pizza stones or large baking sheets coated with cooking spray. Top and bake according to the recipe directions.

For the hummus, place all of the ingredients in a food processor, and process until smooth.

For the toppings and assembly, preheat the oven to 500°F.

Heat the oil in a large nonstick skillet over medium-high heat. Add the onions; cover and cook 10 minutes or until deep golden, stirring frequently. Remove from the heat; set aside.

1 tablespoon balsamic vinegar

⅓ cup (1 ounce) shaved fresh Parmesan cheese

Top each prepared crust with ½ cup of the onions. Sprinkle with the Asiago and feta cheeses. Bake for 8 minutes or until the crusts are crisp. While the pizza is cooking, combine the arugula and the vinegar in a medium bowl. Remove the pizza from the oven; drizzle each with 2 tablespoons of the hummus. Top each pizza with the arugula mixture and the Parmesan cheese. Serve immediately.

Brie, Ham, and Spinach Pizza

MAKES 1 (12-INCH) PIZZA

¾ cup julienned red onion

½ teaspoon chopped garlic

2 teaspoon olive oil, divided

1 (12-inch) prebaked pizza crust

½ cup pizza sauce

1 cup (4 ounces) shredded part-skim mozzarella cheese

3 ounces ham, diced ¼ inch thick

4 ounces Brie, sliced ¼ inch thick

½ teaspoon ground cumin

12 to 15 fresh spinach leaves, stems removed

Preheat the oven to 475°F.

Toss the red onion and garlic with 1 teaspoon of olive oil; roast until soft for 5 minutes. Cool.

Place the pizza crust on a pizza pan or a large baking sheet. Spread the sauce on the pizza crust. Sprinkle the mozzarella over the sauce. Arrange the ham on top of the mozzarella.

Sprinkle the cooled red onion mixture on top of the ham. Arrange the Brie on top, and sprinkle with the cumin. Toss the spinach with the remaining 1 teaspoon of olive oil to coat lightly; arrange on top of the pizza. Bake for 8 to 10 minutes or until the crust is lightly browned.

Classic Potato, Onion, and Ham Pizza

MAKES 1 (16-OUNCE) PIZZA

3 tablespoons butter or olive oil, divided

3 cups potatoes, sliced ¼ inch thick

2 sweet onions, sliced ¼ inch thick

1 tablespoon coarsely chopped garlic

½ teaspoon salt

½ teaspoon pepper

1 (16-ounce) prebaked pizza crust

2 cups (8 ounces) shredded mozzarella cheese

8 thin slices (4 ounces) deli ham

8 slices provolone cheese

½ cup (about 2 ounces) grated Parmesan cheese

¼ cup chopped fresh parsley

Preheat the oven to 400°F.

In a large skillet, heat 2 tablespoons of the butter or oil; add the potatoes, onions, garlic, salt, and pepper. Cook over medium heat for 12 to 15 minutes, turning occasionally. Stir in the remaining butter and cook until the potatoes are golden brown, 5 to 7 minutes.

Place the pizza crust on a pizza pan or a large baking sheet. On the crust, sprinkle the mozzarella; top with the ham slices. Place the potato mixture over the ham; top with the provolone slices. Sprinkle with the Parmesan and parsley. Bake directly on the oven rack for 15 to 20 minutes, or until the cheese is melted.

White Cheddar Pizza with Bacon

MAKES 2 (9-INCH) PIZZAS

PIZZA DOUGH

1 cup water

2 cups all-purpose flour, divided

½ cup cornmeal

1 tablespoon minced fresh sage

1 package quick-rising dry yeast
  (2¼ teaspoons)

1 teaspoon salt

1 teaspoon sugar

2 tablespoons olive oil

TOPPINGS

2 cups chopped smoked bacon

2 cups (8 ounces) shredded
  white Cheddar cheese

1 cup chopped walnuts, toasted

1 cup loosely packed fresh
  Italian parsley leaves

For the dough, heat the water to 120°F to 130°F. Mix 1 cup of flour with the cornmeal, sage, yeast, salt, and sugar. Add the water and oil. Mix until almost smooth. Gradually add enough remaining flour to make a firm dough. Knead 5 minutes. Cover with a damp cloth and allow to rise in a warm place until doubled in size, about 1 hour. Punch the dough down; allow to rise one more time.

For the toppings and assembly, cook the bacon until done, but not crisp. Drain on a paper towel.

Preheat the oven to 500°F. Divide the dough in half; roll or press each half into a 9-inch circle. Place on a pizza pan or large baking sheet. Top each with cheese, bacon, and walnuts. Bake for 8 to 10 minutes or until the dough is lightly browned. Sprinkle with parsley.

Variations: Use prepared focaccia for the crust. For the cheese, choose a blend of four varieties such as Cheddar, Gorgonzola, Asiago, and fontina. Substitute chopped cooked duck for the bacon. To make a vegetarian version, substitute apples or pears for the bacon and use Havarti and Cheddar cheeses.

Gruyère, Asparagus, and Prosciutto Pizza

MAKES 1 (12-INCH) PIZZA

1 (12-inch) prebaked pizza crust

1½ teaspoon chopped garlic

1 teaspoon olive oil

2 cups (8 ounces) shredded Gruyère cheese, divided

3 ounces prosciutto, julienned

5 spears asparagus, trimmed and blanched, cut in 1-inch pieces

½ cup julienned red onion

Preheat the oven to 450°F.

Place the pizza crust on a pizza pan or large baking sheet. Combine the garlic and olive oil and spread on the crust. Sprinkle 1¾ cups of the cheese evenly over the crust. Arrange the prosciutto, asparagus, and red onions over cheese. Sprinkle the remaining cheese over the top. Bake for 9 to 11 minutes or until the crust is lightly browned and the cheese is bubbly.

French Bread Pizza

MAKES 1 (4 X 16-INCH) FRENCH BREAD PIZZA

1 (4 x 16-inch) loaf French bread

2 tablespoons olive oil

1 cup (4 ounces) shredded provolone cheese

½ cup (2 ounces) shredded smoked mozzarella cheese

3 ounces pepperoni sausage, diced

3 ounces ground Italian sausage, cooked

1 medium tomato, diced

½ cup diced Spanish onion

½ cup sliced green olives

1 teaspoon Italian seasoning

6 tablespoons pizza sauce

½ cup diced green bell pepper

Preheat the oven to 400°F.

Cut the top quarter from the bread and remove all but a ½- to ¾-inch layer of bread from inside the crust. Place the bread on a baking sheet. Brush the inside with the oil and bake in the oven or broiler until the edges turn golden and the bread dries slightly. This will only take a few minutes.

Blend the cheeses together in one bowl. In another bowl, combine the sausages, tomato, onion, olives, seasonings, and three-fourths of the cheese blend.

Spread the bread with the pizza sauce. Fill the bread with the sausage mixture, and top with the remaining cheese blend and the pepper. Bake for 15 minutes or until the ingredients are heated through.

Wisconsin Four-Cheese Pizza

1¼ cups crushed tomatoes or sauce tomatoes

3 tablespoons grated Parmesan cheese

¼ teaspoon dried basil, crushed

¼ teaspoon dried oregano, crushed

9 ounces prepared pizza dough

½ cup Italian sausage, crumbled, browned, drained

¾ cup sliced mushrooms

¼ cup (1 ounce) grated Asiago cheese

⅓ cup chopped sweet green peppers

¾ cup (3 ounces) shredded provolone cheese

1 cup (4 ounces) shredded mozzarella cheese

Mix the tomatoes with the Parmesan cheese, basil, and oregano for the sauce.

Preheat the oven to 400°F.

Shape the dough into a 12-inch round crust. Place the crust on a pizza pan or large baking sheet. Ladle the sauce over the crust; spread evenly. Top the pizza with the remaining ingredients. Bake for 18 to 22 minutes until the crust is crisp and golden.

Tip: Instead of making the sauce, you can substitute 2¾ quarts of prepared pizza sauce for the tomatoes, Parmesan cheese, basil, and oregano.

Provolone and Duck Sausage Pizza

MAKES 1 (12-INCH) PIZZA

1 (12-inch) prebaked pizza crust

½ cup pizza sauce

1 cup (4 ounces) shredded mild provolone cheese

1 cup (4 ounces) shredded aged provolone cheese

4 ounces precooked duck sausage, sliced into coins

½ cup sliced shiitake mushrooms

¼ cup diced red bell pepper

¼ cup diced yellow bell pepper

1 tablespoon roasted, chopped garlic

¼ cup chopped chives

Preheat the oven to 450°F.

Place the pizza crust on a pizza pan or large baking sheet. Spread the sauce evenly over the crust. Sprinkle the provolone cheeses over the sauce. Arrange the sausage over the cheese. Arrange the mushrooms and peppers on top of the sausage. Sprinkle the roasted garlic over the top. Bake for 9 to 11 minutes or until the crust is lightly browned. Sprinkle the chives over the top of the pizza.

Sausage Pizza with Onion Confit and Wisconsin Cheeses

CHEF JAN BIRNBAUM

MAKES 1 (12-INCH) PIZZA

ONION CONFIT

¼ cup extra-virgin olive oil

3 medium yellow onions,
   peeled, sliced ¼ inch thick

½ cup white wine vinegar

2 tablespoons white wine

½ tablespoon kosher salt

Pinch of sugar

PIZZA

1 (16-ounce) dough ball or
   1 (12- to 14-inch) prebaked
   pizza crust

Extra-virgin olive oil, for
   brushing crust

¾ cup (3 ounces) shredded
   fontina cheese

¾ cup sun-dried tomatoes in
   garlic-herbed olive oil, patted
   dry, sliced or cut in chunks

4 ounces andouille sausage
   links, sliced ¼ inch thick

¾ cup (3 ounces) shredded
   mozzarella cheese

2 tablespoons grated Parmesan
   cheese

2 tablespoons chopped fresh
   Italian parsley

For the onion confit, heat the olive oil over medium heat in a heavy-bottomed saucepan. Add the onions, stirring to coat with the oil, and separate into rings. Cook until soft over low heat, 5 to 8 minutes. Add the vinegar, wine, salt, and sugar. Stir; bring to a boil. Place the lid on the pan slightly askew; lower the heat to simmer and cook for 30 minutes, stirring occasionally. Remove the lid, keeping at a simmer, and continue cooking 30 additional minutes, or until the onions are very soft and the liquid is reduced. Do not brown or scorch. Remove from the heat; set aside.

For the pizza, preheat the oven to 425°F. If using a pizza stone, place the stone in a cold oven and preheat. If using dough, roll into a 12- to 14-inch circle or a rectangle. Place on a baking sheet to transfer to the stone, or on a pizza pan. Brush the edges of the dough with olive oil. Spread the onion confit over the dough or prepared crust, leaving a ½-inch bare edge. Sprinkle with the fontina. Sprinkle the tomatoes and andouille rounds evenly over the fontina. Sprinkle the mozzarella over the whole pizza. Slide onto the pizza stone or place the baking pan in the oven. Bake the pizza for about 10 minutes, or until golden brown. Sprinkle the hot pizza with Parmesan and parsley.

Buffalo Chicken Pizza

6 ounces cooked chicken breast, sliced ½ inch thick

6 tablespoons hot pepper sauce for buffalo wings (Red Hot brand)

1 (12-inch) prebaked pizza crust

¾ cup sour cream

½ cup (2 ounces) shredded Monterey Jack

¾ cup (4 to 5 ounces) crumbled blue cheese

1 ounce green onions, chopped

1 celery stalk, minced

Toss the cooked chicken with the red pepper sauce and marinate overnight.

The next day, preheat the oven to 475°F.

Place the pizza crust on a pizza pan or large baking sheet Spread the sour cream evenly over the crust. Sprinkle the Monterey Jack cheese over the sour cream. Arrange the marinated chicken on top of the cheese. Bake for 8 to 10 minutes until the cheese is lightly browned and bubbly. Remove from the oven and sprinkle with the blue cheese, green onions, and celery.

Chicken Ranch Pizza

1 (12-inch) prebaked sourdough pizza crust

2 garlic cloves, chopped

2 tablespoons olive oil

2 tablespoons ranch-style salad dressing

1¼ cups (5 ounces) shredded Monterey Jack cheese

¾ cup (3 ounces) shredded aged Cheddar cheese

1 small onion, sliced

3 strips bacon, cooked and diced

4 ounces cooked chicken breast, diced

1 large tomato, diced

Preheat the oven to 475°F.

Place the pizza crust on a pizza pan or large baking sheet. Mix the garlic and oil together and spread over the crust. Spread the salad dressing on the crust; then sprinkle with three-fourths of the shredded cheeses. Layer the onions, bacon, chicken, and tomatoes on top; finish with the remaining cheese. Bake for 8 to 10 minutes.

Chipotle Jack Spicy Chicken Pizza

MAKES 1 (12-INCH) PIZZA

1 (12-inch) prebaked pizza crust

6 tablespoons pizza sauce

1 cup (4 ounces) shredded chipotle Jack cheese

¾ cup (3 ounces) shredded fontina cheese

¼ cup (1 ounce) shredded smoked Gouda cheese

4 ounces cooked chicken, cut ¼ inch thick

½ cup sliced mushrooms

1 small bell pepper, sliced

Preheat the oven to 450°F.

Place the pizza crust on a pizza pan or a large baking sheet. Spread the pizza sauce on the crust. Blend the shredded cheeses together in a bowl; place all but ½ cup on the pizza. Arrange the chicken, mushrooms, and pepper on top. Bake for 9 to 11 minutes. Remove from the oven and sprinkle the pizza with the remaining ½ cup of cheese.

Provolone Pizza with Chicken and Pesto

MAKES 1 (12-INCH) PIZZA

2 tablespoons olive oil

4 boneless, skinless chicken breast halves, cut into strips

1 medium green bell pepper, diced

1 medium red or orange pepper, diced

1 medium onion, thinly sliced

⅓ cup prepared pesto

1½ cups (6 ounces) shredded provolone cheese

1 (12-inch) prebaked pizza crust

Preheat the oven to 400°F.

In a skillet, heat the olive oil over medium-high heat. Add the chicken; sauté until the chicken is browned, 5 to 7 minutes. Add the peppers and onions, and continue to sauté until browned, 4 to 5 minutes. Stir in the pesto.

Place the pizza crust on a pizza pan or large baking sheet. Spoon the chicken mixture on the crust; top with the cheese. Bake for 10 to 12 minutes or until the cheese is bubbly.

Spicy Pepper Jack Cheese and Chicken Pizza

MAKES 1 (12-INCH) PIZZA

1 (12-inch) prebaked thin pizza crust

6 tablespoons pizza sauce

1 cup (4 ounces) shredded pepper Jack cheese

¾ cup (3 ounces) shredded fontina cheese

¼ cup (1 ounce) shredded smoked Gouda cheese

½ teaspoon chipotle seasoning

4 ounces chicken, cooked and cut into ¼-inch pieces

½ cup julienned roasted red peppers, drained

½ cup mushrooms, sliced ⅓ inch thick

2 tablespoon minced fresh cilantro or parsley

Preheat the oven to 450°F.

Place the pizza crust on a pizza pan or large baking sheet. Spread the pizza sauce evenly on the crust. Blend the cheeses and the chipotle seasoning together in a bowl; place all but ½ cup on the pizza. Arrange the prepared chicken, roasted peppers, and mushrooms on top of the pizza. Sprinkle with the remaining ½ cup of blended cheeses.

Bake for 9 to 11 minutes. Remove the pizza to a cutting surface; sprinkle with minced fresh cilantro or parsley.

Fresh Plum, Walnut, and Gorgonzola Pizza

MAKES 12 SERVINGS

12 (8-inch) whole-wheat tortillas

4 tablespoons (½ stick) butter, melted

24 fresh, large plums, pitted and thinly sliced*

¾ cup chopped walnuts

3 cups (18 ounces) crumbled Gorgonzola cheese

* Fresh pears may be substituted for the plums when plums are out of season, using about ½ pear per pizza.

Preheat the broiler.

Brush the tortillas with melted butter, using about 1 teaspoon butter for each. Brown on both sides on a grill or griddle. Arrange 2 plums on top of each tortilla to cover the surface. Sprinkle with the walnuts. Sprinkle about ¼ cup of cheese on each pizza. Broil for 30 seconds to 1 minute, just until the cheese bubbles and starts to brown. Cut into quarters and serve.

DESSERTS

Apple Pie with Wisconsin Cheddar Pastry

MAKES 8 SERVINGS

CRUST

1⅔ cups all-purpose flour

¼ teaspoon salt

1 cup (4 ounces) finely shredded sharp Cheddar cheese

¼ pound (1 stick) butter, chilled

¼ cup ice water

FILLING

5 to 6 cups pie apples (such as Granny Smith, Jonathan, or Winesap), pared, cored, and thinly sliced

½ cup granulated or light brown sugar

1 tablespoon cornstarch

¼ teaspoon cinnamon

⅛ teaspoon nutmeg

⅛ teaspoon salt

2 tablespoons butter

For the crust, preheat the oven to 450°F. Sift together the flour and the salt. Stir in the cheese until thoroughly mixed. Dice the butter, and work it into the flour until the texture resembles cornmeal. Sprinkle in the water, one tablespoon at a time, mixing until all of the flour is moistened and the dough pulls away from the sides of the bowl. Divide the dough in half. Shape into two flattened rounds. Roll on a lightly floured surface until the dough is 2 inches larger than an inverted pie pan. Line a 9-inch pan with one crust, reserving the other for the top.

For the filling, place the apples in a large bowl. Combine the sugar, cornstarch, cinnamon, nutmeg, and salt in a small bowl. Gently stir the sugar mixture into the apples until the apples are well coated. Place the apples in layers in the pastry-lined pan. Dot with butter. Cover with the upper crust and cut slits so steam can escape. Bake for 10 minutes. Reduce the temperature to 350°F and bake an additional 35 to 40 minutes.

Banana Cream Pie

MAKES 6 TO 8 SERVIGNS

1 (9-inch) pastry shell, unbaked

8 tablespoons (4 ounces) cream cheese, softened

1½ cups cold milk, plus 2 tablespoons

1 (3.4-ounce) package instant vanilla pudding and pie filling

2 bananas

2 cups whipping cream

Bake the pastry shell according to the package directions; cool. Set aside.

With an electric mixer, beat the cream cheese until light and fluffy, 1 to 2 minutes.

Add 2 tablespoons of milk, and mix, scraping the sides of the bowl, until the cream cheese is creamy and lump-free. Add the remaining milk; mix well. Add the vanilla pudding mix and beat on the lowest speed for 2 minutes.

Meanwhile, slice the bananas and place in a single layer on the bottom of the cooled pastry shell. Pour the pudding mixture over the bananas. Refrigerate 1 hour.

Whip the cream until stiff peaks form. Pipe or spread the whipped cream onto the pie. Refrigerate 1 or more hours before serving.

Berry Cheese Tart

MAKES 10 SERVINGS

1 sheet refrigerated pie crust pastry

2 cups fresh raspberries

1 cup fresh blackberries

1 cup fresh blueberries

¾ cup sugar

¼ cup quick-cooking tapioca

1 tablespoon lemon juice

STREUSEL TOPPING

1 cup all-purpose flour

½ cup sugar

1 cup (4 ounces) shredded aged Cheddar cheese

4 tablespoons (½ stick) butter

Preheat the oven to 400°F.

Line a 9-inch tart pan with the pastry. Combine the berries, ¾ cup sugar, the tapioca, and the lemon juice; pour into the pastry-lined pan. Set aside.

For the streusel topping, in a medium bowl, combine the flour, ½ cup sugar, and the cheese. Cut in the butter to form crumbs. Sprinkle over the berry mixture.

Bake for 50 to 60 minutes, or until the top is well browned. Cool on a wire rack. Remove the sides of the pan and place the tart on a serving plate.

Cardamom-Scented Wisconsin Cheese and Pear Tart

MAKES 8 SERVINGS

1 sheet frozen puff pastry

¾ cup (3 ounces) shredded Swiss cheese, divided

2 medium Bosc pears, peeled, cored, and sliced

1 tablespoon sugar

½ teaspoon ground cardamom

⅓ cup chopped walnuts

1 egg, lightly beaten

Thaw the pastry for 20 minutes.

Unfold the pastry and cut into two rectangles. Roll each on a lightly floured surface, making one 7 x 15 inches, and the other 6 x 4 inches. Fold the larger piece in half lengthwise, and cut through the folded edge to make slits about 2 inches long and ½ inch apart. Set aside.

Preheat the oven to 350°F.

Place the smaller rectangle on an ungreased baking sheet. Sprinkle half of the cheese down the center, leaving a ½-inch border. Arrange the pears on top. Sprinkle with the sugar, cardamom, and walnuts. Brush the edges of the dough with some of the beaten egg. Place the reserved pastry over the top. Press the edges together with the tines of a fork; brush again with the egg (discard any remaining egg). Trim any excess pastry to make the sides even. Bake for 30 minutes, or until the tart is puffed and golden.

Chocolate Moussecarpone Tarts

MAKES 24 SMALL TARTS

1 cup real milk chocolate chips

1 cup (8 ounces) mascarpone
cheese, at room temperature

24 small chocolate shell cups

24 pecan halves, toasted

Simmer water in the bottom pot of a double boiler. Place the chocolate chips in the top pot and heat over the simmering water, stirring constantly, until melted. Remove from the heat and cool slightly. Add the cheese and mix at medium speed for two minutes. Pipe the mixture into the chocolate cups. Top each filled cup with a pecan half. Chill until ready to serve.

Petite Lemon Meringue Pies

MAKES 22 SMALL PIES

½ cup (4 ounces) mascarpone cheese, at room temperature

2 tablespoons superfine sugar

½ cup prepared lemon curd

22 mini (1¼-inch) phyllo tart shells, baked

1½ cups prepared meringue mixture

22 crystallized edible flowers

Preheat the broiler.

In a medium mixing bowl, whip the cheese with the sugar until creamy. Pipe a scant layer of cheese in the bottom of each tart shell. Top with a scant layer of lemon curd.

Place the filled tart shells, evenly spaced, on a baking sheet. Pipe 1 tablespoon of meringue onto the top of each tartlet. Place under the broiler, 4 to 6 inches from the flame, for approximately 1 minute or until slightly browned. Bring the tarts to room temperature before serving. Garnish each tart with a crystallized flower.

Mini Goat Cheese Tarts with Caramel Drizzle

MAKES 4 TO 6 SERVINGS

15 mini phyllo tart shells (such as Athens brand Mini Fillo Shells), thawed if frozen

⅔ cup (3½ ounces) soft fresh goat cheese, at room temperature

½ cup sugar

¼ cup water

¼ cup pine nuts

Arrange the phyllo cups on a serving plate. Place 2 teaspoons of the goat cheese in each cup. In a small, heavy saucepan, combine the sugar and water. Stir over medium heat until the sugar dissolves. Increase the heat and boil the mixture without stirring until it turns a light amber color, about 6 minutes. Drizzle the hot caramel over the goat cheese in the phyllo cups. Sprinkle with the pine nuts.

Ricotta Tart with Kiwi Raspberry Sauce

MAKES 8 SERVINGS

⅓ cup all-purpose flour

⅓ cup packed light brown sugar

3 tablespoons butter

1 cup flaked coconut

½ cup chopped pecans or macadamia nuts

2 cups (16 ounces) ricotta cheese

½ cup confectioners' sugar

1 teaspoon vanilla extract

1 teaspoon grated lime zest

1 (10-ounce) package frozen raspberries

1 kiwi

Preheat the oven to 350°F.

Combine the flour and brown sugar; cut in the butter until the mixture resembles coarse crumbs. Stir in the coconut and nuts. Press into a 10-inch tart pan or pie plate. Bake the crust for 15 minutes. Set aside to cool.

Combine the cheese, confectioners' sugar, vanilla, and lime zest; process in a blender or food processor until smooth. Spoon into the crust. Chill one hour.

Before serving, thaw the raspberries; process in a blender to a sauce consistency. Strain. Slice and arrange the kiwi in a circle around the top of the tart. Drizzle with half of the raspberry sauce. Serve with the remaining sauce.

Lemon Cheesecake

MAKES 16 SERVINGS

2 cups (16 ounces) part-skim ricotta cheese

2 (8-ounce) packages cream cheese, softened

4 eggs

1 cup buttermilk

½ cup sugar

2 tablespoons cornstarch

2 teaspoons vanilla extract

¼ teaspoon salt

Juice and grated rind of 1 small lemon

Fresh blueberries and raspberries (optional)

Preheat the oven to 375°F.

In a large bowl, beat the cheeses until smooth. Add eggs one at a time, beating well after each addition. Add the remaining ingredients, except the berries. Beat until smooth. Pour into a lightly buttered 9-inch springform pan. Bake for 1 hour. Cool completely before removing the pan rim and serving. Garnish with berries.

Mascarpone Cheesecake with Chocolate Pecan Crust

MAKES 10 SERVINGS

CRUST

1 cup chocolate wafer cookie crumbs

2 tablespoons finely chopped pecans

2 tablespoons butter, melted

FILLING

2 envelopes unflavored gelatin

½ cup cold water

2 (8-ounce) containers mascarpone cheese

1 (8-ounce) package Neufchatel cheese, softened

1 cup sugar

¾ cup milk

1 cup whipping cream, whipped

For the crust, preheat the oven to 400°F. Combine the cookie crumbs, pecans, and butter; pat onto the bottom of a 9-inch springform pan. Bake for 5 to 8 minutes; cool.

For the filling, in a small saucepan, dissolve the gelatin in cold water; heat just until warm. In a large mixing bowl, combine the gelatin, cheeses, and sugar; beat until smooth. Gradually add the milk; mix well. Fold in the whipped cream; pour over the crust, smoothing the top. Chill until set.

Mini Chocolate-Chip Cheesecakes with Raspberry Sauce

MAKES 12 SERVINGS

RASPBERRY SAUCE

¼ cup seedless red raspberry jam

1 teaspoon water

½ pint raspberries

CHEESECAKES

3 eggs

½ cup sour cream

2 cups (1 pound) ricotta cheese

⅔ cup sugar

2 tablespoons all-purpose flour

1 teaspoon vanilla

⅓ cup mini semi-sweet chocolate pieces

12 chocolate wafer cookies

For the raspberry sauce, microwave the jam and the water in a 2-cup bowl on high for 1 minute or until melted when stirred. Fold in the raspberries. Refrigerate until ready to use.

For the cheesecakes, preheat the oven to 350°F. Place the eggs, sour cream, cheese, sugar, flour, and vanilla in a blender container or food processor work bowl fitted with a steel blade. Cover and process until smooth. Stir in the chocolate pieces. Pour into 12 foil cup–lined medium muffin cups; top each with one cookie. Bake for 25 minutes. Remove from the oven and cool to room temperature. When cooled, place in the refrigerator and chill for several hours.

To serve, remove the foil cups from the cheesecakes. Place the cakes cookie side down on a serving plate. Serve with the raspberry sauce.

Sweet Wisconsin Cheese Tart with Raspberry Sauce

MAKES 8 SERVINGS

CRUST

⅓ cup all-purpose flour

⅓ cup packed light brown sugar

3 tablespoons butter

1 cup flaked coconut

½ cup chopped pecans or
macadamia nuts

FILLING

1 cup (8 ounces) ricotta cheese

1 cup (8 ounces) mascarpone
cheese

½ cup confectioners' sugar

1 teaspoon vanilla extract

1 teaspoon grated lime zest

SAUCE

1 (10-ounce) package frozen red
raspberries, in sugar syrup,
thawed

TOPPING

1 kiwi, sliced

For the crust, preheat the oven to 350°F.
In a medium bowl, combine the flour and the brown sugar; cut in the butter until the mixture resembles coarse crumbs. Stir in the coconut and nuts. Press the mixture into a 9-inch pie plate or springform pan. Bake for 15 minutes. Remove from the oven, and cool.

For the filling, in the bowl of a food processor or blender, combine the cheeses, sugar, vanilla, and lime zest; process until smooth. Spoon into the crust; chill for 1 hour.

For the sauce, in a blender, process the raspberries into a smooth sauce.

To serve, arrange the kiwi slices in a circle on top of the tart; drizzle with half the raspberry sauce. Cut the tart into slices; serve with the remaining sauce.

Apple Colby Crisp

2 pounds (about 4 large apples or 5 to 6 cups) tart apples, such as Granny Smith, Winesap, Northern Spy, or Jonathan

2 teaspoons lemon juice

1 cup sugar, divided

½ cup packed light brown sugar

½ cup rolled oats

¼ cup all-purpose flour

½ teaspoon ground cinnamon

¼ pound (1 stick) butter, cut in chunks

¾ cup (3 ounces) shredded Colby cheese

Preheat the oven to 350°F.

Peel, core, and slice the apples into a large bowl. Toss with the lemon juice and ½ cup of the sugar. Spread in an 8 x 8-inch baking dish.

Combine the remaining sugar, brown sugar, oats, flour, and cinnamon in a bowl. Add the butter and mix with a pastry blender or your fingertips until the mixture is crumbly. Stir in the cheese. Sprinkle the mixture evenly over the apples. Bake for 50 to 60 minutes, until the apples are tender and the top is browned.

Cheddar Crunch Apple Squares

MAKES 24 SQUARES

1 (12-ounce box) vanilla wafers (or 3⅓ cups vanilla wafer crumbs)

1½ cups flaked coconut

½ teaspoon ground cinnamon

1½ cups (6 ounces) shredded Cheddar cheese

¼ pound (1 stick) salted butter, softened

2 (21-ounce) cans apple pie filling

Cinnamon ice cream or warmed honey, to serve

Preheat the oven to 375°F.

Using a food processor or a rolling pin, crush the wafers into crumbs, and combine with the coconut, cinnamon, cheese, and butter to form a crumbly mixture. Press half of this mixture firmly into the bottom of a greased 13 x 9-inch baking pan.

Spread the apple pie filling on top of the bottom crust. Top with the remaining crumb mixture; do not press down.

Bake for about 40 minutes or until golden brown. Remove from the oven and place the pan on a wire rack. Place the rack in the refrigerator to cool completely.

To serve, cut into 2-inch squares. Serve with ice cream or warmed honey.

Gouda-Raspberry Swirl Rhubarb Cobbler

MAKES 8 SERVINGS

FILLING

1 cup plus 2 tablespoons granulated sugar, divided

½ teaspoon cinnamon

Pinch of ground cloves

2 tablespoons cornstarch

1 cup water

4 cups chopped rhubarb

COBBLER BISCUITS

1 cup all-purpose flour

2 teaspoons baking powder

1 tablespoon sugar

Salt, to taste

4 tablespoons (½ stick) unsalted butter

⅓ cup milk

2 tablespoons raspberry jam

½ cup (2 ounces) grated Gouda cheese

Cinnamon-sugar, for sprinkling

For the filling, in a small bowl, combine 2 tablespoons of the sugar with the cinnamon and cloves. Set aside.

In a medium saucepan, combine 1 cup of sugar and the cornstarch. Add 1 cup of water and mix well. Add the rhubarb. Cook for 5 minutes, stirring occasionally, until thickened. Reduce the heat to low and keep the filling hot.

For the cobbler biscuits, in a medium bowl, combine the flour, baking powder, sugar, and salt. Cut in the butter until the mixture resembles coarse crumbs. Make a well in the center and add the milk. Stir just until moistened. Turn the dough out onto a lightly floured surface and knead lightly 10 times. Pat the dough into a 12 x 8-inch rectangle. Spread with the raspberry jam and sprinkle with the cheese. Roll up, jelly-roll style, starting from a short side; seal the edges. Cut into 8 slices.

Transfer the hot rhubarb filling to the pan. Immediately place the biscuits on top of the filling. Sprinkle the biscuits with cinnamon-sugar. Bake for about 45 minutes, until the biscuits are golden.

Cheesy Plum Strudel

MAKES 8 SERVINGS

2 (8-ounce) packages cream cheese

½ cup sugar

1 egg

1 tablespoon grated lemon zest

1 cup (4 ounces) shredded brick or Muenster cheese

½ cup slivered almonds, toasted

1 (32-ounce) can plums, drained, pitted, and diced

8 sheets phyllo dough

3 tablespoons unsalted butter, melted

2 tablespoons plain dry breadcrumbs

In medium-sized bowl, mix together the cream cheese and the sugar. Add the egg, lemon zest, shredded cheese, and almonds; mix until just blended. Fold in the plums; refrigerate at least 1 hour.

On a clean work surface, place one sheet of the phyllo dough. Brush with butter and sprinkle with 1 teaspoon of the breadcrumbs. Top with another sheet of phyllo and brush with butter. Place a third sheet of phyllo across the two sheets to create a T shape; brush with butter and sprinkle with 1 teaspoon breadcrumbs. Top with another phyllo sheet and brush with butter. Lay the next sheet in the same direction as the first two sheets; brush with butter and sprinkle with breadcrumbs. Top with another sheet and brush with butter. Repeat the process with the remaining two sheets going in the opposite direction. The final configuration should be a cross with four sheets of buttered phyllo going in each direction.

Preheat the oven to 375°F. Grease a 9-inch pie plate. Center the phyllo cross in the prepared pie plate (the edges will overlap quite a bit). Spoon the plum mixture evenly into the shell; loosely cover the filling with the overlapping phyllo to enclose. Brush the top of the dough with remaining butter.

Bake the strudel for 30 to 35 minutes, or until golden brown and heated through. Let the strudel stand at least 1 hour before cutting into wedges.

Gouda and Apple Pastries

1 sheet frozen puff pastry

¼ cup sugar

¼ cup all-purpose flour

½ teaspoon cinnamon

2 medium Granny Smith apples, peeled and finely chopped to make 2 cups

Juice and grated zest of ½ lemon

8 slices Gouda cheese

Thaw the puff pastry sheet at room temperature for 30 minutes. Preheat the oven to 400°F. In a small bowl, mix the sugar, flour, and cinnamon. In another small bowl, mix the apples, lemon juice, and zest. Combine the sugar-flour and apple mixtures.

Carefully unfold the pastry onto a lightly floured surface. Roll into a 15 x 10-inch rectangle. Brush lightly with water.

With the short side of the pastry facing you, spoon the filling on the pastry and spread to within 2 inches of the short sides and to the edge of the long sides. Starting at the short side, roll like a jelly roll. Cut into 8 (approximately 1½-inch) slices. Place 2 inches apart on a greased baking sheet.

Bake for 20 minutes or until golden. Remove from the oven and place one slice of cheese on each pastry. Return to the oven just until the cheese melts, about 1 minute. Remove from the baking sheet and cool on a wire rack.

Cheddar-Apple Cookies

MAKES 3 DOZEN

1¼ cups all-purpose flour

1 teaspoon baking soda

¼ teaspoon salt

½ teaspoon ground nutmeg

¼ pound (1 stick) butter, unsalted

1 cup light brown sugar, packed

½ cup (2 ounces) shredded Cheddar cheese

2 eggs

1 teaspoon vanilla extract

3 cups rolled oats

⅔ cup prepared applesauce

Preheat the oven to 350°F. In a small bowl, sift together the flour, baking soda, salt, and nutmeg. In a large bowl, cream the butter, brown sugar, and Cheddar cheese. Beat in the eggs and vanilla extract. Stir in the flour mixture. Add the oats and applesauce, stirring well. Drop small spoonfuls of batter onto a lightly greased baking sheet. Bake for 10 to 12 minutes. Remove from the oven and cool on a wire rack.

Sour Cream Cappuccino Brownies with Wisconsin Mascarpone Topping

MAKES 24 BROWNIES

BROWNIES

1 (21- to 24-ounce) package brownie mix

1½ tablespoons espresso powder or freeze-dried coffee

2 tablespoons boiling water

¾ cup sour cream

4 tablespoons (½ stick) butter, melted

2 eggs

MASCARPONE TOPPING

½ cup whipping cream

¼ cup confectioners' sugar

½ teaspoon vanilla

1 cup (8 ounces) mascarpone cheese, softened to room temperature

For the brownies, preheat the oven to 350°F.

Grease the bottom only of 13 x 9-inch baking pan. Place the brownie mix in a large bowl. Dissolve the espresso powder in boiling water; add to the bowl. Add the sour cream, butter, and eggs; mix well. Spread the batter into the prepared pan. Bake for about 25 minutes, or until the brownies begin to pull away from the sides of the pan, and the center is just set (do not overbake). Transfer the pan to a wire rack; cool completely.

For the topping, beat the whipping cream with an electric mixer on medium-high speed until soft peaks form. Beat in the sugar and vanilla. Add the cheese in two batches; beat until smooth and fluffy. Cover and refrigerate until serving time.

To serve, cut the brownies into squares and serve with the whipped topping.

Wisconsin Cheddar Peach Shortcakes

MAKES 6 SERVINGS

1¾ cups all-purpose flour

¼ cup sugar

3 tablespoons cornmeal

4 teaspoons baking powder

¼ teaspoon salt

¼ teaspoon ground nutmeg

4 tablespoons (½ stick) butter, softened

1¼ cups (5 ounces) shredded sharp Cheddar cheese

⅓ cup milk

2 eggs, separated

Additional cornmeal

Additional sugar

1½ to 2 pounds fresh peaches, peeled and sliced (about 4 to 5 cups)

1 cup whipping cream, whipped, lightly sweetened

Preheat the oven to 450°F.

In a large bowl, combine the flour, sugar, cornmeal, baking powder, salt, and nutmeg. Cut in the butter until the mixture resembles coarse meal; mix in the cheese. In a small bowl, mix the milk, 1 egg, and 1 egg yolk with a fork, reserving the remaining egg white for glaze. Add the milk mixture to the large bowl; stir just to blend thoroughly.

Divide the dough into 6 equal portions. Form into 3-inch circles, spaced apart, on a greased baking sheet dusted with cornmeal. Brush with the reserved egg white; sprinkle generously with sugar.

Bake for 10 to 12 minutes until lightly browned. Remove the shortcakes from the pan; cool on a wire rack.

Sweeten the peaches to taste. Halve the shortcakes horizontally; place the bottoms on serving plates. Top each cake with some of the peaches; dollop with whipped cream. Cover each with its shortcake top and more peaches; dollop with more whipped cream.

Orange Cream Trifle

2 (3-ounce) packages instant vanilla pudding mix

1½ cups milk

½ cup frozen orange juice concentrate, thawed

1 cup (8 ounces) ricotta cheese

1 tablespoon grated orange zest

1 cup whipping cream, whipped

1 (10 ½-ounce) package frozen pound cake

¼ cup raspberry preserves

Fresh raspberries (optional)

In a large bowl, combine the pudding mix with the milk, stirring until smooth. Stir in the orange juice concentrate. Add the cheese and the orange zest; mix well. Fold in the whipped cream.

Place 1 cup of the pudding mixture in the bottom of a straight-sided glass bowl. Slice the pound cake into 16 (⅜-inch) slices and spread with preserves. Cut 6 slices in half; arrange around the inside of the bowl. Place 5 slices of cake over the cream mixture. Top with 2 more cups of the cream mixture, 5 slices of cake, and the remaining cream mixture. Chill for 2 to 3 hours before serving. Garnish with raspberries.

Tiramisu

4 egg yolks

²⁄₃ cup sugar

½ cup milk

1 cup (8 ounces) mascarpone cheese

1 tablespoon sweet Marsala wine or 1 tablespoon rum*

1 cup whipping cream

½ teaspoon vanilla extract

18 ladyfingers

1 cup strong coffee or espresso, cooled

1½ teaspoon unsweetened cocoa powder

* You can substitute ⅛ teaspoon rum extract mixed with 1 tablespoon of water.

In a small saucepan, beat the egg yolks lightly with a wire whisk. Add the sugar gradually; beat well. Whisk in the milk until blended. Bring the mixture to a boil over medium heat, about 6 minutes, stirring constantly. Boil for 1 minute, stirring constantly. Remove from the heat; cover the top with plastic wrap to prevent a film from forming. Refrigerate 1 hour until cool.

Remove the egg mixture from the refrigerator. Add the cheese, stirring well to blend. Whisk in the wine or rum. Set aside.

In a chilled non-plastic bowl, beat the whipping cream at high speed, 2 to 3 minutes, until stiff peaks form. Mix in the vanilla. Fold half of the whipped cream into the egg mixture, reserving the other half.

Separate the ladyfinger halves (they come split). Brush both sides of the ladyfinger halves with cold coffee, using a pastry brush. Place half of the ladyfingers in the bottom of an 8-inch square glass baking pan, or a similar-sized bowl.

Spread half of the egg-cheese mixture evenly over the ladyfingers. Top with the remaining ladyfingers and spread the remaining egg-cheese mixture over all. Cover with the reserved whipped cream. Sift the cocoa powder over the whipped cream topping. Refrigerate for at least 4 hours.

Note: It is important to keep this dessert refrigerated before and after serving.

Strawberry and Ricotta Gratin

CHEF MICHAEL SYMON

MAKES 12 SERVINGS

1½ cups (12 ounces) whole milk ricotta cheese

1½ cups milk

1½ cups confectioners' sugar

1½ vanilla beans, halved lengthwise

1 tablespoon cornstarch

3 whole eggs, separated

1½ cups heavy cream

3 pints fresh strawberries, trimmed and quartered

Line a fine-mesh sieve with cheesecloth. Set over a bowl. Place the ricotta in the sieve and refrigerate for 2 hours.

Preheat the oven to 350°F.

Remove the ricotta from the refrigerator and discard the liquid. Whip the ricotta. Set aside.

Bring the milk, sugar, vanilla beans, and cornstarch to a boil. Simmer the mixture, stirring until the cornstarch has dissolved and the mixture has thickened. Remove from the heat. Remove the vanilla beans and discard. Whisk in the egg yolks.

In a deep, narrow bowl, whip the egg whites until stiff peaks form. In another bowl, whip the cream until stiff. Fold the egg whites, cream, and ricotta into the milk mixture.

Divide the strawberries among twelve small, shallow gratin baking dishes.

Pour equal amounts of the custard mixture into each dish. Bake for 15 to 20 minutes. Remove from the oven and heat the broiler; then place the dishes under the broiler until the gratins begin to brown. Remove and serve immediately.

Mascarpone Espresso Mousse

1 tablespoon instant espresso granules*

½ cup cold water

2 envelopes (½ ounce each) unflavored gelatin

2 cups (16 ounces) mascarpone cheese

½ cup confectioners' sugar

½ teaspoon cinnamon

2 ounces unsweetened chocolate, melted

2 teaspoons vanilla extract

2 cups heavy whipping cream, whipped

Additional whipped cream (optional), for garnish

Cocoa powder (optional), for serving

Chocolate shavings (optional), for serving

* Strong brewed coffee or coffee granules may be substituted for the espresso granules.

In a small saucepan, dissolve the espresso granules in water; sprinkle the gelatin over the mixture and cook on low heat until the gelatin dissolves; cool to room temperature.

In a medium mixing bowl, combine the cheese, sugar, and cinnamon; gradually add the chocolate and the vanilla, beating with a wire whisk until well blended. Gradually add the gelatin mixture and continue to beat until well blended. Fold in the whipped cream. Pour into a 6-cup serving bowl or individual dessert dishes; chill 2 to 4 hours. If desired, top with additional whipped cream and sprinkle with cocoa or shaved chocolate before serving.

Mascarpone Savarin with Pears and Chocolate Sauce

CHEF PHILIPPE SCHMIT

MAKES 6 SERVINGS

MASCARPONE MOUSSE

2 ounces pasteurized egg yolk product (equivalent of 4 egg yolks)

½ cup sugar

1 cup (8 ounces) mascarpone cheese

7 ounces pasteurized egg white product (equivalent of 6 egg whites)

POACHED PEARS

2½ cups water

1⅓ cups sugar

1 vanilla bean, split

Juice of 1 lemon

8 pears, peeled

CHOCOLATE SAUCE

¾ cup water

⅔ cup sugar

⅔ cup cocoa powder

BISCUIT

5 eggs

⅔ cup sugar

1¼ cups all-purpose flour

For the mousse, in a small bowl beat the egg yolk product and the sugar with an electric mixer. Combine the cheese with the yolk mixture. In a large bowl beat the egg white product until stiff. Fold the cheese mixture into the egg white mixture. Chill.

For the pears, in a medium saucepan over medium-low heat, combine the water, sugar, vanilla, and lemon juice. Add the pears. Simmer until the pears are tender. Cool in the liquid. Dice 2 of the pears. Set aside.

For the chocolate sauce, in a small pan over medium heat, combine the water, sugar, and cocoa powder. Bring to a boil. Remove the pan from the heat. Strain the sauce into a bowl. Set aside to cool.

For the biscuit, preheat the oven to 400°F. In a medium bowl whisk the eggs and sugar until frothy. Carefully fold in the flour. Spread the batter thinly over an 18 x 12-inch baking sheet. Bake for 8 to 9 minutes. Remove from the oven.

To assemble and serve, cut the biscuit into pieces to line a 10-inch savarin (ring) mold. Add layers of mousse, diced pears, biscuit, and mousse. Chill 2 hours until very cold. Turn out the savarin onto a plate. Cut into six servings. Serve each with a poached pear, and drizzle with the chocolate sauce.

Camembert with Hazelnuts and Apricot Compote

CHEF TODD DOWNS

MAKES 12 SERVINGS

CHEESE

12 (2 x 2-inch) pieces Camembert cheese, rind trimmed

2 cups hazelnuts, toasted, skinned and chopped

DRIED APRICOT COMPOTE

4 cups dried apricots, cut into ¼-inch strips

3 cups Gewurztraminer wine

½ cup sugar

2 vanilla beans, split and scraped

For the cheese, coat the cheese squares evenly with the chopped hazelnuts. Reserve at room temperature, covered, until the cheese softens.

For the compote, combine all of the compote ingredients. Simmer until the apricots are soft and the compote is thickened, about 20 minutes.

To serve, place a piece of Camembert cheese on each of twelve small plates. Top the cheese with a heaping spoonful of compote. Serve.

Creamy Strawberry Dip

MAKES ABOUT 1½ CUPS

1 cup (8 ounces) cream-style large or small curd cottage cheese

1 cup strawberry slices, divided

1 to 2 tablespoons sugar

¼ teaspoon grated orange zest (optional)

Place the cheese, ½ cup of the strawberries, and the sugar in a blender container. Cover and process on high until smooth. Add the remaining strawberries and the orange zest, cover, and process on and off just until the berries are chopped. Chill. Serve as a dip for fresh fruit or over pound cake or angel food cake slices.

Fruit with Wisconsin Mascarpone Honey Sauce

MAKES 2 SERVINGS

½ cup (4 ounces) mascarpone cheese

2 tablespoons honey

1 cup whipping cream, whipped

Strawberries, apple slices, or pear slices, for serving

Combine the cheese and honey; stir until smooth. Fold in the whipped cream. Serve with fruit slices.

Ricotta Gelato

MAKES 12 SERVINGS

1 cup golden raisins

½ cup (4 ounces) light rum or grappa

2½ cups light cream

1 tablespoon grated lemon zest

9 egg yolks

1½ cups sugar

2 teaspoons pure vanilla extract

2 cups (16 ounces) whole-milk ricotta cheese

1 cup (8 ounces) mascarpone cheese

In a saucepan, combine the raisins and rum or grappa. Heat to a simmer, remove from the heat, and set aside until the liquid is absorbed. In a large saucepan, combine the cream and the lemon zest; heat to a simmer. Remove from the heat, cover, and keep warm.

In a large bowl beat the egg yolks; gradually beat in the sugar until it is completely dissolved and the mix is light and lemon colored. Whisk the egg yolk mixture into the warm cream and place the saucepan over medium-low heat; cook, stirring, until the mixture reaches 165°F on an instant-read or candy thermometer. To avoid curdling, do not boil. Strain into a bowl and add the vanilla. Cover and refrigerate.

When the gelato mix is cold but not set, mix in the cheeses until well blended. Pour the mixture into an ice-cream maker and add the raisins. When frozen, transfer the gelato to a chilled container and store in the freezer for at least 3 hours.

Honeyed Fruit with Gingered Wisconsin Mascarpone

MAKES 6 SERVINGS

FRUIT

1 cup white grape juice

¼ cup honey

¼ cup orange liqueur or cream sherry

6 cups mixed seasonal fresh fruits (any variety, except bananas)

CHEESE TOPPING

¾ cup (6 ounces) mascarpone cheese

2 tablespoons honey

1 tablespoon orange liqueur or cream sherry

1 tablespoon finely chopped crystallized ginger

Milk (optional)

For the fruit, in a small saucepan, combine the grape juice and ¼ cup of honey. Bring to a boil, reduce the heat, and simmer, uncovered, for 5 minutes. Stir in ¼ cup of orange liqueur or sherry.

Place the fruit in a large bowl. Pour the warm honey mixture over the fruit. Cover and chill for at least 2 hours or up to 4 hours, stirring occasionally.

For the topping, in a small bowl, combine the cheese, 2 tablespoons of honey, 1 tablespoon of liqueur, and crystallized ginger. Cover and chill until serving time.

To serve, spoon the fruit into dessert dishes. Then spoon the topping over the fruit. (Stir a little milk into the topping, if necessary, to make it smooth and spoonable.) Garnish with additional crystallized ginger, if desired.

Chocolate Wisconsin Mascarpone Fondue

CHEF TREY FOSHEE

MAKES 6 TO 8 SERVINGS

½ pound bittersweet chocolate, chopped

½ pound milk chocolate, chopped

1¼ cups cream

⅓ cup sugar

1 cup (8 ounces) mascarpone cheese

2 ounces bourbon, orange liqueur, or another favorite liqueur

1 cinnamon stick

ACCOMPANIMENTS

Pound cake, cubed

Assorted fresh fruits, such as strawberries, apple chunks, or banana chunks

Marshmallows

Combine the chocolates, cream, sugar, cheese, bourbon, and cinnamon stick in a medium bowl (or the top of a double boiler). Place over a pot of simmering water on the stove burner. Do not allow the bowl to touch the water. Heat until melted, smooth, and warm, stirring often. Remove from the heat. Pour into a fondue or other pot and keep warm. Serve immediately, dipping the accompaniments of your choice.

Pecorino Cheese with Pears, Honey, and Pistachios

MAKES 4 SERVINGS

4 ripe but firm pears (such as Bartlett or Anjou), halved, cored, quartered, each quarter cut into ¼-inch-thick slices

1 (5-ounce) piece Pecorino Toscano or Pecorino Sardo, cut into ¼-inch-thick slices

¼ cup honey

⅓ cup shelled pistachios

To assemble, divide the pear and cheese slices among four plates, slightly overlapping each pear slice with a cheese slice. Drizzle some honey and scatter some pistachios over each plate.

Cream Cheese Frosting

MAKES ABOUT 1½ CUPS

2 cups confectioners' sugar

8 tablespoons (4 ounces) cream cheese, well chilled, cut into chunks

2 tablespoons butter, softened

1 teaspoon vanilla

⅛ teaspoon salt

In the bowl of a food processor or mixer, combine the ingredients; process or mix just until smooth. (Do not overprocess or the frosting will be too soft to spread.)

FIND THE PERFECT PAIRING

CHEESE	SUGGESTED WINE PAIRING	SUGGESTED BEER PAIRING
BRIE AND CAMEMBERT are ivory-colored, soft-bodied cheeses with rich, creamy textures and earthy flavors.	A simple sparkling wine, such as a Moscato d'Asti, offers a crisp, mildly sweet complement.	Apple or pear ciders offer a tart, fruit-flavored complement.
MASCARPONE is a soft, rich, creamy cheese with a clean, sweet finish.	The fresh fruits and acids of a Pinot Gris blend seamlessly with the cheese and refresh the palate.	A delicious Raspberry or cherry fruit lambic brightens the sweetness of the cheese.
MUENSTER is a semisoft, whole milk cheese with mild, sweet cream flavor and a smooth texture.	A wide variety of wines work well with Muenster. Try Sauvignon Blanc for its perfect balance of fruit and acid.	Pilsners, with their mild flavors and slight hoppiness, are a good match.
MONTEREY JACK is a semisoft cheese with a smooth, creamy texture; mild flavor; and a slightly tangy finish.	The apple, pear, and citrus flavor notes of Riesling complement Monterey Jack's tangy finish	The nutty flavors of an easy-to-drink nut brown ale complement the creamy texture of the cheese.
HAVARTI is a creamy, buttery semisoft cheese with a slightly acidic finish.	A bright, young Beaujolais Nouveau will delight with its fresh fruit notes and herbal aroma.	The cocoa and coffee flavors of a mild stout will accentuate the cream and mildly acidic flavor notes.
FONTINA is a whole milk cheese with a buttery texture and earthy, tart flavors.	An "unoaked" Chardonnay is a vibrant companion for this versatile cheese.	A variety of Pilsners offer a good match, with their mild flavors and slight hoppiness.
SWISS AND BABY SWISS vary in texture, but both have a nutty flavor.	Sauvignon Blanc's bright fruit and floral notes complement the nuttiness.	A wheat beer (Weizen/Weiss) elevates the flavor of Swiss.
GRUYÈRE is a semihard cheese with the full, nutty, rich flavors of earth and grass.	Riesling's fresh fruits and acids blend with the cheese and refresh the palate. Gruyère also pairs well with Pinot Noir.	Wheat beer works well, but a stout or porter with big cocoa and coffee flavors provide a more powerful flavor combination.
GOUDA AND EDAM are cheeses with sweet cream–flavor notes. Gouda is made with whole milk, and Edam is made with nonfat milk, resulting in a different texture for each.	A buttery and full-bodied Chardonnay plays off the buttery, sweet cream texture.	A nut brown ale complements the sweet cream flavors and texture. A creamy stout that is not too overpowering will work as well.
AGED BRICK is ivory to yellow in color, with small openings. Its sweet, nutty flavor deepens and intensifies with age.	A Gewürztraminer, both sweet and spicy with a floral aroma, offers a subtle contrast.	The bittersweet flavor notes of bock stand up to aged brick.

WALLA WALLA
RURAL DISTRICT

CHEESE	SUGGESTED WINE PAIRING	SUGGESTED BEER PAIRING
MEDIUM TO AGED CHEDDAR is brothy to beefy in flavor with a creamy to crumbly texture.	Many red wines are a nice complement, but a ruby port or Madeira offers the same great contrast that fruit brings to nuts.	A big, bold stout with rich cocoa and coffee flavors stands up well to the flavor of Cheddar.
PROVOLONE has a few small eyeholes and ranges in color from creamy white to ivory. The flavor is very mild when young and becomes big and piquant with age.	The spicy fruit flavors of Amorone or a classic Chianti match well with the full flavors of the cheese.	An oatmeal stout or a porter, rich in malt flavors, complements the nutty flavors of the cheese.
MOZZARELLA is smooth and elastic in body, with a very delicate, milky flavor.	A fresh Beaujolais, full of fruit flavors, pairs with this quiet-flavored cheese.	The mild flavor of Pilsner complements the delicate flavor of mozzarella.
ROMANO is a hard/firm cheese with a big, nutty, and piquant flavor profile.	The fruitiness found in Chianti provides a playful contrast to Romano.	Apple or pear ciders offer a fruity, tart taste contrast.
PARMESAN is a hard cheese with nutty flavors and notes of salt and sweet milk.	A sweet, late-harvest Riesling or Vin Santo will bring out both the saltiness and the sweetness.	A Scotch ale, with its nutty and hoppy flavors, contrasts with this cheese perfectly.
ASIAGO is a hard cheese that offers a flavor combination between Cheddar and Parmesan. It is nutty with piquant notes.	A sweet, berry-driven Merlot or a Pinot Noir contrasts beautifully.	A delicious raspberry or cherry fruit lambic posts a big fruit contrast to the nutty piquant cheese.
FARMER CHEESE has a semisoft texture and clean, fresh milk flavor.	Keep it clean and simple by pairing with a refreshing Sauvignon Blanc.	Mild Pilsners provide a simple but enjoyable complement.
GORGONZOLA is a soft, creamy, and mild blue-veined cheese with hints of earthiness in its finish.	A rich, fruit-driven Pinot Noir is a classic complement.	A big porter, with its deep flavors, balances the relatively big flavors of Gorgonzola.
BLUE CHEESE has a crumbly texture and is full of sharp, robust flavors.	A big and robust port provides a contrast in flavors.	Raspberry or cherry fruit lambic contrasts the full flavor of blue cheese.

INDEX

Index 479

WALLA WALLA
RURAL LIBRARY DISTRICT